The African Women's Protocol:
Harnessing a Potential Force for Positive Change

First published by Fanele – an imprint of Jacana Media (Pty) Ltd in 2008

10 Orange Street
Sunnyside
Auckland Park 2092
South Africa
+2711 628 3200
www.jacana.co.za

ISBN   978-1-920196-08-0

Cover picture by Annie Bungeroth/Oxfam GB
Cover design by Jacana Media
Set in Sabon 10/12.5pt
Printed by Paarl Print
Job No. 000626

See a complete list of Jacana titles at www.jacana.co.za

The African Women's Protocol: Harnessing a Potential Force for Positive Change

A study commissioned by
Oxfam GB Southern African Region

Rosemary Semafumu Mukasa

Reviewed by Rose Gawaya and Alice Banze

(Zul; Xho; Tso): necessary.
This is a necessary book.

Contents

List of Figures

Acknowledgements

FIRST AND FOREMOST, on behalf of all the researchers I would like to thank Oxfam GB for having the foresight to commission this research and for giving us the privilege of carrying it out. We would like to express out gratitude to Oxfam GB members of staff, particularly Peter Mutoredzanwa (Regional Programme Manager, Pretoria), Cardinal Uwishaka, (who was Country Programme Manager in Mozambique at the time of the study), Alice Banze (Maputo), Ayanda Mivumbi (Programme Coordinator, Johannesburg) and Irungu Houghton. Thanks also to Unaiti Jaime, Gender Advisor (Mozambique) who updated information in the Mozambique section. Special mention must go to Rose Gawaya, (Oxfam's Regional Advisor on Gender) whose diligence, commitment and emphasis on excellence made a world of difference to this undertaking.

I would also like to thank all the members of our advisory team especially Susan Nkomo, whose insight, wisdom and enthusiasm merits special mention. I wish to thank Angela Melo (Special Rapporteur on the Rights of Women) for the critical role she played both at regional level and in Mozambique.

Without the hard work of the national researchers, Alcinda Abreu and Angelica Salomao from Mozambique, Susan Holland Muter from South Africa and Stephen Mukwaya and Matrine Bukku Chulu from Zambia, this report would not possible. We would also like to thank all of the research assistants involved for their tireless efforts and ingenuity in locating and interviewing people who would rather have been left alone to enjoy their end of year vacation/holidays. We will remain forever indebted to all the key respondents at national and regional

levels who took time out of their busy schedules to make an invaluable contribution to this process. They did so with enthusiasm and their thought provoking comments have undoubtedly enriched the content of this research.

I would be remiss if I failed to acknowledge the assistance that I received from Eunice Kigenyi (Uganda Embassy Addis Ababa) in obtaining responses from Addis Ababa. I also wish to thank Ms Chilufya Kasutu for the excellent preparations and logistics that enabled the research to be accomplished at a reasonable speed despite the festive season. Special thanks also goes to Ms Rose Gawaya, for the valuable comments on the draft report. Further thanks go to Ms Charlotte Matempa Wonani, of the University of Zambia, Development Studies Department, for the 'peer review' of the Zambian draft report.

I ardently hope that this research will help make a real difference to the lives of ordinary African women and men. I hope it will be a positive contribution to efforts to make the Protocol to the African Charter on Human and Peoples' Rights on the Rights of Women a truly African Women's Protocol.

– Rosemary Semafumu Mukasa

List of Acronyms

ABC	Abstain, Be Faithful, Condomise
ACHPR	African Charter on Human and People's Rights
AIDS	Acquired Immune Deficiency Syndrome
AMCJ	Associação das Mulheres de Carreira Jurídica
AMME	Associação Moçambicana da Mulher e Educação
AMORADE	Associação Moçambicana da Rapariga e Desenvovimento
ANC	African National Congress
ARVs	Anti-retrovirals
AU	African Union
BESSIP	Basic Education Sub-Sector Investment Program
BIWZ	Beyond Inequalities Women in Zambia
CALS	Centre for Applied Legal Studies
CBOs	Community-Based Organisations
CCJP	Catholic Commission for Justice, Peace and Development
CCMA	Commission for Conciliation, Mediation and Arbitration
CEDAW	Convention on the Elimination of all forms of Discrimination Against Women
CGE	Commission on Gender Equality
CNAM	The National Council for the Advancement of Women
CODESA	Conference for a Democratic South Africa
CSO	Civil Society Organisation

CSO	Central Statistics Office
CSW	Committee on the Status of Women
CTOP	Choice on Termination Of Pregnancy
DHD	Associação dos Direitos Humanos
DHMT	District Health Management Team
DOH	Department of Health
DoJ	Department of Justice
DV	Domestic Violence
DVA	Domestic Violence Act
ECA	Economic Commission for Africa
FAWEZA	Forum for the Advancement of Women's Education Zambia
FGM	Female Genital Mutilation
FHH	Female Headed Households
FRELIMO	Mozambique Liberation Front
FWCW	Fourth World Conference on Women
GBV	Gender-Based Violence
GEAR	Growth, Employment And Reconstruction
GFP	Gender Focal Point
GIDD	Gender In Development Division
GRZ	Government in the Republic of Zambia
HAART	Highly Active Anti-Retroviral Treatment
HIPC	Highly Indebted Poor Countries
HIV	Human Immuno Deficiency Virus
HIV/AIDS	Human Immuno Deficiency Virus / Acquired Immune Deficiency Syndrome
HRC	Human Rights Commission
HSRC	Human Sciences Research Council
ICJ	International Commission of Jurists
ICPD	International Conference on Population and Development
IDASA	Institute for Democratic Alternatives in South Africa
JCIQLSW	Joint Committee on the Improvement of the Quality of Life and Status of Women
KZN	KwaZulu-Natal

LDH   Liga dos Derietos Humanos

MAPODE   Movement of Community Action for the Prevention
              and Protection of Young People Against Poverty,
              Destitution, Diseases and Exploitation
MCWH   Maternal, Child and Women's Health
MDG   Millennium Development Goals
MHH   Male-Headed Households
MINEC   Ministério dos Negócios Estrangeiros e Cooperação
              (Ministry of Foreign Affairs and Cooperation)
MISAU   Ministério da Saúde (Ministry of Health)
MMAS   Ministério da Mulher e Coordenação da Acção Social
              (Ministry of Woman and Social Action)
MMD   Movement for Multiparty Democracy
MOCDSS   Ministry of Community Development and Social
              Services
MOH   Ministry of Health
MP   Member of Parliament
MRC   Medical Research Council
MULEIDE   Mulher, Lei e Desenvolvimento

NCCEMD   National Commission on Confidential Enquiries into
              Maternal Deaths
NCOP   National Council of Provinces
NEPAD   New Economic Partnership for Africa's Development
NGM   National Gender Machinery
NGOCC   Non Government Organisation Coordination Council
NGO   Non Government Organisation
NGP   National Gender Policy
NHAMAI   Associação dos Derietos da Mulher e da Criança
NWLG   National Women's Lobby Groups

OMM   Organização da Mulher Moçambicana
OSW   Office on the State of Women
OVC   Orphans and Vulnerable Children

PAGE   Program for the Advancement of Girls' Education
PAP   Pan African Parliament

PARPA	Plano de Acçao para a Redução da Pobreza Absoluta (Plan for the Absolute Poverty Reduction)
PCAS	Policy Coordination Advisory Services
PENG	Política e Estratégia Nacional de Género (Gender National Policy and Strategy)
PEP	Post Exposure Prophylaxis
PHC	Primary Health Care
PHRC	Permanent Human Rights Commission
PMTCT	Prevention of Mother to Child Transmission
PPASA	Planned Parenthood Association of South Africa
PROMUGE	Organização Moçambicana pap a Promoção da Mulher e do Género
PRSP	Poverty Reduction Strategic Programs
RDP	Reconstruction and Development Plan
RECs	Regional Economic Communities
RENAMO	Resistencia Nacional de Mozambique
SADC	Southern Africa Development Community
SADHS	South African Demographic Health Survey
SALC	South African Law Commission
SANDF	South African National Defense Force
SAP	Structural Adjustment Program
SAPS	South African Police Services
SHEP	School Health Education Program
SOAWR	Solidarity for African Women's Rights
SPANGP	Strategic Plan of Action for the National Gender Policy
SRH	Sexual and Reproductive Health
SRHR	Sexual and Reproductive Health Rights
STD	Sexually Transmitted Disease
STI	Sexually Transmitted Infection
TAC	Treatment Action Campaign
TBA	Traditional Birth Attendants
THPAZ	Traditional Health Practitioners Association of Zambia
TNDP	Transitional National Development Plan
TOP	Termination of Pregnancy
UNDP	United Nations Development Program
UTH	University Teaching Hospital
VAW	Violence Against Women

VCT   Voluntary Counselling and Testing
VSUs   Victim Support Unit

WDF   Women's Development Foundation
WILDAF   Women in Law and Development in Southern Africa
WILSA   Women and Law in Southern Africa
WNC   Women's National Coalition

YWCA   Young Women's Christian Association

ZARD   Zambia Demographic and Health Survey
ZLDC   Zambia Law and Development Commission
ZNBC   Zambia National Broadcasting Cooperation

Section One

Overview

Executive Summary

THIS BOOK IS THE OUTCOME of a policy research that assessed the implications of the Protocol to the African Charter on Human and Peoples' Rights on the Rights of Women, hereafter referred to as the African Women's Protocol. The research was part of Oxfam GB's efforts to promote and protect women's rights and enhance gender equality. The research focused on South Africa, Mozambique and Zambia.

The purpose of the research was to assess the implications of the African Women's Protocol in order to strengthen the popularisation and mobilisation campaigns in three countries – Mozambique, Zambia and South Africa.

The research analysed the African Women's Protocol in light of selected Human Rights instruments. It examines the situation of women and the implications of the African Women's Protocol in Mozambique, South Africa and Zambia focusing on these thematic areas; governance, violence against women and health and reproductive rights. In addition, the research assessed awareness about the African Women's Protocol among policy makers and civil society, and highlights the threats, challenges, best practices and lessons that have been discovered. The research concluded that although the African Women's Protocol is a potential force for change, supporters of women's rights and gender equality must take deliberate and concerted action to ensure its popularisation, ratification, domestication and implementation. The report makes a number of general and country-specific recommendations.

BACKGROUND

On 11 July 2003, the heads of state and government of the African Union (AU) adopted the Protocol to the African Charter on Human and Peoples' Rights on the Rights of Women in Africa. The African Women's Protocol seeks to promote and protect the rights of African women by reinforcing existing international human rights standards and adapting them to address context-specific violations of African women's rights.

The African Women's Protocol seeks to promote and protect the rights of African women by reinforcing international human rights standards and adapting them to address context-specific violations of African women's rights. It commits state parties to combat all forms of discrimination against women through legislative, institutional and other measures. State parties must further commit themselves to modify the social and cultural patterns of male and female conduct through publications, information, education and communication strategies, in order to eliminate harmful cultural, traditional and all other practices based on the idea of inferiority or superiority of the sexes or on stereotyping.

On 8 July 2004, African heads of state and governments adopted a Solemn Declaration on Gender Equality in Africa in which they undertook to sign and ratify the African Women's Protocol by the end of 2004. However, by 31 December 2004, only five countries had ratified the African Women's Protocol, a mere third of the 15 countries required before its entry into force.

Thanks to ongoing campaigns and pressure by non-government organisations (NGOs), the number of ratifications dramatically doubled by 28 February 2005. Ten countries had ratified the African Women's Protocol and duly deposited their instruments of ratification with the AU. The Women's Protocol entered into force on 25th November 2005 after Benin, the 15th country, deposited its instruments of ratification with the AU. The focus then shifted to popularisation, domestication and implementation. Advocacy for ratification is still undertaken by women's rights organisations, in countries that have not done so. The more countries that ratify and domesticate the African Women's Protocol, the more legitimacy it will have.

Oxfam GB has supported a number of activities to promote the African Women's Protocol as part of its drive to protect women's rights and enhance gender equality. Notable among these are the solidarity campaigns for the ratification of the African Women's Protocol and *Pambazuka News* – a weekly online electronic newsletter that advocates for positive social change in Africa. To complement these efforts,

Oxfam GB conducted policy research on the African Women's Protocol. The purpose of this research was to assess its implications in order to strengthen the popularisation and mobilisation campaigns in three countries: South Africa, Zambia and Mozambique.

SIGNIFICANCE

The Protocol is a homegrown instrument developed by Africans for African women. It legitimises the fight against gender oppression as an African struggle. No longer can detractors claim that women's rights are transplants from the western world with no roots in African values and norms.

For the first time, an international human rights instrument addressing violence against women and prohibiting harmful traditional practices like female genital mutilation (FGM), widow inheritance, and child marriages will be implemented. The African Women's Protocol addresses issues hitherto not treated by other instruments, such as health and reproductive rights including HIV and AIDS and the exclusion of rape, sexual slavery and other sexual violence in crimes against humanity. The African Women's Protocol affords protection to vulnerable groups, such as the elderly, widows, nursing women and women in distress.

Like most instruments, the African Women's Protocol is not perfect. It is a compromised document and, naturally, it has its gaps and weaknesses. There are, for example, a number of concerns about weaknesses when it comes to enforcement and uncertainties in the mechanisms for its implementation. There is also dissatisfaction with the manner in which it treats some aspects of marriage, sexuality, reproductive rights and AIDS. In addition to these, it has been unable to specifically address the full range of harmful traditional practices and there are gaps in areas, like bride price (lobola).

Nevertheless, the African Women's Protocol is a potential force for changing the lives of African women for the better. One of the Protocol's greatest strengths is that it is an African instrument that outlaws negative traditional practices and enshrines the right of women to live in a positive cultural context. It can act as a lever to facilitate efforts to harmonise customary and statutory law and tackle the public/private dichotomy in a manner that benefits women.

The African Women's Protocol can strengthen the legal and policy framework of their countries by acting as a standard to which countries are obliged to conform. It promotes equality in marriage by addressing inequalities with regard to decision-making, property and children.

In governance, it demands equal representation in political life and decision-making. Through its specific mention of budgetary allocations for areas such as violence against women, it can serve as a tool for promoting action and bridging the gap between law and policy, on the one hand, and practice and reality, on the other. The Protocol can act as a shield against retrogression, protecting the gains made by women from threats, such as hostile policies and negative change.

Women and NGOs can also make use of the rights to submit individual or group complaints to the African Commission on Human and Peoples' Rights and to the African Court of Justice when it becomes operational. However, this can only be done after domestic remedies are exhausted.

All this notwithstanding, the African Women's Protocol will remain a sleeping lion unless supporters of women's rights and gender equality take deliberate and concerted action to ensure its popularisation, ratification, domestication and implementation.

SCOPE, METHODOLOGY AND EXPECTED RESULTS

The research was conducted at two levels: the regional level and the national level. At regional level, a total of 15 people were interviewed or responded to the questionnaire. At national level, the countries covered were Mozambique, South Africa and Zambia. In South Africa, the total number of respondents and interviewees was 14. In Zambia, 15 people participated, while in Mozambique, there were 11 respondents. The questionnaire that formed the basis for the interviews covered a number of areas including the situation of women with regard to the thematic areas, the strengths, weaknesses, implications of and obstacles to the operationalisation of the African Women's Protocol. It covered the level of awareness among policy makers, civil society and the media, best practices, as well as recommendations for actions and target actors. The methodology involved literature review, questionnaires and interviews. The key interviewees included officials of national governments, and regional intergovernmental organisations, parliamentarians and members of the Pan African Parliament, academicians, representatives of civil society and community-based organisations (CBOs).

The research team encountered a number of problems during the research. The timing, December 2004 to January 2005, coincided with the holiday season making it difficult to interview some respondents. In Mozambique, this situation was aggravated by the national elections.

The expected results were:

- a comparative analysis of the African Women's Protocol in the light of regional instruments, international instruments and national legislations and policies;
- an analysis of national situations and implications for the African Women's Protocol in the thematic areas;
- identification of challenges and best practices;
- recommendations on how to popularise the African Women's Protocol and promote its ratification and implementation.

SUMMARY OF FINDINGS

How does the African Women's Protocol Improve the Existing Framework?

The African Women's Protocol fortifies the framework for the promotion and protection of Women's Rights in a number of significant ways. It focuses on areas that neither the Convention on the Elimination of All Forms of Discrimination Against Women (CEDAW) nor the African Charter on Human and Peoples' Rights addressed, such as violence against women, HIV/AIDS, health and reproductive rights, as well as the exclusion of rape, sexual slavery and other sexual violence from crimes against humanity. It protects the rights of vulnerable women, such as widows, the elderly, the distressed and nursing women, by providing remedies for women whose rights have been violated.

While the CEDAW's effectiveness was undermined in some quarters because it was considered to be a western woman's instrument, the African Women's Protocol is a homegrown instrument developed by African women for African women. On the other hand, where the African Charter on Human and Peoples' Rights (ACHPR) went overboard is in its wholesale embrace of African traditions, values and customs without acknowledging that some of these customs and traditions discriminate against and harm women; the African Women's Protocol outlaws traditions such as FGM, widow inheritance and child marriages.

Furthermore, Article 17 empowers African women by giving them the right to live in a positive cultural context and to enhance participation in the determination of cultural policies. This provision provides African women with a tool to address one of the biggest challenges facing efforts to implement the CEDAW and the Beijing Declaration and Platform for Action, the co-existence of multiple legal systems with customary and religious laws governing personal life and prevailing over positive laws and constitutional guarantees.

Unlike the Beijing Declaration and Platform for Action and the Southern African Development Community (SADC) Gender and Development Declaration (GAD) and its Addendum on the Prevention and Eradication of Violence against Women and Children, the African Women's Protocol is legally binding. It reinforces the CEDAW in a number of areas, such as trafficking of women and addressing inequalities in marriages with respect to decision-making, property and children. By calling for equal representation in decision-making and political life, it further reinforces the CEDAW and is an improvement on the 30 per cent target of the Beijing and the SADC GAD Declaration.

The African Women's Protocol seeks to strengthen the legal and policy framework of countries on gender equality and women's empowerment, helps promote action and bridges the gap between law and policy on the one hand, and practice and reality on the other. It can act as a shield against retrogression, protecting the gains made by women from threats such as hostile policies and negative change. Women and NGOs can also make use of the right to submit individual or group complaints to the African Commission on Human and Peoples' Rights and to the African Court on Human and Peoples' Rights when it becomes operational. However, individuals and other non-state actors do not have direct access to these mechanisms except in rare cases where international instruments once ratified are self-executing.

Implications of the African Women's Protocol in the Thematic Areas

Governance

Article 9 of the African Women's Protocol requires state parties to take specific positive action to promote participative governance and the equal participation of women in the political life of their countries through affirmative action, enabling national legislation and other measures to ensure that participation in elections, electoral processes and the development and implementation of State polices and programmes is non-discriminatory. It also requires State parties to ensure increased and effective representation and participation of women at all levels of decision-making. The call for equal participation in decision-making, and the example set by the AU in respecting the equal participation provision in appointing commissioners and electing women to high level posts (such as the presidency of the Pan African Parliament) augurs well for the political participation of women.

The African Women's Protocol could also be used to strengthen the regulatory framework for the participation of women in decision-making through legislation quotas and other affirmative action measures. In South Africa, great strides have been made in the representation of women in decision-making and political life because of the 30 per cent quota currently applied voluntarily, by the African National Congress (ANC). The institutionalisation of these measures could help protect these strides, which currently depend on the goodwill of the ruling party. It could also result in improvements in other political parties. Similarly, in Mozambique there has been an improvement of the participation of women in decision-making and political participation. Women are represented by 37.6 per cent. In Zambia, NGOs have proposed the introduction of quotas in their recommendations to the Constitutional Review Commission in a bid to enhance the participation of women in politics. The African Women's Protocol could provide leverage for these efforts. In all three countries, the African Women's Protocol could be used to spur progress in areas of governance that have lagged behind, such as local Government, public service, the judiciary, the armed forces and the private sector. Furthermore, the African Women's Protocol would be a useful advocacy tool for efforts to bridge the gap between policy and practice.

Violence against Women

Article 4 of the African Women's Protocol commits state parties to enact and enforce laws to prohibit all forms of violence against women whether it takes place in public or in private. States are also obliged to adopt legal, administrative, as well as social and economic measures, to ensure the prevention, punishment and eradication of violence against women. They commit themselves to provide adequate budgets and other resources for the implementation and monitoring of these measures. This provision will be especially useful in light of the fact that in all three countries resource constraints have been identified as a major challenge. In South Africa, the reference to budgetary resources has been widely lauded. This resource could help enhance the protection of women in Zambia and Mozambique where civil society organisations have been at the forefront of the violence against women struggle.

The article also tackles the problem of the trafficking of women, a pervasive problem in the region, which none of these countries has adequately addressed. The African Women's Protocol will support calls

9

for more research, a stronger legislation policy and attempts to put actions that are more effective in place in this area.

Article 5 prohibits and condemns all forms of harmful practices that negatively affect the human rights of women and that are contrary to international standards. It could greatly improve South Africa's laws, policies and treatment of harmful traditional practices. While its Constitution protects women from violence and harm and protects their rights to life, dignity and health, no detailed policies exist on specific harmful practices such as female genital mutilation (FGM), virginity testing, dry sex, abduction or forced marriage, ukungena (taking over a widow by a male relative without her consent), or the burning and victimisation of women branded as "witches". Women remain the victims of harmful traditional practices in all three countries.

In dealing with harmful traditional practices, it will be important to define and build a consensus on what constitutes harmful traditional practice. While it is clear-cut in some areas, there are practices such as lobola, virginity testing and some initiation rites where there is no clear consensus. More research needs to be carried out and a consensus reached on the circumstances under which some traditional practices become harmful.

Health and Reproductive Rights

Article 14 of the African Women's Protocol seeks to ensure that the health rights of women, including their sexual and reproductive health, are respected and promoted by the State. It provides women with the right to protection against sexually transmitted infections (STIs) including HIV/AIDS. It also authorises medical abortion in cases of sexual assault, rape, incest and where the continued pregnancy endangers the mental or physical health or life of the mother or foetus. In South Africa, the Constitution provides women with more rights than those set out by the African Women's Protocol. However, the African Women's Protocol is an advance on Zambian legislation. In Zambia, a panel of three doctors is required to agree that the mother's health is threatened and it also does not provide for the termination of pregnancy, even in cases of rape, sexual assault or incest. Given the high prevalence of HIV/AIDS in the region, the provisions on protection for women could help improve the dire situation of women, since activists could adopt a rights-based approach, as opposed to a welfare one, in advocating for more effective action. In all three countries, the emphasis on rural areas in the call for adequate, affordable and accessible health services could help bridge the wide disparity between urban and rural women.

The African Women's Protocol could help change the lives of both men and women for the better. Increased participation of women in political life is not just the right thing to do, but will also result in more socially responsible decision-making at all levels. Improved control over their fertility would free women to pursue more productive and fulfilling lives and lead to healthier, more prosperous families. By addressing violence against women and harmful traditional practices that disempower women, the African Women's Protocol will help improve living standards for both men and women alike.

Level of Awareness

At the time of conducting the research (Dec 2004–Feb 2005), the level of awareness about the African Women's Protocol was woefully low. Unfortunately, it was lowest between the two categories of actors that are crucial to its implementation: the media and CBOs. Most CBOs had never heard of it and media coverage of the African Women's Protocol was negligible. In South Africa, not even its ratification managed to catch the news.

The level of awareness was highest among actors (government officials, members of parliament and NGOs) who had been involved in the process of its promotion, adoption and ratification. These actors were knowledgeable enough to use it to advance women's rights. The level of awareness was, therefore, higher in South Africa, which had ratified the African Women's Protocol, at the time of conducting the research. In Zambia, which had not signed the African Women's Protocol at the time and where debate had been limited, most of the officials interviewed were largely unaware of the African Women's Protocol and its contents. A limited number of NGOs were sufficiently conversant with the African Women's Protocol to use it to advance women's rights.

Challenges

A number of challenges must be faced in the process of harnessing the potential force of the African Women's Protocol. These include the gaps and weaknesses in the African Women's Protocol itself, and the absence of a culture of using international human rights instruments. Like most international Human Rights instruments, there are no sanctions for non-compliance. In order to monitor this, the African Women's Protocol relies on states to include a section on its implementation in periodic reports on the implementation of the charter. These reports have thus

11

far not been forthcoming. Given the poor record of compliance of state parties in fulfilling this obligation, women's rights advocates will have to simultaneously pressurise governments on two fronts: first with respect to the preparation of the report on the implementation of the charter and then with regard to ensuring that it contains a meaningful report on the Protocol. It will be helpful for them to draw on the CEDAW's experiences with the reporting process and devise measures such as NGO shadow reports and indicators to help mitigate this weakness.

Regarding implementation, there will be a need to clearly define the relationship between the court and the commission in order to iron out uncertainties with respect to competence. It is not yet clear how the merger of the Court on Human and Peoples' Rights and the AU Court of Justice will affect its capacity to promote and protect human rights. Countries will also have to make a declaration accepting the competence of the court to receive individual complaints before their citizens enjoy this protection. In addition, unless adequate resources are provided, the court will share the problems the commission experienced in its early years.

The weakening of the women's movement in Africa in the last decade and the weakness of key partnerships and alliances are hurdles that women must seek to overcome. The lack of political will to address gender issues and the weakness of key gender machinery in terms of power, resources and skills are some of the other challenges with which we must grapple. Other issues include the strength of patriarchy, tradition, culture and religion, the co-existence of multiple legal systems, and the public/private dichotomy, which restricts women to the private sphere. Finally, threats in the policy environment ranging from the diversion of resources away from other causes to the fight against terror, the implementation of structural adjustment measures, which limit government spending on social services, and the rise in religious and cultural fundamentalism could revoke the gains made by women over the years.

Lessons

Adopt a Holistic Approach

> To ensure maximum impact synergy, and follow through, efforts to promote ratification, popularisation and implementation should be part of a national plan or strategy.

Take the African Women's Protocol to the Grassroots

> The African Women's Protocol must be unpackaged and repackaged in a manner that makes it available, accessible and user friendly to different actors.

Promote its Domestication and Effective Use

> If the African Women's Protocol is to be effectively implemented it must be incorporated in the domestic laws of a country as well as in its sector policies, programmes and plans at local, provincial and national level.

Break the Private/Public Dichotomy and Move the Mountain of Tradition

> Efforts to popularise the African Women's Protocol must target the actors and institutions that control the private domain where many women spend most of the their lives.

Transform Targets for Change into Agents of Change

> Efforts to popularise and implement the African Women's Protocol must target crucial actors in the campaign for popularising the African Women's Protocol, such as the media and cultural leaders, as both subjects and potential agents for change.

Start Early

> Efforts for popularising the African Women's Protocol must target girls and boys at the stages before their opinions become formed.

Maximise the Opportunities Provided by Technology

> Efforts for popularising the African Women's Protocol must make maximum use of the information revolution, while being mindful of the new threats it presents and of the need to bridge the digital divide between grassroots women and the rest of the world.

CONCLUSION

The African Women's Protocol legitimises the struggles for gender equality and the promotion and protection of women's rights as an African struggle. Despite its imperfections, it is a potential force for positive change. If properly harnessed, it can serve as an effective empowerment tool for African women. Empowering African women, who make up more than half of the continent's population, will have a positive multiplying effect that will result in happier, healthier, wealthier and more harmonious families and societies.

SUMMARY

Chapter One of the research report analyses the African Women's Protocol in relation to instruments like the CEDAW, the African Charter for Human and Peoples' Rights, the Beijing Declaration and Platform for Action and the SADC GAD and its addendum on the prevention and eradication of violence against women and children. It highlights the role the African Women's Protocol can play in strengthening the framework for promoting and protecting women's rights. Chapter Two examines the situation of women. Chapter Three examines the implications of the African Women's Protocol for the three countries in three thematic areas: governance, violence against women, and health and reproductive rights. Chapter Four examines the level of awareness among policy makers, civil society and the media in the three countries. Chapter Five outlines major challenges and threats. Chapter Six highlights best practices that have been implemented in a number of areas in some countries. Chapter

Seven sums up the lessons and conclusions. The report then makes general and country-specific recommendations on how to popularise, promote the ratification and ensure the implementation of the African Women's Protocol. It concludes by identifying possible areas for future research.

The Situation of Women

THE SADC REGION: A PANORAMIC VIEW

OVER THE LAST DECADE, the SADC region has witnessed a number of notable achievements with regard to the situation of women. In politics, there have been great strides with respect to the participation of women in decision-making. Electoral reforms in Malawi, Mozambique and South Africa have resulted in an increase in parliamentary representation over and above the required 30 per cent target set by the SADC GAD. The region has seen ground breaking appointments of women to high level posts such as prime minister and deputy president, speakers of parliament and ministers to cabinet portfolios that were hitherto the domain of men, such as Foreign Affairs, Finance and Defence.

All countries in the SADC region have ratified the CEDAW and there have been legal reforms that aim at promoting gender equality in many countries. With the exception of Swaziland, Angola and Mozambique, most countries had adopted National Gender Polices with implementation plans by 31 December 2004. Many countries have also adopted specific strategic plans to promote gender equality in fields such as health, education, agriculture and labour. In the field of education, a critical area for empowering women, the adoption of policies, such as the drive for 50/50 enrolment at primary school level, free primary education, programmes to enhance the self-esteem and self-confidence of the girl child and affirmative action at tertiary level, have significantly improved the lot of women and girls.

There have been efforts to improve the financial position of women through entrepreneurship programmes, the establishment of women's

16

banks, credit institutions and development funds. Trade policies have been revised to improve women's access to credit and a number of countries have begun land reforms that, among other things, aim to improve women's access to land.

Unfortunately, the region's health has deteriorated as a result of the HIV and AIDS pandemic. The plight of women and girls is further aggravated by the fact that they also bear the multi-faceted burden of home-based care to those living with AIDS. In addition, poverty has increased dramatically in the region's population. At 70 per cent, women make up an unacceptably high percentage of those living in extreme poverty. The increased number of poor households led by women under an atmosphere of food and nutritional insecurity reflects this feminisation of poverty.

By removing safety nets, such as access to essential services, without substantially enhancing their capacity to compete in the free marketplace, structural adjustment programmes have left women in double jeopardy in many of the region's countries. Micro-credit, small-scale loans and income generating projects, though helpful, have not succeeded in permanently lifting women out of the vicious cycle of poverty (Lomoyani, 2005: 2).

Violence against women has been recognised as a human rights issue and there have been some efforts to address it. Nevertheless, it remains a major challenge in the region. Trafficking in women and children is on the increase but is yet to be seriously addressed. While the women's movement has weakened over the decade, patriarchy and societal attitudes that disadvantage women have remained largely unchanged. Gender machineries remain weak in terms of financial resources, skills and power (ECA, 2004: 5–8; Lomoyani, 2005: 3–5).

While advances have been made in efforts to improve gender equality and women's rights, there is much that remains to be done to improve the plight of the majority of women in the region. It is against this backdrop that Oxfam undertook the research in South Africa, Zambia and Mozambique.

THE THREE COUNTRIES: AN OVERVIEW

In many ways, the three countries under examination are very different. They have different national historical experiences, economic situations and challenges. Mozambique is a former Portuguese colony where a bloody civil war followed the struggle for independence. Zambia, a former British colony, has only known the impact of conflict indirectly as it plays host to fleeing refugees, while South Africa suffered a unique institutionalised form of oppression under the apartheid system.

Yet, despite these differences, threads of similarity closely knit them. All three countries are undergoing a process of transformation. South Africa is grappling with the onerous task of transforming the apartheid legacy. Zambia is still struggling to come to grips with its metamorphosis from one of the richest countries in Africa to one of the poorest. And Mozambique is struggling to overcome the aftermath of conflict. All three countries are attempting to entrench the democratic process.

Unfortunately, another thread that firmly binds all three countries together is the fact that despite their differences, discrimination against women remains a pervasive reality. Their national experiences may differ and their standards of living may vary, but in all three countries, a lot remains to be done to improve the lot of women.

South Africa

The unbanning of the ANC in 1990 after decades of resistance to apartheid rule marked the beginning of a new South Africa. A process of transformation unfolded that resulted in the establishment of a democratic state on 27 April 1994.

Following difficult negotiations under the Convention for a Democratic South Africa (CODESA), and the multi-party negotiation process, a new Constitution was adopted in December 1996. It is widely acclaimed as one of the most progressive and inclusive constitutions of our time. The Constitution asserts that the democratic state is founded on the values of human dignity, the achievement of equality, of human rights and freedoms, non-racism and non-sexism. The Equality Clause in the Bill of Rights advances gender equality. This positive framework was the result of highly organised lobbying and advocacy by the Women's Coalition. Two issues clearly illustrate this struggle: the successful rebuttal of attempts to exclude the principle of non-sexism from Constitutional principles, and the successful challenging of moves by traditional leaders to exclude customary law from the Bill of Rights, especially the Equality Clause.

The Equality Clause provides for protection against unfair discrimination (direct or indirect) on one or more grounds, including race, gender, sex, pregnancy, marital status, ethnic or social origin, colour, sexual orientation, age, disability, religion, conscience, belief, culture, language and birth. The Constitution also provides for the creation of statutory bodies supporting constitutional democracy. Six bodies were formed, including the Commission for Gender Equality

(CGE) and the Human Rights Commission (HRC).

The new Constitution was set up at a time when women were preparing for the Fourth World Conference on Women in Beijing, which enabled the gender dimension of the Constitution to be influenced by the process. It also led to another noteworthy development. The South African government ratified the CEDAW without reservation, a move that had hitherto been opposed by the former ruling National Party. This provided additional weight by legally binding the government to take steps to ensure gender equality (Holland-Muter, 2005: 10).

Zambia

With its rich reserves of copper and an income of US $1200 per capita, Zambia was regarded as one of the richest and most promising countries in sub-Saharan Africa when it gained independence in 1964. Unfortunately, plummeting commodity prices and poor policy choices combined to drastically change the situation. Today, Zambia is one of the poorest countries in the world and is counted among the highly indebted poor countries (HIPC).

However, Zambia did not escape the wave of democratisation that swept over many countries on the continent in the post-Cold War era. The victory of the Movement for Multi-party Democracy in the country's 1991 elections brought an end to the United National Independence Party (UNIP) one-party rule.

Zambia has a plural legal system. Statutory law, which is based on English common law, is applied side by side with customary law and practice. Article 2 of the Constitution embodies the principle of equality. Article 11 enshrines the right of Zambians to enjoy fundamental rights and freedoms without distinction to race, place of origin, political opinion, colour, creed, sex or marital status. Article 23 reinforces this. However, this protection is contradicted by the fact that the same Constitution permits discrimination against women in terms of personal law in areas such as marriage, divorce and property rights. The High Court applies statutory law while the lower courts apply customary law. Customary law, which treats women as minors, applies to most cases regarding personal relations, property rights and ownership. The situation is even worse in villages where headmen or chiefs in local courts hear disputes. The net result is that, in terms of personal law, the Constitution has defined a power relationship between women and men that disadvantages women in terms of access to and control over productive resources and benefits in the private sphere of life. This translates into gender-based inequalities in the public sphere, in areas such as education, training employment, business enterprise, politics and decision-making (Muyakwa, 2005: 11–14).

Mozambique

Mozambique is a poorly developed country where women constitute 52 per cent of the population. 72.2 per cent of these women live in rural areas. The country's population suffered at the hands of a bloody civil war that followed independence in 1975. It raged on until 1992 when a peace agreement was signed between the Government and rebels from the Resistencia Nacional de Mozambique (RENAMO). The country is struggling to consolidate peace and national unity, to promote development, reduce poverty and entrench democracy. Mozambique has just concluded an election that was widely hailed as a sign of the strengthening of democracy in the SADC region.

Mozambique ratified the CEDAW and submitted is first report in 2007 to the CEDAW's Committee in fulfilment of its reporting obligations. The provisions and spirit of the CEDAW are being domesticated and this can be seen in reforms of the areas of land law, and its labour, family, penal and civil codes. Mozambique has a plural legal system where statutory law, which is based on Portuguese civil law, is applied alongside customary law. The Mozambique Constitution was revised in December 2004 and now enshrines the principle of gender equality.

THE THREE COUNTRIES: NATIONAL MACHINERY, GENDER POLICIES AND POSITION ON AFRICAN WOMEN'S PROTOCOL

National Machinery

Figure 1.1 (see page 23) presents the current situation with respect to the national machinery promoting the rights of women in the three countries. The creation of these extensive structures is a welcome and positive development. However, national machinery has suffered a number of plagues that have seriously undermined their effectiveness as the catalyst institutions for the promotion and protection of women's rights. This is further discussed in the section on challenges.

National Gender Policies

South Africa, Zambia and Mozambique all have National Gender Policies. Zambia adopted the National Gender Policy in 2000 and its Strategic Action Plan in 2004. Mozambique adopted its National Gender Policy (2006) and is in the process of revising the new National Plan for the Advancement of Women (2007–2011).

Current Position on the African Women's Protocol

Zambia

Zambia signed the African Women's Protocol on 3 August 2005 and ratified it on 2 May 2006. Furthermore, Zambia had begun a process of domesticating the CEDAW. The decision to domesticate the CEDAW is a welcome development.

Mozambique

Mozambique ratified the African Women's Protocol on 15 December 2005. Women's rights organisations are lobbying their government to domesticate the provisions of the Protocol in their national legislation and policy frame works.

South Africa

South Africa has ratified the African Women's Protocol. It deposited its instrument of ratification with the Secretary General of the AU on 14 January 2005. It did so with three reservations and two interpretative declarations.

South Africa made reservations to Articles 4(j), 6(d) and 6(h). Article 4(j) obliges state parties to take effective measures to ensure that if the death penalty exists, death sentences are not carried out on pregnant or nursing women. In its reservation, the government states that the death penalty has been abolished and the article finds no application in South Africa. Its existence in the African Women's Protocol should not be construed as an inadvertent sanctioning of the death penalty in other state parties, since South Africa is opposed to it in principle since it conflicts with Article 2 of its Constitution.

South Africa entered a second reservation to Article 6(d), which requires all marriages to be recorded in writing and registered in order for them to be recognised. The South African government does not consider itself bound because section 4.9 of the Customary Marriages

Act of 1998 stipulates that failure to register a customary marriage has no effect on its validity. This is considered protection for women married under customary law.

The third reservation was made to Article 6(h) on the grounds that it subjugates the equal rights of men and women with respect to the nationality of children to national legislation and national security interests. This could deny children their inherent right to citizenship and nationality.

South Africa made two interpretative declarations on Articles 1 and 31. With respect to Article 1, South Africa basically restricts the definition of discrimination against women to the scope contained in section 9 of its Constitution as the Constitutional Court may interpret it. With regard to Article 31, on the status of the Protocol, the South African government says the South African Bill of Rights should not be seen to offer less favourable protection than the Protocol even though, unlike the Protocol, it provides for limitations under certain conditions.

While the three reservations are progressive, in that they are made in the best interest of South African women, the same cannot be said for the two interpretative declarations.

Figure 1.1
National machinery

ZAMBIA

Executive	Legislature	Independent	Civil Society
Gender in Development Department (GIDD) Established: 1996 Location: Cabinet Office Functions: Policy formulation, guidelines on gender activities, coordination, liaison and networking, monitoring and evaluation. Gender Focal Points (GFP) Location: Sector ministries, some public institutions, provincial administration	Committee on Legal Affairs, Governance, Human Rights and Gender Matters Established: 1999 Functions: Scrutinises Government activities to ensure gender is prominent.	Gender Consultative Forum (GCF) Established: 2003	Non Governmental Organisation Coordinating Council (NGOCC) Established: 1985 Functions: NGO umbrella organisation, coordination of affiliated NGOs.

SOUTH AFRICA			
Executive	Legislature	Independent	Civil Society
Office on the Status of Women (OSW) Established: 1997 Location: Presidency Functions: Coordination, policy formulation, support in gender mainstreaming to government departments and public sector bodies, monitoring implementation of mainstreaming.	Joint Committee on the Quality of Life and the Status of Women (JCIQLSW) Established: 1996 Functions: Monitors and assesses progress with respect to status and quality of life for South African women, government compliance with national and international commitments, mainstreaming, including budgets and fiscal framework.	Commission on Gender Equality (CGE) Established: 1997 Functions: Independent, statutory advice and research body, monitoring and evaluating policies and practices of government, the private sector and other organisations, reviewing legislation, public education, monitoring and reporting on compliance with international commitments and investigating inequalities and complaints in the field of gender.	No umbrella body. About 60 NGOs attend national machinery meetings. Strongest networks operate in field of violence against women.

SOUTH AFRICA			
Executive	Legislature	Independent	Civil Society
GFP Location: Sector ministries, provincial administration Functions: Ensuring civil service transformation to guarantee gender equity, mainstreaming gender in development policies and programme implementation.	Women's Empowerment Unit (WEU) Location: Speaker's Forum Functions: Forum for speakers for national and provincial legislatures, training and skills development.		

Mozambique			
Executive	**Legislature**	**Independent**	**Civil Society**
Ministry of Women and Social Action (MMAS) Established: 2000 Functions: Coordinate implementation of women's empowerment and development policies. National Directorate of Women Established: 2001 Functions: Define and promote implementation of support programmes. National Focal Points	Social Gender and Environmental Affairs Commission Functions: Mainstreaming.	National Council for the Advancement of Women (CNAM) Functions: Oversight, monitoring and promoting implementation of government policies and programmes.	Women's Forum Network of NGOs Functions: To lobby government, capacity building for various organisations.

2

Comparative Analysis of the Protocol to Selected International Instruments and Policy Documents

THIS SECTION ANALYSES the African Women's Protocol in relation to the CEDAW, the African Charter on Human and Peoples' Rights, the Beijing Platform for Action, and the SADC GAD and its Addendum on the Prevention and Eradication of Violence against Women. It highlights the strengths and weaknesses of each instrument. Together they complement each other and serve as a framework for the protection and promotion of women's rights. The section highlights the ways in which the African Women's Protocol fortifies the framework for protecting and promoting women's rights. It also looks at the lessons we can draw from the experience with other commitments as we move towards the implementation of the African Women's Protocol.

THE INSTRUMENTS

The Convention on the Elimination of all Forms of Discrimination against Women (CEDAW)

The CEDAW was adopted in 1979 and entered into force in 1981. It was the first instrument to bring together all women's human rights, which had hitherto been scattered in various instruments, into the ambit of a single Human Rights instrument. It has thus, been widely hailed as the first Bill of Rights for women. Within 179 State parties, it has attained near universal ratification.

In 30 articles, the CEDAW seeks to eliminate any distinction, exclusion, or restriction made on the basis of sex, which has the effect or purpose of impairing or nullifying the recognition, enjoyment, or exercise by women on a basis of equality with men of human rights and fundamental freedoms in the political, economic, social, cultural, civil or other fields.

In Article 2, state parties commit themselves to ensure that government organisations comply with the CEDAW regulations by taking legislative and other appropriate measures to eliminate discrimination in public institutions and by any personal organisation or enterprise, and to modify or abolish discriminatory laws, regulations, customs and practices. Article 4 authorises the adoption of special measures creating temporary inequality in favour of women aimed at accelerating de facto gender equality and protecting maternity.

Articles 5 through 16, which outline substantive political, civil, economic and social rights, basically reiterates rights contained in other Human Rights instruments. The rights upheld cover public participation, citizenship, employment, education, health care, special needs of rural women, domestic relations, leisure, prostitution and human trafficking.

Part IV of the Convention establishes the duties of the Committee on the Elimination of all forms of Discrimination Against Women, and outlines modalities for its operation. The committee monitors compliance with the CEDAW through periodic reports submitted by state parties. They are considered through a non-contentious process of constructive dialogue. Article 21 of the Convention empowers the committee to make recommendations, observations and suggestions to interpret, clarify, and promote the implementation of certain articles or specific subjects relating to the Convention. In addition, part VI covers dispute settlements and procedural details on entry into force, ratifications and reservations (Semafumu, 1999: 176–178). An optional protocol, which entered into force in 2000, provides women with a means of redress for violations of rights protected under the Convention. (Figure 2.1 on page 31 summarises the strengths and weaknesses of the CEDAW.)

Lessons Learnt From the CEDAW

Ratification

The CEDAW was adopted on December 1979. It entered into force on 3 September 1981 in a record time of less than two years, making it the fastest human rights instrument to enter into force at the time. The speed of ratification was accelerated by the five conferences on women that take place annually. In fact, the adoption of the Convention itself on December 1979 was, in part, the result of pressure to have it presented to the Copenhagen Conference in July 1980. When it was presented, 64 States signed it and two ratified it.

Another factor worth noting is the different roles of NGOs and Government in the elaboration and adoption of the CEDAW and the African Women's Protocol. During the seventies, when the CEDAW was adopted, NGO participation in the elaboration of international instruments had not attained the level of acceptability that we witness today. Governments were the dominant player, which proved to be a double-edged sword. On a positive side, it meant that there was more buy in from the organisations and individuals responsible for the pushing of ratification. Once the Convention was signed, it was easy to push it through the national ratification processes. On the downside, once it was ratified, someone had to educate NGOs who were crucial to its implementation.

In the case of the African Women's Protocol, the NGOs played a pivotal role in its initiation, elaboration and subsequent adoption. In fact, when the Protocol was not tabled for adoption in 2002 at the launch of the AU as had been expected, feverish lobbying by NGOs for its inclusion played a crucial role in its adoption by the Assembly of Heads of State and Government in 2003 (Wandia, 2004: 2). The downside to this is that once it was adopted, countries had to work backwards to obtain buy in from the government organisations responsible for its signature and ratification. The advantage, however, is that these countries have a pool of NGOs who are familiar with the African Women's Protocol and can facilitate its implementation.

Implementation

The CEDAW has strengthened the legal framework for de jure equality. As a result of its impact, many constitutions and regulatory frameworks have provisions that guarantee equality and prohibit discrimination on the grounds of sex. It has provided the standard for the repeal of discriminatory provisions in civil, penal and personal status codes and spurred the adoption of equal opportunity acts to improve the de facto position of women. The CEDAW has contributed to the strengthening of the institutional frameworks that act as a catalyst for the promotion and protection of women's rights.

Courts and judicial procedures are gradually becoming more attuned to requirements of the Convention and a jurisprudence of gender equality guided by the Convention is developing. This notwithstanding, judges are often reluctant to base their decisions on international treaties, such as the CEDAW. If a country has ratified the CEDAW, they usually have the authority to consider it either as part of national law or as an aid to interpreting national law. Precedents, or examples where other countries have applied the CEDAW and other human rights instruments, are helpful persuasive tools. In Africa, examples of such cases include Ephrohim vs. Pastory (Tanzania) and Longwe vs. Intercontinental Hotel vs. Attorney General and Unity Dow (Zambia). These cases will be discussed in greater detail under best practices (Llana Landsberg-Lewis: 1998).

A study on the impact of the CEDAW undertaken in 2000 (McPherson et al, 2000: 17) identified a number of problems that have hindered its effective implementation. The co-existence of multiple legal systems with customary and religious law governing personal and private life and prevailing over positive law and even constitutional guarantees of equality remain major hurdles. The persistence and resilience of discriminatory cultural practices, traditions, social norms and stereotyping, insufficient political will, lack of resources and ignorance by women about their rights as well as insufficient redress for violations are among the other obstacles identified.

Notwithstanding this environment, the study identified a number of factors that promote or hinder its effective use. (See Figure 2.2.)

Figure 2.1

The strengths and weaknesses of the CEDAW

Hallmarks	Strength	Weakness
• First document to bring together all earlier piecemeal provisions into a single comprehensive instrument (Bill of Rights) on rights of women. • Considered ethnocentric in some quarters.	**Content** • Covers political, civil, economic, social, cultural rights. • Covers both the public and private spheres. • Provides for special measures creating temporary inequality to attain de facto gender equality. • Requires states to modify behaviour and culture in addition to refraining from committing these violations themselves. **Implementation** • Elaborate reporting system. • Near universal ratification. • Introduction of procedure for inquiries and individual complaints.	**Content** • Omissions such as violence against women, FGM, sexual and reproductive rights, the rights of widows and other vulnerable groups like the elderly, people infected with HIV/AIDS, etc. **Implementation** • No procedure for rejecting ratifications incompatible with its object and purpose. • Inadequate resources for its implementation mechanism. • Like most international human rights instruments, it lacks the sanctions to back it.

THE AFRICAN CHARTER ON HUMAN AND PEOPLES' RIGHTS

The African Charter was adopted in Nairobi in 1981. But, it only entered into force five years later in 1986. The charter seeks to address the gap in existing international human rights instruments when it comes to addressing human rights from an African perspective. It attempts to combine African values and traditions with international norms. The African Charter promotes individual duties and collective rights in addition to individual rights.

The charter covers internationally recognised individual rights, civil and political rights, such as non-discrimination, equality before the law, the rights to dignity and freedom, liberty and the security of person, as well as the right to a fair trial. It provides for the rights to freedom of conscience, worship and religion and the rights to receive information and freedom of expression. Other freedoms upheld by the charter include the freedom of association, assembly and movement. In addition, it also provides for the right to participate in government and equal access to the public service.

With regard to economic, social and cultural rights, the regional instrument upholds the right to own property, to work under equitable conditions and to receive equal work for equal pay. In addition, it protects the rights to physical and mental health, education and freedom to participate in cultural activities. Under the charter, African families enjoy the rights to protection and to assistance from the state. The charter spells out special measures for the protection of the aged and the disabled. It briefly touches on discrimination against women and children's rights.

The charter covers group or community rights; including the right to determine their mode of governance and the development of their economies, the right to peace and security and the right to a clean environment. Part II of the charter sets out safeguard measures. It establishes the African Commission on Human and Peoples' Rights, whose functions are to promote human rights, protect human rights, interpret the charter and undertake consultative activities. It must also perform any other duties that the Assembly of Heads of State may request.

Strengths and Weaknesses

Substantive Rights

The major strength of the charter lies in its contribution of concepts of

African values, collective rights and individual duties to the international human rights regime. The charter is comprehensive in scope, covering political, civil, economic and social rights and collective rights. In terms of content, its main weaknesses are omissions with respect to the right to privacy and collective bargaining and the unsatisfactory manner in which it deals with women's rights.

Implementation

The three most important tasks of the protection mandate of the African Commission on Human and Peoples' Rights are the consideration of state reports, inter-state complaints and individual complaints. Unfortunately, the commission was initially plagued with problems. "Paper tiger", "toothless", "invisible" are some of the ways in which the commission was described as it struggled to carve out a role for itself in very difficult circumstances in its first eight years of its existence. It had a shoestring budget, no full time professional staff and not enough meeting time to carry out its functions. Its independence was often called into question because government officials as opposed to experts represented it. It had little zeal for the promotion and protection on human rights. As a result of the interpretation, its work was shrouded in secrecy. To aggravate the situation, between 1986 and 1993 no women were elected to the commission (Nmehielle, 2004: 4).

In the next 10 years of its existence, the tide has turned in the commission's favour. Through creative interpretation, the charter was empowered to receive individual complaints. The wording of Article 58 would seem to imply that the commission may only consider communication when it reveals a series of serious and massive violations of human rights and after the Assembly of Heads of State requests it to do so. In practice, the commission considers every violation even if it is only a single violation. Furthermore, in emergency situations, the commission may, under rule 111 of its rules and procedures, adopt provisional measures urging the state to refrain from any action that could cause irreparable damage until the commission hears the case (OAU: 4-5).

As a result of its innovation, Africa now has Special Rapporteurs and Focal Points on a number of human rights issues such as the rights of women and refugees. There has been a dramatic increase in the number of complaints because of the increase in the level of openness. Another positive development in recent years has been the progressive and pragmatic application of the admissibility requirements, particularly the

Figure 2.2
Factors that influence the effectiveness of CEDAW

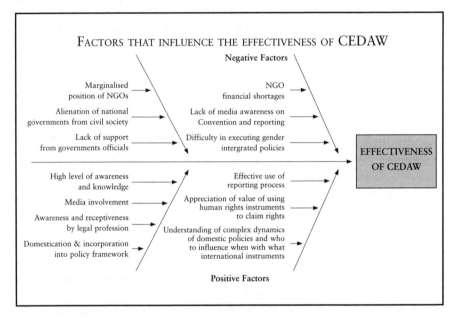

FACTORS THAT INFLUENCE THE EFFECTIVENESS OF CEDAW

Negative Factors

Marginalised position of NGOs

NGO financial shortages

Alienation of national governments from civil society

Lack of media awareness on Convention and reporting

Lack of support from governments officials

Difficulty in executing gender intergrated policies

EFFECTIVENESS OF CEDAW

High level of awareness and knowledge

Effective use of reporting process

Media involvement

Appreciation of value of using human rights instruments to claim rights

Awareness and receptiveness by legal profession

Understanding of complex dynamics of domestic policies and who to influence when with what international instruments

Domestication & incorporation into policy framework

Positive Factors

exhaustion of local remedies rule (Nmehielle, 2004: 10).

Despite these positive developments, the charter did not have an effective remedial mechanism. Even where it found a violation on the part of a state party, this did not afford a remedy to the victim. To address this gap the Protocol to the African Charter on Human and Peoples' Rights on the Establishment of a Court on Human and Peoples' Rights was adopted in Ouagadougou in June 1998. It entered into force on 25 January 2004; however, its implementation was delayed by a decision to postpone the appointment of judges until July 2005. Unless governments are persuaded to make the declaration under Article 34.6, accepting the competence of court to receive individual complaints from their citizens at the time they sign the Protocol, the ability of their citizens to enjoy this protection will be adversely affected. There is a need to clearly define the relationship between the court and the commission. Furthermore, unless adequate resources are provided, the court like the commission may spend the better half of its first decade struggling to become relevant.

The Protection of Women's Rights Under the Charter

It is worthwhile to briefly examine the level of protection afforded to women under the charter. Article 2 of the charter provides for non-discrimination and includes sex as one of the grounds on which the individual's enjoyment of the rights spelt out in the charter shall not be impaired. Article 3 provides for equality and equal protection before the law. Article 18(3) of the charter undertakes to ensure the elimination of every discrimination against women and to ensure the protection of women and children as stipulated in international declarations and conventions. Under the charter, the ACHPR is empowered to go beyond the provisions of the Protocol and "draw inspiration from international human rights law, including the Convention on the Elimination of Discrimination Against Women (CEDAW)". The appointment of a Special Rapporteur on the Rights of Women is one of the major ways in which the charter promoted women's rights (FEMNET, 2003: 64).

Gaps

The charter does not address the experiences and special needs of women resulting from their gender and the manner in which gender roles have been constructed. It is, therefore, silent on areas in marriage, such as the right to consent and equality of the spouses during and after marriage. It did not address special women's concerns in areas like the workplace or in conflict.

Article 18.3 prohibits discrimination only under the context of the family. To aggravate the situation it comes just after Article 18.2, which describes the family as the custodian for morals and traditional values, recognised by the community. This raises concern about the implications for women's rights.

Another area of inadequacy stems from the charter's warm and wholesale embrace of African tradition and customs, without taking into account the fact that some of these very traditions discriminate against women. The charter extols "the virtues of historical tradition and the values of African civilisation", without addressing its vices, which include FGM, child marriages and widow inheritance. The charter does not address issues like violence against women, health and reproductive rights, HIV/AIDS, inheritance or the rights of vulnerable women.

THE PROTOCOL TO THE AFRICAN CHARTER ON HUMAN AND PEOPLES' RIGHTS ON THE RIGHTS OF WOMEN IN AFRICA

The Protocol is the first regional, legally binding instrument on women's rights elaborated by Africans for African Women. It attempts to combine international standards with African values. The Protocol is divided into three sections. The preamble outlines the rationale for its elaboration. The second part begins with a general undertaking by governments in Articles 2 and goes on to outline substantive rights in Articles 3 through 24. The final part (articles 25 to 32) addresses the modalities for adoption, implementation, monitoring and amendment.

In the preamble, heads of state and government recognise that despite the Charter and a number of other human rights instruments, women remain victims of discrimination and harmful traditional practices. They resolve to "ensure that the rights of women are promoted, realised and protected" (AU, 2003: 3).

The second part of the Protocol outlines substantive rights covering civil and political rights, economic, social and cultural rights, and the rights to development and peace as well as reproductive and health rights. The areas addressed in this section include:

- Dignity, integrity and the security of person;
- Elimination of harmful traditional practices;
- Marriage;
- Access to justice and equal protection before the law;
- Equal participation in the political and decision-making processes;
- Conflict;
- Education and training;
- Economic and social welfare;
- Health and reproductive rights;
- Food security;
- Adequate housing and sustainable environment;
- Positive cultural context;
- Sustainable development;
- Inheritance; and
- Protection of women with special needs.

The final part of the Protocol deals with implementation. It addresses the manner in which the Protocol will be adopted, monitored and amended. Article 25 calls for effective remedies, determined by efficient, impartial and competent forums.

Substantive Content

Strengths of the African Women's Protocol

The African Women's Protocol is comprehensive in scope. It covers all categories of human rights in both the private and the public sphere. In addition to calling for legislative reform, it emphasises the need for effective policies. The African Women's Protocol outlaws harmful traditional practices such as FGM, child marriages and widow inheritance. It protects the rights of vulnerable women, such as widows, the elderly, the distressed and nursing women. It addresses issues hitherto not treated in legally binding international instruments, such as violence against women, health and reproductive rights, the impact of HIV and AIDS, and the exclusion of rape, sexual slavery and other sexual violence in crimes against humanity. The African Women's Protocol promotes equality in marriage by addressing inequalities with regard to decision-making, property rights and children. In governance, it demands equal representation in political life and decision-making. It gives women the right to live in a positive cultural context and to participate in the determination of cultural policies. As an instrument developed by Africans for Africans, it legitimises the struggle against gender oppression as an African struggle.

Weaknesses

There is dissatisfaction with the manner in which the African Women's Protocol treats sexuality, polygamy and maternity. The African Women's Protocol equates being a woman with reproduction and, thus, emphasises reproductive health concerns at the expense of reproductive rights. Sexuality is only mentioned as a public health issue in terms of protection from and control of STIs, HIV and AIDS. With regard to maternity, the African Women's Protocol has been criticised for not going far enough to provide protection from dismissal and provision of child care facilities.

There are concerns about gaps in the African Women's Protocol with respect to prostitution and sexual exploitation, the rights to privacy, freedom from forced labour and access to legal aid. (Akina Mama, 2004: 21). Groups of people, who are socially marginalised and thought to engage in taboo sexual relations, notably lesbians, sex workers and young girls, are disregarded (Holland-Muter, 2005: 54).

Implementation

Strengths

In article 25, state parties commit themselves to providing appropriate remedies determined by competent judicial, administrative or legislative authorities for women whose rights or freedom, under the African Women's Protocol, have been violated. This is a positive development. Article 4.2 calls on states to provide adequate budgetary allocations for areas like violence against women. In addition, Article 31 enables women to enjoy the law favourably in cases where national legislation is stronger than the African Women's Protocol.

Weaknesses

Like most international human rights instruments, the African Women's Protocol has no sanctions for non-compliance and no enforcement mechanisms. Article 26 of the Africa Women's Protocol commits states to indicate the legislative and other measures undertaken for the full realisation of the rights in the African Women's Protocol, when they submit their periodic reports on the implementation of the charter. Unfortunately, the record of states in complying with this obligation has so far left a lot to be desired (see Figure 2.3).

By May 2003, 19 countries had not bothered to submit a single report to the commission (ACHPR-Commission, 2004). Given the poor record of compliance of State parties in fulfilling this obligation, women's rights advocates will have to pressurise governments simultaneously on two fronts. First with respect to the preparation of the report on implementation of the charter and then with regard to ensuring that it contains a meaningful report on the African Women's Protocol. It will be helpful for them to draw on the CEDAW's experience with the reporting process and devise measures, such as NGO shadow reports, to help mitigate this weakness.

Under the charter, women can submit individual complaints when their rights have been violated. However, they must comply with the rule that local remedies must first be exhausted. Even though the commission has interpreted this rule quite liberally and there has been an increase in the number of complaints it has handled of late, most grassroots women would not have the resources, confidence or sophistication to use this procedure. The issues surrounding the competence of the court, access by individuals and relationship between the court and the commission when the former becomes operational, have already been dealt with in the section under the charter.

THE BEIJING DECLARATION AND PLATFORM FOR ACTION

The Beijing Declaration and Platform for Action was adopted in 1995. It aims at accelerating the implementation of the Nairobi Forward Looking Strategies for the Advancement of Women and at removing all the obstacles against women's active participation in all spheres of public and private life through a full and equal share in the economic, social, civil and political decision-making. The Platform for Action calls upon governments, the international community and civil society to take action in 12 critical areas of concern: poverty, education and training, health, violence against women, armed conflict, the economy, power and decision-making, institutional mechanisms, human rights, the media, the environment and the girl child.

One of the hallmarks of the Beijing process is the five yearly review process at national, regional and international level. Through this process, countries highlight achievements and obstacles in each of the 12 critical areas of concern and adopt further actions and initiatives to give impetus to the implementation of the Beijing Declaration and Platform for Action.

Strengths and Weaknesses

The major strengths of the Beijing and Dakar processes lie in the NGOs' active participation in the five yearly review process. In many countries, NGOs participate actively in their formulation, implementation, monitoring and evaluation. In fact, ordinary women are more likely to have heard of the term 'Beijing' than of the CEDAW or any other process for the promotion of women's rights. The five yearly review process provides an opportunity for the international community to take stock of progress, or the lack thereof, in each of the 12 critical areas of concern. It also enables the Beijing process to keep abreast of, and address, emerging issues. Its main weakness is that it is not legally binding and depends on goodwill for its implementation.

THE SADC DECLARATION ON GENDER AND DEVELOPMENT

The SADC Declaration was adopted in 1997 in Blantyre, Malawi, as part of the follow up of the Beijing and Dakar processes. This declaration commits countries to:

- Reach the target, of at least 30 per cent, of women in political and decision-making structures by 2005.
- Promote women's full access to, and control over, productive resources in order to reduce the level of poverty among women.
- Repeal all laws, amend Constitutions and change social practices that still subject women to discrimination.
- Take urgent measures to prevent, and deal with, the increasing levels of violence against women.

Figure 2.3
Nineteen countries that hadn't submitted a single report by May 2003

Botswana	Central African	Comoros	Côte d'Ivoire
Djibouti	Republic	Ethiopia	Eritrea
Gabon	Equatorial	Kenya	Liberia
Madagascar	Guinea	Niger	São Tomé &
Sierra Leone	Guinea Bissau	Zambia	Príncipe
	Malawi		
	Somalia		

The Addendum to the Declaration on the Prevention and Eradication of Violence against Women and Children was adopted in Mauritius, in 1998, in response to growing concerns over the increase in violence and the inadequacy of existing preventative measures.

There is a process to transform the GAD Declaration and its addendum on Violence Against Women (VAW) into a fully-fledged binding protocol. The draft SADC protocol contains a road map to overcome sex inequality. It is a result of a process that started in 2005, with the audit of the SADC Declaration on Gender and Development and its addendum on VAW. It addresses a range of issues that affect women in the SADC region, including constitutional and legal rights, governance, education, gender-based violence (GBV), health, HIV and AIDS, peace building and conflict resolution. The draft protocol also requires SADC member states to have constitutions that protect gender inequality and ensure that customary laws adhere to the constitution by 2015.

Strengths and Weaknesses

On the upside, the GAD Declaration and its addendum on violence against women and children are homegrown sub-regional commitments. Commitments like the 30 per cent target for women in decision-making areas benefit from stronger peer pressure when made at the regional level. In addition, the existing sub-regional institutions and mechanisms, such as regular policy organisation meetings, can monitor their implementation. Unfortunately, like the Beijing process they are not legally binding. Until the GAD Declaration is turned into a binding protocol, little can be done to enforce its effective implementation.

HOW DOES THE AFRICAN WOMEN'S PROTOCOL IMPROVE EXISTING FRAMEWORK?

The African Women's Protocol fortifies the framework for the promotion and protection of women's rights in a number of significant ways. It addresses areas that neither the CEDAW nor the African Charter on Human and Peoples' Rights addressed, such as VAW, HIV/AIDS, health and reproductive rights, as well as the exclusion of rape, sexual slavery and other sexual violence in crimes against humanity. It also protects the rights of vulnerable women, such as widows, the elderly, the distressed and nursing women, by providing remedies for women whose rights have been violated.

While the CEDAW's effectiveness was undermined in some quarters because it was considered to be a Western women's instrument, the African Women's Protocol is a homegrown instrument developed by Africans for African women. On the other hand, while the ACHPR went overboard in its wholesale embrace of African tradition, values and customs without acknowledging that some of these customs and traditions discriminate against and harm women, the African Women's Protocol outlaws traditions such as FGM, widow inheritance and child marriages.

Furthermore, Article 17 empowers African women by giving them the right to live in a positive cultural context and to enhance participation in the determination of cultural policies. This provision provides African women with a tool to address one of the biggest challenges for efforts to implement the CEDAW, and the Beijing Declaration and Platform for

Action, the co-existence of multiple legal systems with customary and religious law governing personal life and prevailing over positive law and even the constitutional guarantees.

Unlike the Beijing Declaration and Platform for Action and the SADC Declaration and its Addendum on the Prevention and Eradication of violence against women and Children, the African Women's Protocol is legally binding. It reinforces the CEDAW in a number of areas, such as trafficking of women, and addressing inequalities in marriage with respect to decision-making, property and children. By calling for equal representation in decision-making and political life, it further reinforces the CEDAW and improves on the 30 per cent target of the Beijing process and the GAD Declaration. Through its specific mention on budgetary allocations, for areas such as VAW, it can serve as a tool for promoting action by bridging the gap between law and policy on the one hand, and practice and reality on the other.

The African Women's Protocol seeks to strengthen the legal and policy framework of countries, help promote action and bridge the gap between law and policy on the one hand, and practice and reality on the other. It can act as a shield against retrogression, protecting the gains made by women from threats, such as hostile policies and negative change. Women and NGOs can also make use of the right to submit individual or group complaints to the African Commission on Human and Peoples' Rights, and to the African Court on Human and Peoples' Rights when it becomes operational. However, individuals and other non-State actors do not have direct access to these mechanisms except in rare cases like Namibia where international instruments, once ratified, are self-executing.

3

Implications of the Protocol[1]

INTRODUCTION

THIS SECTION LOOKS at the implications of the African Women's Protocol in Mozambique, South Africa and Zambia in the three thematic areas of governance, VAW and health and reproductive rights. It highlights the relevant provisions, briefly examines the prevailing situation of women in these countries and identifies the ways in which the African Women's Protocol could help improve it.

In governance, it focuses on the participation of women in politics, with particular attention being paid to areas where participation has lagged behind and the challenges that the implementation of women's participation faces in these areas including the need to go beyond women being seen as just numbers.

In the area of VAW, this section concentrates on rape, defilement, VAW, trafficking of women and children and harmful traditional practices. With regard to health and reproductive rights, the section focuses on maternal mortality, HIV and AIDS and abortion.[2]

Governance

What the African Women's Protocol Says:

Article 9: Right to Participation in the Political and Decision-Making Process

1. State parties shall take specific positive action to promote participative governance and the equal participation of women in the political life of their countries through affirmative action, enabling national legislation and other measures to ensure that:

   a) Women participate without any discrimination in all elections.

   b) Women are represented equally at all levels with men in all electoral processes.

   c) Women are equal partners with men at all levels of development and implementation of state policies and development programmes.

2. State parties shall ensure increased and effective representation and participation of women at all levels of decision-making.

The Situation

In all three countries, an effort has been made to improve the participation of women particularly in the higher echelons of decision-making. Both Mozambique and South Africa have surpassed the 30 per cent minimum requirement of the SADC GAD Declaration with regard to representation in parliament. Figure 3.1 shows the situation as of early 2005, with respect to the percentage of women's participation at the various levels.

Figure 3.1
The 2005 situation with respect to the percentage of women's participation

COUNTRY	MPS	CABINET	DEPUTY MINISTERS	LOCAL GOVERN-MENT[3]
ZAMBIA	12 per cent	25 per cent	9.8 per cent	7 per cent
SOUTH AFRICA	32.75 per cent	42.8 per cent	47.6 per cent	23 per cent
MOZA-MBIQUE	37.6 per cent	29 per cent	-	13.2 per cent

Ironically, women have found it difficult to break into the governance structures at local government level. Following the 2001 local government elections in Zambia, men made up 93 per cent of elected councillors, 90 per cent of the elected mayors and 100 per cent of the town clerks. This is unfortunate because representation at this level is crucial for service delivery. It is often at this level where decisions crucial to the day-to-day lives of rural women, such as the location of boreholes and health centres, are made and implemented. In both Mozambique and Zambia, where community courts administer customary law, the importance of representation of women at these levels takes on a new and critical significance.

However, as of 2006, the above scenario seems to have changed in Zambia and Mozambique. During the 2001 tripartite elections two women joined the race for republican president out of 11 presidential candidates but performed very badly in all parts of the country; however, the precedent was set for women to contest the presidency. In the 1996 presidential and parliamentary elections, 59 women were adopted by various political parties as candidates out of which only 13 were elected to parliament. On the other hand, 106 women were adopted by various political parties to stand as parliamentary candidates in the 2006 presidential and parliamentary elections. Of the 106 women adopted only 22 were elected as members of parliament. This represents an increase of nine percentage points in the number of women elected in parliament.

At the level of Cabinet, there were a total of 20 Ministers out of which six were females, which represented 25 per cent prior to the September

2006 presidential, parliamentary and local government elections. As of 30 October 2006, out of 24 members of Cabinet only five were women, indicating 20.8 per cent women representation. This shows a reduction from the previous Cabinet, which stood at 25 per cent. At deputy minister level, current statistics show that only 10 per cent were women while at provincial minster level all were males.

In the civil service, female representation is similar to that observed in the political arena. At permanent secretary level, female representation stands at 19 per cent. At director level, women only account for 23 per cent, while at deputy director level and equivalent female representation is 43.66 per cent. Female representation at assistant director level is 20.91 per cent.

The number of female parliamentarians in the Assembleia da República (3.7.6 per cent) and the number of female ministers (29 per cent) is very encouraging and paves the way to lobby for more reforms.

Implications

Legal and Policy Framework

In Article 9.1, state parties commit themselves to take specific positive action to ensure equal participation of women in the political life of their countries through affirmative action. The African Women's Protocol could be used to strengthen the regulatory framework for women's participation. In all three countries, there are no institutionalised quotas to promote the participation of women. South Africa's ruling party, the ANC, currently has a self-imposed quota of 30 per cent. This has contributed immensely to the increased participation of women in politics. Unfortunately, it depends on the goodwill of the ruling party and does not bind other political parties. Neither the Constitution nor the Electoral Act specifies a quota for women in parliament or cabinet. This raises sustainability concerns. The Women's Protocol could be used to institutionalise a binding quota system that would apply to all political parties. It could strengthen the campaign to lobby political parties to improve their representation of women and to ensure their manifestos speak to women's needs and interests.

In Mozambique, women are well represented in Parliament and Cabinet. This is, in part, a result of the fact that the ruling party, Mozambique Liberation Front (FRELIMO), came from a socialist ideological background that encouraged women's participation. As in the case of South Africa, this positive situation depends on the goodwill of the ruling party. It is therefore, important for gender activists to strike while the iron is still hot and crystallise this goodwill while it lasts.

Zambia currently does not have a quota system to promote the representation of women in decision-making. Submissions to the Constitution Review Commission and the Electoral Reforms Technical Committee (ERTC) include the introduction of a quota system. The African Women's Protocol could be a useful advocacy tool for women activists in their efforts to ensure that the proposal is adopted. The Protocol could also be used to lobby for more women friendly electoral processes and practices.

The African Women's Protocol could also be applied by women's rights advocates to push for change in areas that are vital for the realisation of women's rights where women's representation has lagged behind. This can be capitalised on during any forthcoming elections. In addition to local government, other areas that need to be addressed include public service, the judiciary, the armed forces and the private sector. In South Africa, the civil society initiated and driven 50/50 campaign seeks to implement a 50 per cent representation of women in all three spheres of government. Making use of the African Women's Protocol as an advocacy tool could strengthen this. It could also help women to push governments to address some of the challenges women's participation faces.

Challenges

In all three countries, a number of factors continue to discourage and prevent women from actively participating in public life. These include gender biased cultural beliefs, myths, negative traditional practices and stereotyping, problems with balancing women's multiple roles and the conflict between work, domestic and community responsibilities. The situation is aggravated by the fact that the structures and electoral processes of most political parties do not support the effective participation of women. In Zambia and Mozambique, high levels of female illiteracy (currently above 42 per cent in Zambia and 68 per cent in Mozambique), poor resource bases in terms of financial resources, information and tangible assets, and poor media coverage of women role models in power and decision-making areas were identified as additional barriers.

At the level of local government, the combination of the electoral system, the perception of inept female councillors, and the hostile and negative environment towards women, discouraged women in all three countries from increased participation in politics. It would be worthwhile to explore how the electoral laws could be amended to encourage the participation of women.

Beyond the Numbers

In Article 9.2, state parties commit themselves to ensure increased effective representation and participation. In countries that have attained high levels of representation, like South Africa and Mozambique, the need to go beyond the numbers and the 'politics of presence' was emphasised. It is true that irrespective of any other considerations, women should participate on an equal footing with men at all levels of decision-making because it is the just and the right thing to do. This notwithstanding, it is not unreasonable to expect women in these positions to make a positive difference in the struggle for gender equality and women's rights. There is a sense of frustration regarding this because in many cases this is not happening.

While it is widely accepted that the mere presence of women does make a positive difference, and can even result in some practical changes in how business is done, merely increasing the number of women in the different spheres of government will not necessarily translate into women benefiting from policies and programmes.

As one South African interviewed remarked about the link between women's representation and effective delivery for women constituents, "People are asking questions about gender impact at two levels: one level is the numbers issue in the representation of women. The second level is the bigger, harder question – how do you actually transform the conditions of unemployment and poverty, how are you going to transform lives?" (Holland Muter, 2005). Hon. Bwambale, the then chairperson of the Pan African Parliament (PAP) Committee on Gender and Disability agrees.[4] She says, "There are too many women who occupy positions but do nothing to improve the situation of women". Women in decision-making levels must stress the importance of efforts to improve the situation of women.

The challenge is to make sure that the women who have been appointed take gender issues seriously and actually take action to mainstream gender equality in the sectors they head. Two areas that merit further research is how women in decision-making positions at all levels can be made more responsive and more effective in promoting gender equality and supporting other women, and how they can contribute to the promotion and protection of women's rights without compromising their party or other loyalties.

Violence against Women
What the Protocol Says:

Article 1: Definitions

'Violence against women' means all acts perpetrated against women which cause or could cause them physical, sexual, psychological and economic harm, including the threat to take such acts; or to undertake the imposition of arbitrary restrictions on or deprivation of fundamental freedoms in private or public life in peace time or during situations of armed conflict or of war.

Article 4: The Right to Life, Integrity and Security of the Person

1. Every woman shall be entitled to respect for her life and the integrity and security of her person. All forms of exploitation, cruel, inhuman or degrading punishment and treatment shall be prohibited.

2. State parties shall take appropriate and effective measures to:

   a) Enact and enforce laws to prohibit all forms of violence against women including unwanted or forced sex [regardless of] whether the violence takes place in private or public;

   b) Adopt such other legislative, administrative, social and economic measures as may be necessary to ensure the prevention, punishment and eradication of all forms of violence against women;

   c) Identify the cause and consequences of violence against women and take appropriate measures to prevent and eliminate such violence;

   d) Actively promote peace education through curricula and social communication in order to eradicate elements in traditional and cultural beliefs, practices and stereotypes which legitimise and exacerbate the persistence and tolerance of violence against women;

   e) Punish the perpetrators of violence against women and implement programmes for the rehabilitation of women victims;

f) Establish mechanisms and accessible services for effective information, rehabilitation and reparation for victims of violence against women;

g) Prevent and condemn trafficking of women, prosecute perpetrators of such trafficking and protect those women most at risk;

h) Prohibit all medical or scientific experiments on women without their informed consent;

i) Provide adequate budgetary and other resources for the implementation and monitoring of actions aimed at preventing and eradicating violence against women;

j) Ensure that, in those countries where the death penalty still exists, not to carry out death sentences on pregnant or nursing women;

k) Ensure that women and men enjoy equal rights in terms of access to refugee status, determination procedures and that women refugees are accorded the full protection and benefits guaranteed under international refugee law, including their own identity and other documents.

Article 5: Elimination of Harmful Practices

State parties shall prohibit and condemn all forms of harmful practices, which negatively affect the human rights of women, and which are contrary to recognised international standards.

State parties shall take all necessary legislative and other measures to eliminate such practices, including:

a) The creation of public awareness in all sectors of society regarding harmful practices through information, formal and informal education and outreach programmes;

b) Prohibition, through legislative measures backed by sanctions, of all forms of FGM, scarification, medicalisation and para-medicalisation of FGM and all other practices in order to eradicate them.

Figure 3.2

A panoramic view of level of compliance of selected articles

Degree of Compliance	Zambia	South Africa	Mozambique
Art. 4.2(a): Enact, enforce laws to prohibit violence, private and public	Low. No specific laws. Penal Code applicable.	High compliance, Domestic Violence Act 1998.	Low. No specific laws. Penal Code applicable.
Art. 4.2(b): Adopt laws, administrative & other measures to prevent, punish and eradicate violence	Victim support unit & sex crimes units in police.	46 family violence, child protection and sexual offences units.	Gender unit in Police.
Art. 4.2(i): Adequate budgets	Poor.	Poor.	Poor.
Art. 4.2(e): Punish perpetuators	Low, reporting & low conviction rates.	High reporting, fair conviction rates.	Low, reporting & low conviction rates.
Art. 4.2(e), 4.2 (f): Victim reparation and rehabilitation	Low. No reparation, rehab mainly by civil society.	Low. No reparation, rehab mainly by civil society.	Low. No reparation, rehab mainly by civil society.
Art. 4.2(d): Active promotion of peace education	Poor.	Poor.	Poor.

Degree of Compliance	Zambia	South Africa	Mozambique
Art. 4.2(g): Trafficking: Prevention, prosecution of perpetrators, protection of victims	Legislation in place.	No specific legislation.	No specific legislation.
Art. 5: Harmful Traditional Practices: prohibition backed by sanctions, public awareness	No specific laws or policies.	Has Traditional Leaders Act.	No specific laws or policies.

Rape, Defilement and Domestic Violence

In all three countries, women and children continue to suffer the scourges of rape, defilement and domestic violence despite efforts made to address violence against women. South Africa has one of the highest incidences of VAW worldwide. The government has recognised it as a priority issue. The country has made extensive progress with respect to the development of laws, policies and plans, as well as the creation of institutional mechanisms, in areas of domestic violence, rape and sexual harassment. The Domestic Violence Act goes as far as outlawing marital rape, a step few countries have ventured to take. The NGOs in this sector are probably the most highly organised in civil society.

Mozambique and Zambia do not have specific legislation dealing with VAW. However, both countries have Bills related to domestic violence (DV) in place. Women's rights NGOs are advocating for the enactment of DV Acts. In Zambia, the penal code is the law applicable to cases of rape, assault and DV. There is no remedy for victims and implementation remains weak. A Bill on Gender Violence and Sexual Offences is in the offing. In Zambia, special units have been formed in the police services such as the Sex Crimes Unit and the Victim Support Unit. NGOs have established drop-in centres and shelters for battered women and children. They also provide counselling services to both victims and perpetrators of violence. The provisions of the African Women's Protocol could be used to strengthen the Zambian legal and policy framework in the context of the ongoing law reform process. Despite the absence of reliable statistics in Mozambique, studies undertaken show that VAW is a serious problem in all parts of the country. A Gender Unit was established to deal with violence against women and children, train police officers in the investigation of crimes against women and girls and promote gender mainstreaming. In addition, in some police stations, there are special units to deal with women and children victims of abuse that provide support to the victims.

In Zambia, rape and defilement are on the increase. In 2004, only 27.6 per cent of defilement cases and 37.5 per cent of rape cases reported resulted in convictions. A serious flaw in the system allows the parents of some victims to opt for compensation at the expense of punishing perpetrators. Rape and defilement often take place at the very hands of those in whose care the children have been entrusted. In South Africa, 33 per cent of rape victims under 15 years of age say that the perpetrators were their schoolteachers. The advent of AIDS has introduced a new and deadly dimension to this gross injustice against the girl child.

Challenges

In Zambia, a number of factors that exacerbate VAW have been identified. These include their low socio-economic status, the strength or patriarchal and societal attitudes, cultural beliefs and practices like initiation ceremonies and payment of bride price.

The main mechanisms for enforcement of sanctions for VAW are: courts, traditional structures (chiefs), the Director of Public Prosecutions, prisons and the police. A number of challenges adversely affect the rights of women during their attempts to seek redress. These include:

- Lack of privacy and confidentiality in court proceedings, which discourages victims of violence from going to court. This is compounded by the prohibitive costs of litigation.
- Limited sentencing power among magistrates who handle the bulk of these cases. The maximum sentences that a class I magistrate can impose for rape is seven years. In most cases, the convicts receive lesser sentences. Consequently, this has not deterred perpetrators of these crimes.
- Gender insensitive magistrates and court environments.
- Lack of compliance on the procedures set out in the Juveniles Act. Juveniles' rights to be heard on camera, to bail, to be represented by a guardian, juvenile inspector or legal counsel throughout the proceedings and to be incarcerated in an exclusively juvenile institution, are frequently disregarded.

In Mozambique, efforts by women's rights organisations at addressing VAW have given visibility to the issue. Difficulties encountered by women in their attempts to seek justice include:

- Poor coordination within the criminal justice system and with women's rights NGOs.
- Low socio-economic status of women.
- Long distances to access the justice system.
- The strength of patriarchal and societal attitudes.
- Cultural beliefs and practices, like initiation ceremonies and payment of bride price.
- Fragmented service provision between the justice and health sectors.
- And inadequate support services (i.e. lack of trained gender sensitive personnel; attitude of those responsible for enforcing the

legislation often leaves a lot to be desired; lack of understanding of gender violence dynamics and sometimes they themselves are perpetuators of domestic violence, making it difficult for them to provide support.

- Traditional beliefs, attitudes, stereotypes and myths that justify or blame women for violence against them.

In South Africa, women continue to be victims of violence and to suffer secondary victimisation at the hand of the law enforcement and administration of justice sectors. In the areas of domestic violence, barriers encountered include:

- Fragmented service provision within the criminal justice system; fragmented service provision between the justice and health sectors.
- Inadequate support services i.e. the lack of trained gender sensitive personnel is a major impediment. The attitude of those responsible for enforcing the legislation often leaves a lot to be desired. Many times, they simply do not understand the dynamics of gender violence. They frequently share the negative traditional beliefs, attitudes, stereotypes and myths that justify or blame women for violence against them. At times, they themselves are perpetuators of domestic violence, making it difficult for them to be honest brokers for justice. Unfortunately, efforts to address these deep-seated attitudes through training have not been effective as the courses are too short and they are given in piece-meal fashion.

Resource Constraints

Notwithstanding the fact that South Africa is comparatively richer than Zambia and Mozambique, resource constraints adversely affect efforts to enforce the Domestic Violence Act and programmes addressing rape and sexual assault. With respect to domestic violence, the Department of Social Development was only able to provide support to less than half of the shelters run by NGOs. The demand for services far exceeds supply. Battered women are only allowed to stay in a shelter for a three-month period – a period that is shorter than the time it takes for courts to hear their cases.

In Zambia, civil society organisations have been at the forefront of the struggle against VAW. The Young Women's Christian Association (YWCA), churches and religious organisations have provided support services, such as shelters and areas of safety for battered women, in Zambia. Since these cannot effectively cater for all the women in need, government needs to play a greater role in supporting organisations that protect women from violence. Sadly, the situation is no better in Mozambique. In light of the fact that the lack of resources is a serious obstacle to the implementation of South Africa's legislation and policy framework and guidelines for VAW, Article 4(j) of the African Women's Protocol, which obligates state parties to provide adequate budgetary and other resources for implementation was warmly welcomed.

Trafficking of Women and Children

Implications

Trafficking of women (and children) is an area that is severely under-reported and under researched. In all three countries, there are no specific laws to address this problem. Information is limited and more research is needed. In South Africa, trafficking is currently dealt with under the Sexual Offences Bill (approved by parliament but not yet law as of September 2007). It is clear that the absence of specific legislation on trafficking undermines efforts to protect women and child victims of trafficking and dents efforts to arrest and prosecute offenders. The need to strengthen South Africa's legislation in this area was highlighted by the CEDAW Committee in its concluding comments on South Africa's report in 1998. In Zambia, it is hoped that the ongoing law reform process will result in a legislation dealing with the trafficking of women and children. The Protocol could be a useful tool in strengthening the legal and policy framework in this respect.

In South Africa, a recent stakeholder's conference revealed that trafficking was more pervasive than previously thought. The country is both a transit and destination point for trafficking women. Intra-country trafficking of women takes place, mostly from rural to urban areas. Issues that still need further research include the extent to which South Africa is a source of trafficked women, the actual extent to which women are trafficked into and through South Africa, and for what purposes.

In Mozambique, a study carried out by IOM in 2002–2003 revealed that victims were mostly between the age of 14 and 24, and many of them ended up in Johannesburg. They were employed as domestic or sex workers and were paid about R500 a month. The victims were tortured at the borders of Komati Port and Ponta de Ouro. After a night in a transit hotel, they were "raped as a form of initiation to the sex work that awaited them". In Johannesburg, some were sold to brothels for R1000; some were turned into private slaves, while mine workers bought other as wives for the going price of R800. OIM estimates that through this exploitation, traffickers gained about an annual amount of a R1 000 000 for every 1000 victims that were trafficked (Government of Mozambique, 2005: 19).

Article 4.2(g) of the African Women's Protocol calls on states to take appropriate and effective measures to prevent and condemn the trafficking of women, prosecute perpetrators and protect women at risk. If properly used by gender activists, it could help highlight the plight of victims, enhance legal and other protection for women and children and contribute positively to efforts to bring the perpetrators to book.

Harmful Traditional Practices

The following traditional practices were identified as harmful: FGM, virginity testing, dry sex, abduction or forced marriage, ukungena (taking over a widow by a male relative without her consent), burning and the victimisation of women considered to be "witches". In addition to these, Zambia identified the payment of lobola and certain initiation ceremonies as practices that can be harmful to women. South Africa identified the practice of virginity testing.

There is a debate as to whether FGM is currently practised in South Africa. It has been argued that it may be present as a result of increasing immigration to South Africa of people from communities who practice it. At the same time, with changing approaches to Islam, the practise might be present in some sections of the Muslim community. Considering this uncertainty, the Department of Health has been called upon to conduct research to establish the prevalence of FGM in South Africa.

'Virginity testing' to determine whether a girl has lost her virginity is still performed in some provinces, including the Eastern Cape and Limpopo. It has recently been revived in KwaZulu-Natal (KZN). In the current context of HIV/AIDS, this practice has taken on new proportions. It is popularly seen as means to 'protect' young girls from potential HIV infection. However, in light of the 'virgin myth' (the belief that having sex with a virgin will cure you of HIV/AIDS), the practice might actually place young girls who are 'proven' virgins at an increased risk of sexual violence or exploitation, and possible infection. Furthermore, women's and human rights organisations have argued that the practice denies young girls their right to autonomy and dignity especially given that no similar practices promote the virginity of young boys.

'Dry sex' is a common practice in South Africa and Zambia. It entails applying astringents or douches to the vagina prior to sex to make it dry, in order to, reportedly, increase male sexual pleasure. Some of the substances used are harmful to the vaginal mucosa and cause ulceration. Apart from making sexual relations painful for women, it has been associated with higher HIV and other STI transmission rates as it is more likely to result in vaginal abrasions during sexual intercourse.

Article 5 on the elimination of harmful practices could be used to improve South Africa's laws, policies and treatment of harmful traditional practices. The Constitution protects women from violence and harm and protects their rights to life, dignity and health. However, no detailed policies exist on specific harmful practices such as FGM, virginity testing, dry sex, abduction or forced marriage, ukungena, or the burning and victimising of women who are branded 'witches'.

In dealing with harmful traditional practices, it will be important to define and build a consensus on what constitutes harmful traditional practices. While it is relatively clear-cut in some areas, there are practices, such as lobola, virginity testing and some initiation rites where there is no clear-cut consensus. More research needs to be done and a consensus has to be built on the circumstances under which some traditional practices become harmful and a strategy need to be established regarding how women can be protected.

Article 4.2(d) calls on states to actively promote peace education and to raise issues of how culture and tradition, gender stereotypes promote and condone VAW. This constitutes an advance on the legal and policy framework of all three countries.

Health and Reproductive Rights
What the Protocol Says:

Article 14: Health and Reproductive Rights

1. State parties shall ensure that the right to health of women, including sexual and reproductive health, is respected and promoted. This includes:

   a) The right to control their fertility;

   b) The right to decide whether to have children, the number of children and the spacing of children;

   c) The right to choose any method of contraception;

   d) The right to self protection and to be protected against STIs, including HIV/AIDS;

   e) The right to be informed on one's health status and the health of one's partner, particularly if infected with STIs, including HIV/AIDS, in accordance with internationally recognised standards and best practices;

   f) The right to have family planning education.

2. State parties shall take all appropriate measures to:

   a) Provide adequate, affordable and accessible health services, including information, education and communication programmes to women especially those in rural areas.

   b) Establish and strengthen existing pre-natal, delivery and post-natal health and nutritional services for women during pregnancy and while they are breastfeeding.

   c) Protect the reproductive rights of women by authorising medical abortion in cases of sexual assault, rape, incest, and where the continued pregnancy endangers the mental and physical health of the mother or the life of the mother or the foetus.

Introduction

One of the greatest benefits that women can derive from the African Women's Protocol in the area of health and reproductive rights is that it provides a tool to enable them to adopt a rights-based approach to addressing some of the social injustices at the root of their plight. Although the situation with respect to the other thematic areas remains unsatisfactory, there is greater recognition of the human rights dimension. In the area of health and reproductive rights, the welfare approach remains dominant. Even in South Africa, where sexual and reproductive rights are legally covered, one observes major contradictions.

On the one hand, there is positive legislative and policy framework in the field of sexual and reproductive rights. On the other, women often battle to exercise these rights within the family, the community and in relation to the government. Traditional gender norms and practices, along with the unequal status of women, reduce women to a position where they are regarded as primarily responsible for contraception and childcare, and have little power to negotiating when, with whom and why to have sex.

Figure 3.3

Maternal mortality: Immediate causes and underlying factors

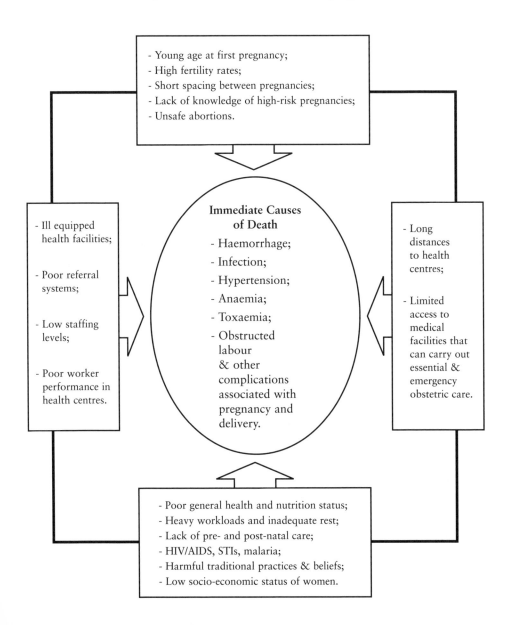

Nowhere are the consequences of the welfare approach to women's rights more tragic than in the area of maternal mortality. In Mozambique, the figures are uncertain but estimates range between 500 and 1500 deaths per 100 000 births. In Zambia, the figures are on the increase. The maternal morality rate shot up from 649 per 100 000 live births in 2001 to 729 death per 100 000 in 2003. In South Africa, the figures are comparatively low at 150 deaths per 100 000 live births because of the country's superior infrastructure and health service system. However, a breakdown of this figure by race reveals that maternal mortality, for the most part, has a black face. African women account for 92 per cent of maternal deaths, mostly occurring during the postpartum period. In all three countries, the risk of maternal mortality is highest in rural areas. The tragedy is, that many of the factors that cause or exacerbate these unacceptably high maternal mortality rates are easily preventable. (Figure 3.3 illustrates the immediate causes and underlying factors of maternal morality.)

In many cases, a post-mortem would probably indicate hemorrhage, infection, hypertension, anaemia, toxemia, hypertension, obstructed labour or complications associated with pregnancy and delivery as the cause of death. In reality, many women die because of underlying factors such as poverty, ignorance and discrimination.

Articles 14.2(a) and 14.2(b) commit member states to provide adequate, affordable and accessible health services, including information, education, and communication programmes to women especially, in rural areas, and to establish and strengthen existing pre-natal delivery and post-natal health and nutritional services for women. Adopting a rights-based, instead of a welfare, approach might help save the lives of countless, nameless, faceless women who quietly become maternal mortality statistics on an annual basis.

HIV and AIDS

The HIV and AIDS pandemic is a major challenge in all three countries. Gender inequality is a key factor in the spread of AIDS. Women bear the brunt of the HIV and AIDS pandemic – in terms of levels of infection, as well as shouldering the burden of care of those living with HIV and AIDS. Women and girls are more vulnerable to HIV transmission than men and boys. In addition to biological reasons, social, cultural and economic inequalities create conditions whereby the HIV prevalence rate is higher for women and girls than it is for men.

The vulnerability of women is heightened by the fact the policies for the prevention of HIV and AIDS do not take into account the unequal power relationship between men and women. The emphasis is usually on lifestyle changes and, because of this, the high levels of sexual coercion and rape or the difficulties of negotiating condom use for women whose partners have multiple sexual partners or for young girls whose partners are older men are disregarded. The introduction of home-based care services for HIV and AIDS cases without an adequate support system has shifted the burden from hospitals to women who, as the primary caregivers in the home, now have an increased workload as they spend additional time and energy taking care of the chronically ill.

In Zambia, the national HIV prevalence rates among adults (15–49) have been estimated at 17 per cent with infection rates being substantially higher among women. The HIV prevalence among pregnant women ranges between ten per cent in some areas to 30 per cent in others. Younger women 25–34 years are at much higher risk of HIV infection than men in the same age group. The prevalence rates are 12.7 per cent in young women compared to 3.8 per cent in young men (UNAIDS, 2006). Some traditional and cultural practices place women at a higher risk of contracting HIV/AIDS and/or STIs. These include the practice of 'dry sex', sexual cleansing and polygamy. In addition to this, women have limited control over their sex lives and are taught from early childhood to be obedient and submissive to their husbands. There is an urgent need to re-examine the impact that traditions such as circumcision, initiation ceremonies and cleansing, are having on the AIDS pandemic.

In both Zambia and Mozambique, there is a need for greater involvement of young people and men in the design, implementation, monitoring and evaluation of reproductive health programmes. Since many adolescents engage in sexual activities at an early age, with limited guidance on sexuality and inadequate information on reproductive health services they are exposed to a greater risk of contracting HIV and other STIs, having unplanned pregnancies and unsafe abortions. The exclusion of men from health programmes, especially reproductive health programmes, undermines its acceptance and effective use by women who believe that the absence of their partner's consent might result in gender violence or divorce. In Mozambique, the HIV/AIDS prevalence rate is an estimated 16.6 per cent of the adult population. The virus infects an estimated 1.14 million people. Rites of initiation, polygamous marriages, rites of passage (cleansing), taboos, traditional medicine, ignorance regarding the ways of prevention and transmission of the disease, lack of power to negotiate safe sex, sexual abuse and poverty are some of the reasons that contribute to the high levels of HIV and AIDS rates.

South Africa's prevalence rate for HIV/AIDS is one of the highest in the world. In 2005, the Human Sciences Research Council study showed that 10.8 per cent of the study population was HIV positive (PEPFAR, 2007).

Article 14.1(d) empowers women with the right to self-protection and to be protected from sexually transmitted infections, including HIV and AIDS, as well as the right to be informed of one's health status and that of one's partner. This is the first time that HIV/AIDS is addressed in a legally binding women's instrument. For all three countries, this is a welcome improvement on national legislation and policy. Article 14(e) stipulates that women have the right to be informed of their health and that of their partner, particularly if they are affected by sexually transmitted infections. This has generated much debate around the difficulties in implementation that the African Women's Protocol will face.

In Zambia, there are no laws that specifically protect women from HIV/AIDS or give them control over their sexuality. Culture and religion discourage contraceptive use and teach women to be submissive towards men. The payment of lobola aggravates the situation. The situation is similar in Mozambique.

South Africa also does not have laws to protect women from HIV infection. The South African government is updating the 2000–2005 HIV/AIDS/STI strategic plan with the National Strategic Plan 2007-2011. The former recognises the vulnerability of women but only mentions women's rights in the context of sex workers and victims of sexual assault. By not mainstreaming the gender dimensions of the AIDS issue, but rather encouraging the women's sector to develop its own policies, it could marginalise gender concerns. Despite limitations, such as the omission of a right to treatment, the African Women's Protocol is a timely advance on the legal and policy framework in the three countries. As in the case of maternal mortality, every effort should be made to ensure that a rights-based approach is adopted in efforts to fight against HIV and AIDS.

Termination of Pregnancy/Abortion

Article 14.2(c) calls upon member states to protect the reproductive rights of women by authorising medical abortions in cases of sexual assault, rape, incest and where the continued pregnancy endangers the mental and physical health of the mother or the life of the mother or the foetus. In South Africa, the Choice of Termination of Pregnancy Act of 1996 makes termination legal up to the 12th week of pregnancy. It is also legal between the 13th and the 20th week under certain conditions, especially upon recommendation of a medical practitioner or midwife, who takes into account factors such as the socio-economic condition of the woman, rape, incest and health risks. Article 14.2(c) is, therefore, more restrictive than South African legislation. On the issue of sexuality, many people have expressed the concern that provisions in this area actually reinforce traditional gender stereotypes and expectations that equate women with reproduction.

On the other hand, the article is an advance on Zambian legislation, which requires a panel of three doctors to agree that the mother's heath is threatened and does not provide for termination even in cases of rape, sexual assault or incest. In Mozambique, women do not have the right to an abortion and the issue is considered a taboo subject. It is likely to be among the major bonds of contention during the debate on the ratification of the Protocol. By September 2007, the law on safe abortion was in parliament for consideration. However, there are concerns in Mozambique as abortion is considered a taboo subject and there was opposition from religious leaders.

PROTECTION FROM RETROGRESSION

There is currently a rise in international and national conservatism and religious fundamentalism that could threaten to undermine the gains made by women over the last few decades. This is reflected in trends like the Bush administration's reduction of support for family planning programmes. There is an emphasis on a return to family values, moral regeneration and abstinence. While the emphasis on moral regeneration is in itself a positive development, every effort should be made to ensure that it does not take place at the expense of women's hard-won gains. The onus must not be put on women to promote family values and prevent HIV and AIDS but must recognise that it is an equal partnership between the genders. The African Women's Protocol could play a positive role in protecting some of the gains women have made and in the process harmonise customary law and statutory law in a manner that benefits women. Women should take full advantage of Article 17, which enshrines the right to live in a positive cultural environment and to participate at all levels in the determinations of cultural policies.

CONCLUSION

The African Women's Protocol can be a useful tool for improving the lot of women in all three countries by strengthening legislative and policy frameworks. In areas where they are adequate, it can help bridge the glaring gap between laws, policies and the actual situation by giving impetus to their implementation. The Protocol is an additional tool that can help ensure the harmonisation of customary and religious law with statutory law, in order to advance the rights of women. As a shield from retrogression, it can help protect the rights of women when changes in national and international policies and actors threaten to revoke hard-won gains. In all the three thematic areas, the Protocol will need to help address a number of challenges if it is to improve the lot of women. These seemingly daunting challenges should be used as starting points for action.

Notes

[1] This section is based on an analysis of the national reports, the country reports for the Beijing +10 and interviews.

[2] The South African context uses the concept of termination of pregnancy, whereas Mozambique and Zambia use abortion. There is a fluid relationship between the concepts of abortion and termination of pregnancy. This article has used the two concepts interchangeably depending on the context.

[3] The figures for South Africa and Zambia for local government refer to councillors. Those for Mozambique refer to district administrators.

[4] Interview with Hon. Bwambale.

4

Awareness about the Protocol[1]

Figure 4.1

Awareness about the African Women's Protocol[2]

		SOUTH AFRICA		
I		Weak	Medium	Strong
N **F** **L**	**Strong**	Media CBOs		MPs working with Protocol
U **E** **N** **C**	**Medium**		Other academicians and NGOs	NGOs and academicans working with Protocol
E	**Weak**		Sectoral ministries	National machinery

AWARENESS

	ZAMBIA		
I N F L U E N C E		Weak	Medium	Strong
	Strong	Media MPs CBOs		
	Medium	Other academicians and NGOs		NGOs working with Protocol
	Weak	Sectoral ministries	National machinery	

AWARENESS

INTRODUCTION

USING A SCALE of one to five, the level of awareness of the African Women's Protocol was assessed among the various actors. One was considered to be the least, while five was the highest. This matrix (Figure 4.1) maps out the levels of awareness of the different actors against their capacity to reach grassroots women as of February 2005. On the whole, the level of awareness about the African Women's Protocol was woefully low. Unfortunately, it was lowest between the two actors that are crucial to its implementation: the media and CBOs. Most CBOs had never heard of it and media coverage of the African Women's Protocol was negligible. In South Africa, not even its ratification managed to catch the news.

The level of awareness was highest among actors (government officials, members of parliament and NGOs) who have actually been involved in the process of its promotion, adoption, and ratification. They were knowledgeable enough, to use it to advance women's rights. The level of awareness was, therefore, higher in South Africa, which has ratified the African Women's Protocol. In Zambia, which had not signed the African Women's Protocol (Zambia has now ratified the Protocol) and where debate had been limited, officials interviewed apart from the line department were largely ignorant of the African Women's Protocol and its content. A limited number of NGOs were sufficiently conversant with the African Women's Protocol to use it to advance women's rights. Under the circumstances, the popularisation of the African Women's

Protocol must remain high on the agenda if it is to be an effective tool for change.

South Africa

Policy Makers

Three of the gender machinery representatives rated themselves with a grade of 5 (high), indicating that they were able to use the African Women's Protocol to promote women's rights. One of the three relevant sector ministry interviewees rated himself a five. The other two knew of its existence but could not speak to its relevance for their particular sectors.

Civil Society Organisations

All seven of the civil society representatives interviewed could use the African Women's Protocol to promote women's rights. However, one of the interviewees rated human rights NGOs and academics as a two (two is at the lower end of the scale). This denotes that she believed that civil society organisations might (at best) know of its existence, but were ignorant of its content. This level of knowledge and awareness decreased to a one (lowest) in reference to CBOs and the media, denoting that she believed that, in general, these organisations had heard of it.

Discussions were held within the country with regards to the African Women's Protocol. These revealed limited participation of NGOs on the formulation and popularisation of the African Women's Protocol. In general, government functionaries, apart from those who participated in the processes of negotiation, signature or ratification, were ignorant of the actual content of the African Women's Protocol. This, however, was not the case with members of parliament who would had participated in discussions of the African Women's Protocol during the parliamentary sessions. However, the members of the Portfolio Committees on Justice and Constitutional Development and Foreign Affairs, and members of the governmental delegation who participated in the actual negotiation process, would have a degree of in-depth knowledge of the African Women's Protocol and its applicability.

Mass Media

All interviewees remarked that the mass media has not covered the Protocol, and none of them had read or heard anything about it via these means. There has been information circulating via emails and email list servers, but on the whole, the South African public in general was ignorant of the African Women's Protocol's existence, never mind its content.

The lack of fanfare or public announcement with regard to the government's decision to ratify the Protocol was a missed opportunity to popularise and promote the existence of the Protocol. However, this is a general difficulty with respect to persuading the mass media of the newsworthiness of issues that pertain to women and gender relations.

Zambia

Policy Makers

The few policy makers interviewed in the course of this research project exhibited serious gaps in their knowledge of the African Women's Protocol. The interviewee from the Gender in Development Division (GIDD) showed the highest level of awareness of the Protocol, since the interviewee was aware of its existence but was unsure of its content. The respondents from the Justice Ministry and the Deputy Minister from the Ministry of Community Development and Social Services exhibited complete ignorance about the African Women's Protocol. The Ministry of Foreign Affairs was not ready to give an interview by the time the report was written.

Civil Society Organisations

The regional civil society organisation, Women and Law in South Africa (WLSA), appeared the most conversant with the African Women's Protocol and could use it to promote women's rights. An independent gender consultant was equally conversant with the Protocol and appeared to have read it. Other civil society organisations appeared completely ignorant of the Protocol.

Mozambique

The fact that the African Women's Protocol was adopted in Maputo did not have any significant effect on the levels of awareness in the Mozambican population. As in the other countries, very few people outside those that have actually been directly involved with the Protocol knew anything about it.

CONCLUSION

In all three countries, awareness about the Africa Protocol was low. Even in South Africa, where the level of awareness was highest, it was high only among people who worked with the Protocol or had been directly involved with its implementation. In Zambia, very few people knew about the Women's Protocol and very few policy makers; civil society organisations and academics were fully conversant with its provisions. This would confirm that one of the major points of any work around the Protocol must be to popularise it and promote its usefulness to government officials, the public, CBOs and civil society in general. The popularisation of the Protocol should therefore remain high on the agenda if it is to be an effective instrument of change.

However, as of September 2007, the level of awareness among the various actors was relatively high. A number of women's rights NGOs were involved in the popularisation and advocacy for the implementation of the African Women's Protocol.

Notes

[1] Awareness as of February 2005.
[2] Influence refers to the capacity of actors to reach grassroots women.

5

Threats and Challenges

Introduction

THIS SECTION IDENTIFIES ten challenges that must be faced in efforts to operationalise the African Women's Protocol. Some of them are rooted in the weaknesses of the Protocol and of international human rights law. Others are endemic of the struggle to protect and promote women's rights.

Gaps, Ambiguities and Weaknesses in the African Women's Protocol Itself

The weaknesses of the African Women's Protocol (as mentioned in Chapter Two) could discourage its use as tool for the advancement of women's rights. It is important to sell it realistically, making it clear what the African Women's Protocol can do and what it cannot do. In South Africa, the perception that it does not offer any significant gains or advances to the current legislative and policy framework in most areas could undermine its use as a tool for advancing women's rights.

General Lack of Awareness about the International Human Rights Regime

There is a general problem with regards to knowledge and use of human rights instruments. In South Africa, the culture of using international agreements, as leverage in support of calls to improve the legislative or policy framework and/or their implementation, is quite weak. To illustrate this, the South African government did not submit its second CEDAW report to the committee, and is currently combining its second and third report. Women's organisations did not protest this, so it would appear that they do not even seem to be monitoring government's compliance. In the same vein, the recommendations from the UN Committee to the South African government were not used as a strategic entry points to build a programme of action. In fact, women's organisations do not even seem to know what these recommendations are. A similar pattern can be found in terms of the International Conference on Population and Development (ICPD) and Beijing processes.

When asked if they would use the African Women's Protocol in domestic cases in their day-to-day practice, advocates who were interviewed in other capacities, such as parliamentarians or representatives of academic institutions, said they probably would not and did not think that other lawyers would[1]. Advocate Madasa, a PAP member pointed out that most lawyers do not know when a country had ratified an international instrument or when it had been entered into force. They would rather rely on national law. This underscores the need for domestication and the use of test cases to help create awareness about instruments like the Protocol in judicial systems.

The Weakening of the Women's Movement in Africa

The regional review of the Beijing +10 for Southern Africa identifies the weakening of the women's movement in Africa over the last decade as one of the challenges in efforts to realise the Beijing Goals (ECA, 2004: 12). In Mozambique, the general strengthening of the women's movement and the re-establishment of the network fighting VAW ranked high among the recommended priority actions. In South Africa, the disintegration of the 'women's movement' has resulted in the lack of a coordinated and cohesive response and challenge to government's performance (calling for accountability to its commitments made to women). The weakening of the women's movement in South Africa has been influenced by a negative funding environment, the dependence on priorities and flavours of the day of donor funding, and a lack of policy and advocacy skills in most women's rights NGOs to promote effective change for women.

The importance of a strong women's movement cannot be over emphasised. When all is said and done, there can be no substitute for the women's movement as the forerunner for the protection of women's rights. The need to build a constituency cannot be ignored as a prerequisite for the success of efforts to get the African Women's Protocol implemented. It will, however, be difficult to build constituency on the back of a weak women's movement. The area of the state of the women's movement in Africa and how to strengthen it in the face of the current global environment is an area that has not received sufficient attention and merits further research.

However, there are new emerging women's rights Civil Society Organisations (CSOs) with emphasis to monitor and evaluate government's commitment on implementing women's human rights instruments in the region. For example, the Africa Gender Monitor is a new regional women's rights NGO with an activist agenda to hold governments accountable to the implementation of women's human rights instruments. The focus on re-invigorating the women's movement in the SADC region was initiated by OSISA, HIVOS and the SADC Parliamentary Forum. A three-day conference was held that developed strategies for re-invigorating the women's movement in October 2006.

Lack of Political Will on the Part of Governments

The lack of political will on the part of governments to move beyond the rhetoric and implement gender policy was cited as a major problem in Zambia and South Africa. It has been raised as a major hurdle in the implementation of the CEDAW and the Beijing process. The problem of political will is closely linked to the state of the women's movement. Political indifference will continue to be a threat until the women's movement can organise itself into a credible constituency.

The Strength of Patriarchy, Tradition, Culture and Religion

Old habits die hard and changing negative cultural aspects is always an uphill task. Yet, this is perhaps the most important level from which to work if one is to transform commitments from paper to reality. There has not been a fundamental change in the mindset of society. Generations of deeply rooted traditional beliefs, knowledge and practices, in relation to women and gender relations remained almost untouched by the constitutions, laws and policies of the countries. Unfortunately, this challenge has, more often than not, been met with gender training or training in specific laws and policies. However, undoing a mindset and transforming approaches takes time, and training programmes are generally under funded and have short durations. Training, in and of itself, is of limited value if the system and 'way of doing business' is not transformed as well.

In all three thematic areas (governance, VAW and health and reproductive rights), negative traditional gender norms and beliefs remain major obstacles. However, culture, religion and tradition are not static and every effort must be made to influence its evolution in a manner that benefits, rather than harms, women.

The Public/Private Dichotomy and the Multiple Systems of Law

The strength of patriarchal structures in society is aggravated by the public/private dichotomy. Although in most areas, the women's place has moved beyond the kitchen, the public sphere is still seen as a place that belongs primarily to men. Women are seen as belonging to the private sphere. Even where gender equality is guaranteed by the Constitution, the Constitution allows exceptions in private law areas, such as customary law, personal law and family law. It is in these areas where many violations of women's rights, such as VAW, take place. In Zambia, Article 11 protects women against discrimination. However, Article 23 (4) negates this guarantee by allowing discrimination in matters of personal law. The Constitution permits discrimination in areas of the law that most affect women amongst which include aspects related respect to marriage, divorce and distributing of property. Customary law, which is unwritten and variable, tends to treat women as minors. The situation is similar in Mozambique where customary law is applied side by side with statutory law, which is based on Portuguese civil law.

The Weakness of Key Institutions

The problem of weak institutions is endemic to the struggle for the promotion of gender equality. It has been observed in regional gender departments and units; national machinery for women's rights; national, regional and community-based NGOs. The marginalised position of NGOs in the political system was identified as one of the barriers in the way of the effective implementation of CEDAW. At the regional level, two institutions that need to be strengthened urgently are the Gender Directorate of the AU and the Office of the Special Rapporteur on the Rights of Women in Africa. These institutions are pivotal to catalysing action and spearheading the process of partnership and alliance building. While the degree of weakness varied in all the countries researched, all the key institutions were identified as too weak when it came to mainstreaming gender issues.

In South Africa, tension and confusion related to roles, responsibilities and loyalties between the different components of the gender machinery, have undercut its effectiveness. The situation has been aggravated by factors such as insufficient budget; lack of (skilled) personnel; low level of authority and legitimacy to effectively promote gender equality and the ineffective use of existing mechanisms to call government to account for its poor performance.

Resources, Resources, Resources

In all the countries examined, weaknesses that resulted from inadequate financial resources, skills and logistics were typical. It should be noted that this is a general problem when it comes to addressing gender issues. In Zambia and in Mozambique, the insufficient budgetary allocation to the implementation of the gender policy was identified as one of the main obstacles gender inequalities must address. The MMAS is the least funded though it is mandated to take care of women, orphans and vulnerable children (OVC) and elderly related issues.

In South Africa, the insufficient budget allocated to the National Gender Machinery (NGM) and to the implementation of polices relating to the key themes under discussion (governance, GBV and sexual and reproductive health rights [SRHR]) was highlighted as a major challenge. It has been influenced by two issues: firstly, the adoption of Growth, Employment and Reconstruction (GEAR), whose underlying principles and values have created severe structural limitations to prioritising government spending that is pro-poor and pro-women. Secondly, the decision to move away from a gender budget (which provided the government with a means to allocate monies in a consciously gender disaggregated manner), to gender-responsive budgeting has undermined the government's ability to ensure that the budget is being spent on women's needs and interests. In addition, the absence of a governmental plan of action, which has integrated gender concerns with clear objectives, programmes, indicators and monitoring mechanisms in an environment of limited resources to respond to multiple interests and needs, has created a condition in which gender can slip off the agenda and subsequently the budget as well (Holland-Muter, 2005: 27).

Weak Partnerships and Alliances

Strong and smart partnerships are essential for the implementation of the African Women's Protocol. Unfortunately, a number of problems constitute serious barriers that stand in the way of its implementation. These include: the alienation of national governments from civil society; the lack of support given to NGOs from government officials; infighting; competition over resources and unclear mandates for different actors responsible for the promotion of gender equality. These are just some of the problems that have been identified as obstacles that must be overcome in order to build a strong, effective women's movement.

Not enough attention has been paid to building cross-sector alliances, nor have solid alliances between CBOs, trade unions, women's NGOs and other social movements been built. The ability to hold government to account on the promotion of gender equality has been further undermined by a weak, fragmented relationship between civil society (especially women's organisations) and NGM.

The challenge is to build partnerships at all levels: between civil society organisations and governments; regional continental organisations and Regional Economic Communities (RECs) and national machineries and sector ministries. There is a need for mechanisms where information can be shared. This will help create synergy and, thus, make efforts at attaining gender equality more effective (Holland-Muter, 2005: 57).

Threats in the National and International Policy Environment

The focus on the war of terrorism means that there will be fewer resources for issues such as gender equality. Globalisation, liberalisation and the information revolution present both opportunities and threats. The privatisation of essential services leaves women in double jeopardy, as cost sharing removes their safety net without enhancing their capacity to compete in a free marketplace. Access to essential drugs for diseases like HIV/AIDS is severely hampered by the intellectual property rights regime, which values the profits of pharmaceutical companies above the rights and well being of human beings.

Furthermore, there is presently a rise in religious fundamentalism and conservatism that could revoke some of the gains achieved by women. The treatment of reproductive rights at the Beijing + 10 Review Conference in New York clearly illustrates this danger and highlights the importance of legally binding instruments as shields guarding against retrogression.

While the information revolution has made communication easier through the Internet and cell phones, it has also facilitated new forms of exploitation. The widening digital divide threatens to further marginalise women who have no access to basic services, let alone computers.

CONCLUSIONS

In many areas, the challenges that threaten to undermine the African Women's Protocol are the very reasons it was initiated, negotiated and adopted in the first place. Though they are difficult to surmount, they help us to identify priority areas. Addressing these areas will enable us to make inroads in the fight for gender equality and women's rights.

Notes

[1] Ms Boogie Khutsoane and Adv. Madasa.

6

Best Practices

POPULARISING INTERNATIONAL INSTRUMENTS

ONE OF THE BEST PRACTICES identified was the Solidarity for African Women's Rights (SOAWR) campaign promoting the ratification of the Protocol. The dramatic increase in the number of ratifications is an indication that the campaign is bearing fruit. The publication and dissemination of a handbook by Akina Wa Afrika entitled, *The Protocol to the African Charter on the Human and Peoples' Rights on the Rights of Women in Africa: A Review of the Protocol and Its Relevance to Women in Uganda*, was another beneficial practice identified. The two best practices identified by the experience that Women Law and Development in Africa (WILDAF) have had with the CEDAW were the simplification and translation of the instrument into local languages and the use of popular drama to raise awareness among magistrates. After women who WILDAF had educated on women's rights had their claims thrown out of court by gender insensitive magistrates, WILDAF organised and invited magistrates to a satire depicting the injustices that women suffered at the hands of the judiciary. The impact on the magistrates who saw themselves depicted in this light was overwhelming.[1]

CREATION OF AN ENABLING LEGAL POLICY AND INSTITUTIONAL FRAMEWORK

South Africa

The victory of women's organisations in lobbying to ensure the inclusion of non-sexism in the founding principles of the Constitution; the Bill of

Rights, especially the Equality Clause and the fact that the Constitution takes precedence if there is a conflict between customary law and the Constitution, is well worth emulating. In addition, the Constitution promotes freedom from violence occurring in public and private sources and the right to health services, including reproductive health services.

Progressive laws and policies adopted which promote women's autonomy in the areas of governance, GBV and SRHR, include the:

- National Policy Health Act, No. 116 of 1990.
- Labour Relations Act, No. 66 of 1995.
- Choice on Termination of Pregnancy Act, No. 92 0f 1996.
- The South African Schools Act, No. 84 of 1996.
- The Employment Equity Act of 1997.
- Domestic Violence Act, No. 116 of 1998.
- Recognition of Customary Marriages Act, No. 120 of 1998.
- Electoral Act, No. 73 of 1998.
- The Promotion of Equality and Prevention of Unfair Discrimination Act, No. 4 of 2000.
- The Employment of Educators Act, No. 53 of 1998, amended in 2000.

Cabinet has adopted the National Policy Framework for Women's Empowerment and Gender Equality, and a considerable number of government departments have developed gender policies, addressing the gender concerns of their particular sector.

Mozambique

Progressive laws and policies adopted that promote women's autonomy in the areas of governance, GBV and SRHR, include the:

- Land Law: the land law allows women to own land.
- The Family Law: Prior to December 2003, Mozambique had four official systems of marriage: customary, religious, civil and mutual consent union/cohabitation. By the time of Mozambique's independence in 1975, the Portuguese had established common laws that had little regard for local customs, as the majority of Mozambicans regulate their lives along customary practices. Both legal systems contained legislation and practices that disadvantage women. The new Family Law, which was introduced in 2003, has

made progress in reconciling the two sets of laws, introducing legislation that will protect women from discrimination. The new Law guarantees Mozambican women a broad range of rights which were previously non-existent. The minimum age for marriage has been raised to 18 years for both men and women. Prior to the legal reforms in December 2003, the minimum age for marriage was 14 years for females and 16 years for males. The new law allows women to inherit property in the case of divorce and legally recognises traditional marriages, which constitute the majority of marriages in Mozambique (Oxfam America, 2006: 1).

Test Cases Using International Instruments

Tanzania, Ephrohim Vs. Pastory

Holaria Pastory challenged a Haya customary law that prevented her from selling clan land that she had inherited from her father. Her nephew attempted to have the sale cancelled on the grounds that it was prohibited in terms of the Tanzanian Declaration of Customary Law. The Tanzanian High Court relied on the fact that government had ratified the CEDAW, and other international instruments to confirm that women were constitutionally protected from discrimination, when it ruled that the rules of inheritance in the Tanzanian Declaration of Customary Law were unconstitutional and contravened international conventions that Tanzania had ratified.

Zambia: Longwe Vs. Inter-Continental Hotel

In 1984, Sara Longwe asked a Zambian ombudsman to order a hotel to stop discriminating against women after she was denied entry on the grounds that a male escort did not accompany her. Despite the ruling, the hotel did not change its policy and in 1992 she went to the Zambian High Court arguing that the policy violated her right to freedom from discrimination on the basis of sex as enshrined in the new Constitution, as well as Articles 1, 2, and 3 of CEDAW. The court relied on the Constitution to rule in her favour, but stated that Zambia's ratification of CEDAW meant that courts should look to the Convention when situations that were not covered by domestic law arose (Llana Landsberg-Lewis, 1998).

DEVELOPMENT OF MONITORING AND EVALUATION TOOLS

The Economic Commission for Africa (ECA) has developed an African Gender and Development Index that should be adapted as a monitoring tool for the African Women's Protocol.

GOVERNANCE

At the regional level, the AU's verdict that women commissioners must make up 50 per cent of memberships is a good example of how the organisation is implementing the African Women's Protocol's provisions. It is now in a good position to urge member states to emulate its example at national and regional levels. However, women must build on these improvements.

THE USE OF QUOTAS

In South Africa, the quota system adopted by the ANC to promote women's representation in political and public life has undoubtedly contributed to the high representation of women within national and provincial parliaments, and is a commendable policy. Tanzania has gone even further to institute these quotas in their Constitution. This way gender representation does not depend on the goodwill or programme of the party that wins elections. Meaning that whichever party comes to power, women will be guaranteed minimum representation. The challenge is now to increase this percentage.

VIOLENCE AGAINST WOMEN

In South Africa, specialised Sexual Offences Courts, Family Courts and Equality Courts have been established as one-stop centres that respond to the needs of women and children suffering from domestic violence, rape and sexual assault. Although these are, in effect, too few to meet the demand, are under funded and staffed by personnel who require more training, they are beginning to turn the tide on VAW.

In most countries that have addressed VAW, governments take action in reforming penal codes and other relevant laws and policies but leave the provision of support structures, such as shelters for battered women to NGOs, churches and other sectors of civil society. In Mauritius, however, the government has played an active role in establishing and maintaining support mechanisms.

BUDGETING

In South Africa, the Portfolio Committee on Finance introduced the Women's Budget Process, which aimed at analysing the government's budgets from a gender perspective to ensure that government can be pressured to allocate money to women's empowerment and development schemes. Although this has now been changed to gender responsive budgeting, it would be a useful practice to emulate in light of the resources necessary for the implementation of the African Women's Protocol.

BUILDING PARTNERSHIPS AND ALLIANCES

In South Africa, the University of Pretoria's Centre for Human Rights has developed a programme to support the work of the Special Rapporteur on the Rights of Women. Unfortunately, it has not yet received sufficient support. In the Western Cape, the City of Cape Town and the Department of Local Government's incipient development of a gender network, including the CGE and the OSW, together with women's NGOs and organisational networks, such as the network on VAW, is a noteworthy attempt to address the bottlenecks and obstacles facing the effective implementation of public policies.

INVOLVEMENT OF MEN

Several government departments, the NGM, particularly the OSW, and women's organisations have encouraged the participation of men in their efforts to transform unequal gender relations. These have mainly concentrated on male-based organisations that are confronting men to stop exercising and supporting GBV. By promoting safer sex and responsible sexuality, these organisations are creating alternative visions and constructions of positive opinion of male support for gender equality. The FEMNET programme of men against gender-based violence is an example of the kind of gender partnership that is crucial to promoting gender equality and women's rights.

Notes

[1] Interview with Gladys Mutukwa.

7

Lessons and Conclusions

LESSONS

Adopt a Holistic Approach

> *To ensure maximum impact and follow through, efforts to promote the popularisation and implementation should be part of a national plan or strategy.*

THE STRATEGY SHOULD TAKE INTO ACCOUNT the situation on the ground of each country in a process driven by lead organisations in government and civil society. It should include links to the country's other relevant obligations such as international instruments and commitments like NEPAD and the Millennium Development Goals and national policies, such as Mozambique's Plan for Absolute Poverty Reduction (PARPA) and Zambia's Poverty Reduction Strategic Programme.

Take the African Women's Protocol to the Grassroots

> *The African Women's Protocol must be unpackaged and repackaged in a manner that makes it available accessible and user friendly to different actors.*

Efforts at making the Protocol user friendly must start with the name of the Protocol. By any standards, the full name "The Protocol to the African Charter on Human and Peoples' Rights on the Rights of

Women" is quite a mouthful. Imagine trying to sensitise a group of rural women or to generate media interest using this title. The Protocol itself needs to be simplified so that policy makers and implementers can internalise key aspects and explain it easily. It must then be translated into local languages so that it can be accessible to ordinary women who are supposed to benefit from it. Activists must ask how they will monitor its implementation and how women will use it to claim their rights if it remains in a language they cannot read. Simplified versions and handbooks must also be developed to enable leaders like parliamentarians and government officials to internalise and disseminate key aspects of the Protocol.

Promote its Domestication and Effective Use

> *If the African Women's Protocol is to be effectively implemented, it must be incorporated in the domestic laws of a country, as well as in the local provincial and national sector policies, programmes and plans.*

Break the Private/Public Dichotomy and Move the Mountain of Tradition

> *Efforts to popularise the African Women's Protocol must target the actors and institutions that control the private domain where women live most of their lives.*

Women must claim the right to live in a positive cultural environment and to participate at all levels in the determination of cultural policies, which Article 17 of the Protocol enshrines. Well thought through campaigns, which seek to build alliances with traditional, cultural and religious leaders must be launched to promote understanding and convince religious and traditional authorities to support, or at least not stand in the way of the implementation of the Protocol. The Protocol should also be used to help harmonise contradictory positions in statutory and customary law.

Transform Targets for Change into Agents of Change

> *Efforts to popularise and implement the African Women's Protocol must target crucial actors in the campaign, such as the media and cultural leaders seeing as both these actors are subjects and potential agents for change.*

The media and traditional, religious and cultural leaders must be persuaded not only to change their own attitudes, but must also become agents of change in communities or organisations. For example, a traditional leader in an area where FGM is practised must not just be persuaded to stop believing in it, but must also become sufficiently sold the idea that he is able to sell it to others. The media is one of the most critical pillars in any popularisation campaign. Yet, it remains one of the critical areas of concern of the Beijing process. It must be persuaded not only to refrain from stereotyping and portraying women negatively, but must also be persuaded to effectively disseminate the African Women's Protocol's message.

Start Early

> *Efforts at popularising the African Women's Protocol must target girls and boys at an age before their opinions become formed.*

Most gender training and sensitisation targets adults whose opinions and belief systems have long been formed and are, therefore, hard to change. Education about the Protocol and other human rights instruments should be included in school curricula as early as possible. Most of it is currently focused on people at the tertiary level, by which time it is more difficult to change a person's opinion.

Maximise the Opportunities Provided by Technology

> *Efforts at popularising the African Women's Protocol must make maximum use of the information revolution, while being mindful of the new threats it presents and of the need to bridge the digital divide between grassroots, the Protocol, and information technology.*

CONCLUSIONS

South Africa

Despite the perception that the Protocol does not significantly advance South Africa's legislative and policy framework, the Protocol provides the opportunity to revitalise discussion and debate, around women's oppression in the country, within government and civil society. Popularising the Protocol, and discussing its provisions and clauses, will inject civil society and government with renewed enthusiasm and impetus.

The Protocol can provide benchmarks and indicators for the definition of national priorities, by being a lens through which to analyse the particular problems experienced by women in South Africa. Popularising the Protocol will give government and civil society the opportunity to see international conventions, Protocols and plans of action as tools that need to be used to support calls for accountability for the lack of implementation of existing government policies. An important consideration is the emphasis the Protocol places on ensuring adequate mechanisms and budgets for addressing concerns about VAW.

The Protocol provides the opportunity to promote the principle that the responsibility for promoting gender equality, eradicating VAW, improving women's sexual and reproductive health and improving the conditions for women's participation in politics and public life, is everyone's responsibility. This includes all government departments, parliament, all members and organisations of civil society (organisations working around land rights, worker's rights, right to health and other socio-economic rights etc.) and in so doing, this will ensure that it is not just the responsibility of women's organisations or the gender machinery. This would also provide a challenge to women's organisations and the gender machinery to define a common agenda, and use it to construct meaningful alliances with other sectors of civil society who have common concerns.

At the same time, popularising the Protocol will provide the opportunity for women's organisations and government to consolidate efforts to promote gender equality at a regional level. It lends itself to promoting and consolidating networks and alliances, by sharing strategies, actions, best practices and the building of a common regional agenda. It provides South African civil society with the opportunity to see the AU as an important arena and resource in their efforts to promote gender equality, both in South Africa and the region (Holland-Muter, 2005: 61–62).

Zambia

Zambia, like many other African countries, is a highly patriarchal society. Issues of gender equality and women's empowerment receive little or no attention in public policy and even less attention in terms of implementation. Nevertheless, there are strong gender-based civil society organisations that have been instrumental in advocating the need to establish gender machinery, adopt a gender policy and promote all human and women's rights. Some of them recognise the value of the Protocol as a tool that Zambian women and men can use to bring about gender equality (Muyakwa, 2005: 39).

Although the focus is currently on domesticating CEDAW, Zambia must be persuaded that CEDAW and the African Women's Protocol complement each other and strengthen the framework to promote and protect women's rights. Efforts to operationalise the African Women's Protocol must, therefore, be pursued side by side with efforts to domesticate CEDAW.

Mozambique

In Mozambique, there are efforts to domesticate the African Women's Protocol. Women's organisations are working to disseminate the Protocol either at community level or training law enforcements to apply it.

General

The African Women's Protocol legitimises the struggles for gender equality, and the promotion and protection of women's rights as an African struggle. Despite its imperfections, it is a potential force for positive change. If properly harnessed, it can serve as an effective empowerment tool for African women. Empowering African women, who make up more than half of the continent's population, will have a positive multiplier effect that will result in happier, healthier, wealthier and more harmonious families and societies.

8

Research Recommendations

THE AFRICAN UNION
The African Union Should:

- Promote the continent-wide ratification and implementation of the African Women's Protocol.
- Strengthen institutions responsible for the implementation of the Protocol, such as the Office of the Special Rapporteur on the Rights of Women and the Gender Directorate.

The Pan African Parliament Should:

- Promote the continent-wide ratification of the African Women's Protocol.
- Use the budget's oversight function to help ensure that adequate resources are earmarked to strengthen institutions that play a vital or catalytic role in the implementation of the Protocol, such as the Office of the Special Rapporteur on the Rights of Women and the Gender Directorate.
- Keep the issue of the ratification of the African Women's Protocol in countries that have not yet done so and its implementation high on the AU's agenda.
- Encourage its members to serve as champions for the African Women's Protocol in their own countries by spearheading the drive to promote it.

The Commission Should:

- Help ensure that the issue of the African Women's Protocol is kept high on the AU's agenda.
- Conduct research and undertake studies to promote the implementation of the Protocol.
- Arrange meetings, seminars and workshops that bring together key stakeholders.
- Develop indicators to enhance monitoring and evaluation of the Protocol.
- Ensure that the Protocol is used as a reference point and framework for work in other sectors of the AU.

NATIONAL GOVERNMENTS

Governments should, in partnership with civil society organisations, develop plans of action to promote the African Women's Protocol. The plans should link actors, actions and targets and should include the following key elements:

- Champions (individuals) and key drivers (institutions) to spearhead the process of popularisation and domestication must be identified. Notwithstanding the role of different structures and their combined importance, there needs to be public faces/ champions, from both men and women, who become emblems of the African Women's Protocol.
- Strategies must be tailored to each country's circumstances. Its targets should include parliament; government officials; women at all levels in decision-making positions; grassroots; NGOs; law enforcement agencies; the judiciary; the legal profession, including law society, civil society organisations; schools; traditional leaders; religious organisations; the media and the general public.
- There must be meetings between key stakeholders to map out action plans. These could include key ministries such as Gender; Foreign Affairs; Justice, Parliamentary Affairs; parliament, the judiciary; NGOs; local and provincial administrations; cultural and religious leaders; academics and the media.

- Sector by sector analysis of the implications of the African Women's Protocol to national policies, programmes and processes at the national, provincial and local levels to facilitate mainstreaming must be made.
- Media campaigns and face-to-face "meet the people" tours to sensitise women at the grassroots level must be conducted.

In applying these key elements, governments should strengthen institutions responsible for the implementation of the African Women's Protocol, such as gender machinery.

CIVIL SOCIETY

Civil society organisations should develop tools for the dissemination of the Protocol. These could include:

- Pamphlets of simplified versions of the African Women's Protocol.
- Translations of the African Women's Protocol into local languages and official languages, such as Portuguese.
- Handbooks on the African Women's Protocol and its relevance to women in the particular country.
- Websites on the African Women's Protocol, its relevance and how individuals and organisations can get involved in the campaign for its implementation.
- Creation of posters and a slogan to help focus the campaign.
- Indicators to monitor and evaluate the Protocol once it enters into force.
- Relevant research, analysis, position papers and studies.
- Model curriculum for use in schools and institutions.
- Seminars for academics; policy makers; government representatives and civil society organisations.

Civil society organisations should undertake and support activities to popularise the African Women's Protocol and ensure its domestication. These could include:

- Media campaigns using T.V., radio, newspapers.
- The use of popular culture, such as drama, music, soap operas and art, to popularise the African Women's Protocol.
- Seminars for academics; policy makers; government representatives and civil society organisations.
- Campaigns that lobby policy makers and other significant actors.
- Test cases and strategic litigation using the African Women's Protocol.

Civil society organisations should develop and strengthen cross-country alliances between NGOs at regional level, the AU and sub-regional gender structures to support efforts to promote the African Women's Protocol.

AREAS THAT MERIT FURTHER RESEARCH

- The implications of Article 17, on the right to a positive cultural context, participation in the determination of cultural policy and how it could be best utilised to change women's lives. This should include research into how it relates to cultural practices such as lobola, virginity testing and initiation ceremonies. It could also include its relationship to issues of sexuality.
- The situation with regard to the trafficking of women in the region.
- The state of the women's movement in Africa in the 21st Century: how can we strengthen it? This should include studies on the link between the growing numbers of women in public office to the actual situation of women, and on making women in decision-making positions, at all levels, more responsive and more effective in promoting gender equality.

9

Country Recommendations

MOZAMBIQUE

Domestication

Establish a pressure group for the popularisation and implementation of the Protocol. (Lead organisations include Liga dos Direitos Humanos (LDH), Mulher, Lei e Desenvolvimento (MULEIDE), Associação dos Direitos da Mulher e da Criança (NHAMAI), women lawyers association and WLSA.

Policies

- Devise a strategy for the popularisation and implementation of the African Women's Protocol.
- Lobby for the adoption and implementation of the Gender National Policy and Strategy.
- Incorporate gender issues in the Poverty Reduction Strategic Programmes (PRSP).

Institutions

- Strengthening mechanisms for promoting gender equality.

Networks and Alliances

- Build and strengthen strategic alliances.
- Re-activate the network on violence against women.
- Build partnerships with the media to gather support for efforts to sensitise the public on women's rights.
- Strengthen collaboration between NGOs and the Ministry of Gender and Social Welfare.
- Involve men to popularise the African Women's Protocol.
- Create networks to lobby government, with each group focusing on a specific thematic area.

Unpacking the African Women's Protocol

- Translate the Protocol into local languages.
- Establish the interpretation of the Protocol in a national context.

Tools

- Plan and conduct surveys and research on traditional rights and community practices in a bid to promote understanding of the situation at grassroots, and to differentiate between positive and negative practices and traditions.
- Support the development of gender indicators, and other monitoring and evaluation instruments, to periodically assess progress.

Advocacy

- Advocate for the inclusion of more women in decision-making and governing bodies, as well as for better access to education for women.
- Campaign for the extension of health services in rural areas.
- Lobby for the introduction of peace education and gender equality in schools.

Sensitisation

- Increase awareness on women's rights.
- Promote disseminate and market the new Family Law.

SOUTH AFRICA

Popularisation of the Protocol/Unpacking Implications of Provisions

ACTOR	PROPOSED STRATEGIES AND ACTIVITIES	TARGET GROUP
ALL POLITICAL PARTIES	Inform their constituencies of the existence of the African Women's Protocol. Make links between local and regional issues. Use any upcoming elections to promote the provisions of the Protocol, especially as they relate to the promotion of women's right to participate in elections and to represent their constituencies, on the one hand, and the need for government policies and programmes to respond and cater to women's interests, on the other.	• Political parties' constituencies • Local government wards
OSW (NATIONAL AND PROVINCIAL)	Develop conceptual document that draws the linkages between the African Women's Protocol and the Gender Policy Framework and discuss it in the Coordination Forum of the NGM, distribute IEC material for popularisation campaigns. Discuss the Protocol and the implications for their particular sectors with the Gender Focal Points (GFPs).	• Coordination Forum of the NGM • National and provincial GFPs
OSW JOINTLY WITH THE DEPARTMENT OF COMMUNICATIONS	Inform all the organs of state and government departments about the existence of the Protocol and the implications of the provisions for their particular sector.	• The presidency; commissions involved with rights of children and people with disabilities • All government departments

Actor	Proposed Strategies and Activities	Target Group
OSW Departmental GFPs	Promote the existence of the Protocol and unpack the implications for each sector during government cluster meetings and Director General (DG) forums; holding forums, disseminating information on the implications of the Protocol for their particular sector and to raise it during planning and evaluation of government department projects.	• Government Clusters, especially Justice, Social Development • Director General forums • All government departments
Joint Committee on the Improvement of the Quality of Life and Status of Women (JMCIQLSW) with Foreign Affairs	Promote discussion of the African Women's Protocol and disseminate IEC material in parliament and parliamentary committees.	• Parliament • Portfolio committees
JMCIQLSW	Hold meetings with relevant sector ministers to promote existence of Protocol and to assess the implications of the Protocol for their particular sectors. Provincial legislatures and local councils should also receive information. The speakers should be approached and convinced of the importance of the Protocol.	• Ministers • Provincial legislature

Actor	Proposed Strategies and Activities	Target Group
NGOs and CGE	Hold meetings with chief whips from each political party. Hold roundtables, dialogues with representatives of the different political parties to inform, educate and obtain buy in.	• Chief Whips • Representatives of different political parties
	Hold meetings to discuss existence and relevance of Protocol with mayors and local councillors.	• Mayors • Local councillors. • Local councils
	Hold gender dialogues and public hearings to popularise Protocol and discuss implications of Protocol for promoting gender equality in SA.	• NGOs; CBOs; communities; private sector; government.
CGE	Lobby the other Chapter Nine bodies on the relevance of the Protocol for their work, as well as explore the possibility of joint campaigns.	Chapter Nine bodies, especially human rights and electoral commissions.

Actor	Proposed Strategies and Activities	Target Group
NGOs	Develop a 'commentated publication' that highlights general provisions and principles of the Protocol and its importance for promoting gender equality in the context of South Africa and the region. This should be followed by a detailed exploration of the implications of the Protocol for different sectors and for people's daily lives. Case studies of concrete issues in people's lives and how they relate to the provisions should be used. Accessible and user friendly.	• CBOs • NGOs • Trade unions • Social movements • Government departments • Policy makers • Media
	Develop position papers on the different provisions in the Protocol, which examine the implications of the provision for each sector and analyse how it's being implemented in the current South African context. These would be useful materials on which to base advocacy campaigns as well as on which to base discussions with policy makers.	
	Develop fact sheets, pamphlets, and posters to popularise the Protocol and its application/relevance for NGOs, government departments and private sector. These could also be distributed to the media.	
	Develop educational material directed at people with a lower level of education, such as photo comics.	

Actor	Proposed Strategies and Activities	Target Group
NGOs, CGE and Dept of Communications	Conduct media campaigns promoting the Protocol and the relevance of its provisions for different sectors and the person on the street. This could include publishing the above material in one's own publications; the Womensnet web page, Gender Stats; the government and CGE web page. Participate in radio talk shows, community radio, posting radio adverts and inserting the material in a popular form in local television soaps.	• General public • CBOs • NGOs • Government • Private sector
Training NGOs and CGE	Develop training material/guides on the Protocol and its relevance. This could be both an informative training manual, as well as a guide to how to use the Protocol for advocacy purposes. It could include basis information on the AU and its structures and processes, the different provisions of the Protocol and its relevance to each sector (including case studies); guidelines on how to use it as an advocacy tool, including the monitoring procedures and avenues available for accountability. The above-mentioned educational material, such as fact sheets, position papers and commentated publications, could be included in informational resources. It would need to be developed for a number of audiences, notably community organisations, NGOs and government departments.	• CBOs • NGOs • Trade unions • Social movements • Media • Government departments

Actor	Proposed Strategies and Activities	Target Group
NGOs AND DEPT OF EDUCATION	Promote that formal educational institutions include the Protocol in their curricula, as well as consider it in their research projects, which could be carried out by the Departments of Legal Studies; Public Policy; Political Science; Gender Studies and African Studies; Schools.	• University students • Academics • Schools
NGOs	Promote that the Protocol be included in short courses run by winter and summer schools.	• CBOs • NGOs • Social movements
OSW	Include Protocol in the curricula of the South African Management Development Institute (which trains all managers within the public service).	• Public service managers

Actor	Proposed Strategies and Activities	Target Group
SA parliamentarians who participate in regional AU committees	Ensure that Protocol is used as a reference point and framework for work of regional AU committees in order to develop common strategies to combat common problems (e.g. equity and access to services).	Relevant sector AU Regional Committees
Parliamentarians	Integrate the Protocol provisions and specific implications for their particular sector, in their political party's existing programmes of action.	• General public • Political party constituencies
NGOs; OSW; GFPs; CGE	Use the Protocol as a resource and a strategic, political tool – a standard or checklist. Use Protocol as a tool to promote discussion and debate, to refine understanding and analysis (e.g. a woman's right to the free development of her personality). A useful notion as it refers to issues of personal empowerment, of fulfilling human potential. Use Protocol to inform our political demands and organisational strategies; to lobby for advances in the normative framework; to refine and close the gaps around incomplete law reforms and to promote the actual implementation of existing policies.	• NGOs • Government

Actor	Proposed Strategies and Activities	Target Group
Sector specific NGOs (**SRHR; VAW; HIV/AIDS;** land rights; men's training networks/forums)	Integrate Protocol in existing campaigns. Sector specific NGOs should popularise the Protocol and use the pertinent provisions in support of current campaigns. A few examples include the 50/50 campaign, the 16 days of activism for violence against women and the inclusion in the Women's Dialogues.	• CBOs • NGOs • Government departments • Private sector
NGOs, CGE and OSW	Integrate the provisions in the Protocol into monitoring and evaluating frameworks that are used to measure government's compliance with international conventions (CEDAW); international programmes of action, for example Beijing Platform for Action; the International Conference on Population and Development (ICPD) Programme of Action and Millennium Development Goals (MDGs).	• NGOs • CGE • OSW • Coordinating Forum of the NGM

Integration of the African Women's Protocol into Existing Ongoing Activities

ACTOR	PROPOSED STRATEGIES AND ACTIVITIES	TARGET GROUP
NGOs	Develop and promote common legal strategies and arguments to address common problems/barriers to gender equality. Examples of these are the inclusion of marital rape in domestic violence or sexual assault legislation; denial of women's access to land rights and the primacy of customary law over constitutional law.	• Regional NGO legal networks
	Developing a database where successful judgments are posted to act as a resource for similar litigation in other countries.	• Regional NGO networks
	Conduct strategic litigation training, at a regional level, on how to advance women's rights in the region by using regional and international human rights standards.	• Feminist/women's legal rights NGOs
WOMEN'S LEGAL RIGHTS NGOS; SECTOR SPECIFIC NGOS AND THE CGE	Lobby and litigate to domesticate particular sections of the Protocol that are not included in South Africa's current legislative framework.	• SA legal system
NGOS; TRADE UNIONS; SOCIAL MOVEMENTS	Take up specific campaigns on key problems in South Africa, around issues highlighted in the Protocol. Focus on improving service delivery and compliance with existing legislation and policies. Issues could include the slow distribution of Anti-Retrovirals (ARVs); lack of funding for family courts; poor service attention, the poorly equipped facilities for survivors of domestic and sexual abuse, and the lack of funding for NGM.	• CBOs • NGOs • Local, provincial and national government

ZAMBIA

- The government must provide adequate resources, both human and financial to implement the National Plan of Action for the Gender Policy. These resources must be provided for in the National Budget and timely disbursements should be ensured; a well resourced monitoring and evaluation system of the budget and the deliverable outputs should accompany this. These actions should be in line with provisions of the African Women's Protocol and the CEDAW on provision of adequate budgetary and human resources to implement women's empowerment programmes.

- Leading women's NGOs and other development and civil rights NGOs should continuously lobby government to implement the gender policy effectively and efficiently and should hold government accountable for its implementation. These should undertake programmatic initiatives that link work on VAW, sexual and reproductive health services and livelihoods to the Protocol.

- Government, through the Ministry of Justice, should quickly domesticate the provisions of all international, regional and sub regional instruments, for instance the CEDAW, the African Women's Protocol and the SADC GAD in order to enhance the existing policy and legal framework that will result in ensuring the protection of women's rights.

- The government should popularise the Africa Women's Protocol. This will help strengthen the existing national legal and policy framework. Popularisation of the Protocol should be done through a joint effort amongst the major stakeholders which include Ministries of Justice and Foreign Affairs as well as the Ministry of Gender and Women in Development and the Gender In Development Division (GIDD), the Ministry of Community Development and Social Welfare and other stakeholders like the women's movement, women's rights organisations and other civil society organisations.

- Oxfam GB Southern Africa should support efforts to popularise the AU Women's Protocol in Zambia.

Figure 9.1
Countries that have ratified the African Women's Protocol, as of 26 May 2007

Section Two

South African Country Report
Susan Holland Muter

Summary

SITUATIONAL ANALYSIS

SOUTH AFRICA HAS RATIFIED (without reservations) the CEDAW (1979) and is a signatory of the Beijing Platform for Action and Cairo Program of Action (along with their relevant subsequent five year action plans). South Africa has incorporated many of the provisions included in the international commitments and programmes of action in its Constitution (1996), as well as a range of its laws and policies. On the whole, there is a positive gender enabling legislative and policy framework within the country.

South Africa has a very extensive and sophisticated NGM comprising of the OSW and Gender Focal Points in the Executive; the Joint Committee on the Improvement of Quality of Life and Status of Women and an independent statutory body (the Commission on Gender Equality). South Africa's efforts to promote gender equality are loosely governed by the National Gender Policy on Gender Equality and Women's Empowerment (2000), which is spearheaded by the NGM but whose responsibilities for implementation lies with its stakeholders.

At the formal level of the legislative framework, policies and statements, South Africa has demonstrated political will to implement its international and national commitments to promote gender equality. However, it has fallen short of demonstrating the will to ensure that these are effectively implemented through the provision of an inadequate budget; the lack of skilled human resources assigned to implement its gender programmes; not paying enough attention to ensure that gender is successfully integrated into its cluster objectives and departmental

109

programmes and not ensuring that a strong message for promoting gender equality is heard by government functionaries.

The lack of an overall gender action plan with measurable targets and indicators, connected to government priorities, has made it difficult to ensure coordinated and effective mobilisation of the little resources that exist. At times, actions take place in a haphazard way, with each component of the gender machinery operating within its own imperatives, which has made it difficult to ensure that government actions effectively address the needs of (poor, black, rural) women. It also lacks the coordinated action and leverage to ensure that government complies with the gender policy framework and its international commitments. Using a number of frameworks, policies, international conventions and action plans, causes understandable confusion when it comes time to plan and measure any progress achieved. It is highly recommended for the NGM to create a single framework, based on the priorities and problems faced by South African women, with measurable benchmarks and indicators. In addition, monitoring and evaluation information could be maintained in a central database and accessed as, and when, necessary by various members of the NGM.

TRANSLATING POLICIES INTO PRACTICE: GOVERNANCE, VIOLENCE AGAINST WOMEN AND SEXUAL AND REPRODUCTIVE HEALTH AND RIGHTS OF WOMEN

Governance

A potential weakness in ensuring women's representation in public office is that there are no laws that make it mandatory to have a quota for women's political participation and representation. However, the ANC's organisational policy, ensuring a 30 per cent quota for women, has gone a long way to improving women's political participation and representation. The last national elections, in April 2004, saw women constituting almost a third of the National Assembly (32.75 per cent). This high level of women's representation is echoed at provincial level with women occupying 35.18 per cent of the permanent members. Local government continues to demonstrate a low level of women's representation, with women constituting only 23 per cent of the legislature in 2003. The lack of women's representation is echoed in the public service, judiciary, armed forces and police services.

Barriers to women's effective political participation and representation (especially at local government level and within the public service) continue to be seen in the negative attitudes towards and suspicion of women's abilities to hold public offices, in the traditional gender norms and practices (including the gender division of labour) and in the (local government) electoral system.

Violence Against Women

South Africa has one of the highest incidences of VAW in the world. Statistics reveal a systematic pattern of women abuse, including sexual harassment; rape; battery; economic abuse; emotional and psychological abuse; femicide; trafficking of women; and harmful traditional practices. Although a range of laws and policies have been developed to combat VAW across the departments, the implementation has been hindered by the lack of sufficient budget, the lack of appropriately trained and skilled personnel and the lack of provision of additional human and other resources (e.g. police cars, shelters). Legal and policy gaps are to be found in the area of the trafficking of women (legislation of trafficking of women is in the process of development) and in harmful traditional practices.

Women's Sexual and Reproductive Health and Rights

South Africa's legislative and policy framework promotes women's SRHR, with a range of sexual and reproductive health services being offered free of charge at primary health care level. However, incomplete restructuring of the health services at provincial and district level, poor health care worker performance, staff shortages and burnout, combined with patriarchal traditional, cultural and religious beliefs and practices, severely undermine women's abilities to take advantage of these laws and services. HIV and AIDS is a particular problem in South Africa, as the country has one of the highest prevalence rates in the world. Women and girls are disproportionately represented in the HIV statistics, and bear the burden of care. The South African government's response to HIV and AIDS, particularly the provision of care and HIV and AIDS treatment, has been marred by political controversy.

THE AFRICAN WOMEN'S PROTOCOL

The South African government ratified and deposited the Women's Protocol, subject to the reservations expressed in Articles 4(j), 6(d) and 6(h) and a number of interpretative declarations. The Minister of Foreign Affairs signed the Protocol on 16 March 2003, it was adopted by the National Assembly on the 17 November 2004, and was officially ratified on 17 December 2004. It was deposited with the Chairperson of the Commission of the AU on 14 January 2005.

Implications for South Africa's Legal and Policy Framework

On the whole, South Africa's legislative and policy framework complies with, and in many instances exceeds, the provisions laid out in the Women's Protocol. The South African Constitution recognises, promotes and protects a wide range of human and women's rights and there are extensive numbers of laws and policies promoting women's autonomy, their political participation, attempts to deal with VAW and women's SRHR. Thus, the Women's Protocol does not offer much in the way of improvement for South Africa's legislative and policy framework. However, it could contribute to enhance the policy development in areas, such as harmful traditional practices, and deepen discussions around the implications of living a positive cultural life. In addition, it could also be used to inform ongoing development of policies and guidelines.

The benefit and value of the Women's Protocol for South Africa lies in that efforts to popularise its existence, promote its implementation. This could provide the much needed impetus to renew broad based discussions and organisation (within civil society and government circles alike) around the slow and uneven implementation of governmental policies. At regional level, it strengthens the legal framework promoting gender equality; contributes to harmonising culture and tradition with international human rights law; highlights the specific challenges facing African women and provides tools to help bridge the gap between policy and practice. Ensuring its adoption and implementation provides opportunities for the consolidation or development of regional alliances and strategies.

Awareness of the African Women's Protocol

By January 2005, there was limited knowledge of the existence of the African Women's Protocol, amongst policy makers and NGOs alike. A range of concrete recommendations (actors, actions and target group) was provided, specifically to promote its ratification (at the time), to popularise its existence and promote its implementation at national and regional levels.

10

Introduction

AFRICAN HEADS OF STATE took the groundbreaking decision to adopt the ACHPR on the Rights of Women in Africa (hereafter referred to as the Women's Protocol) at the July 2003 Maputo Summit in Mozambique. It had long been the contention of gender activists and government officials alike, that the African Charter (Banjul) on Human and People Rights, adopted in June 1981 by heads of state, did not effectively address the rights and concerns of women.

The African Women's Protocol potentially provides the women of Africa with an Africa specific tool to promote the rights of women on the continent and to hold governments to account. The 32 articles contained in the Protocol commit African states to eliminate discrimination against women and to promote their right to dignity, life, integrity and security. It highlights particular economic, social, cultural and political measures necessary to ensure the rights of women, including the pre-requisite legal frameworks, mechanisms and budgetary resources.

The African Women's Protocol holds a political and symbolic value for the African continent, for both women's organisations and governments. For the first time there is a regional instrument that spells out the specific issues confronting African women, issues that to a large degree have been absent from other international agreements like the CEDAW. This provides African women with a relevant political tool to negotiate with governments and regional bodies in order to ensure that these issues are dealt with. Significantly, the Women's Protocol is also the outcome of a political negotiation process between African heads of state, giving it an added degree of legitimacy and credibility in comparison to other international agreements – it is an instrument that has been developed by

Africans for Africans. This would go a long way to undermine arguments that gender concerns and women's disadvantages are Western imported concerns, and provides gender activists with a tool in the face of an increasing general backlash against gender concerns and feminism.

South Africa's ratification of the African Women's Protocol is one of the many steps that the South African government has taken to promote women's rights in the country. This research report contributes to discussions assessing the implications of this decision in the South African context, and maps out the best method for popularising the existence and promoting the implementation of the provisions contained in the Women's Protocol. Considering the Women's Protocol contemplates a wide-ranging number of provisions, three issues have been prioritised for discussion: namely governance, VAW and sexual and reproductive health and rights.

Based on a literature review and supported by interviewee's contributions where necessary, the first section of this report will highlight the international and regional instruments promoting gender equality signed and ratified by the South African government. Consideration will be given to how the national legislation and policy frameworks have domesticated these international and regional commitments. Particular attention will be paid to the development of the national gender policy framework and its implementation through a discussion of the national gender machinery.

The South African section will draw attention to the current situation of women in the key thematic areas under investigation. Attention will be paid to domestic legislation, policy frameworks, programmes and institutional mechanisms that have been established to promote women's participation in leadership and decision-making structures to prevent, respond to and support (women) victims of violence and to promote women's sexual and reproductive health and rights. The discussion of each of the thematic areas will include an analysis of the strengths and weaknesses in current policy and programmes, and will highlight the obstacles standing in the way of their implementation.

South Africa's position and background to the signing and ratification of the Women's Protocol will then be described. The specific concerns and national discussion will be examined, notably the gaps, ambiguities and controversies within the Women's Protocol that could hinder its use as a tool to promote gender equality in South Africa and the region. Attention will also be paid to South Africa's reservations and interpretative declarations to the Women's Protocol.

114

Following this, the implications of the African Women's Protocol for the key thematic issues under investigation will be examined in the South African context, paying particular attention to comparing the provisions contained in the Women's Protocol and how they speak to South Africa's domestic legal and policy framework and its implementation efforts. In order to assess the extent of the need to popularise the Women's Protocol, interviewees' perception of levels of awareness of the Women's Protocol, notably that of policy makers and civil society organisations, will then be discussed. This will be followed by a discussion of the challenges that South Africa faces in promoting gender equality and transforming women's condition and position. Best practices regarding this will also be highlighted. To wrap the report up, concluding comments will be followed by concrete steps and recommendations on how to take forward national and regional efforts to popularise and implement the provisions contained in the Women's Protocol.

11

Methodology

THIS REPORT FORMS PART OF a study undertaken in three countries: South Africa, Mozambique and Zambia. The research team is comprised of three country researchers (one per country), headed by a lead researcher. A local Oxfam programme officer, who provided logistical and other support, supported each national researcher.

The country research reports are based on secondary literature and key informant interviews. The literature review included articles; reports; policy guidelines and organisational annual reports relating to the key thematic areas under investigation (governance, gender-based violence and sexual and reproductive health and rights[1]), as well as committee minutes of the Justice and Constitutional Portfolio Committee including the attendant reports and inputs presented to the committee.

The researcher and the Oxfam functionary identified key informants from government, NGOs and academics. Considering the governmental sector, heads of Parliamentary Portfolio Committees, who would have been involved in national discussions of the African Women's Protocol, as well as those implicated in its popularisation and implementation, were prioritised. These included Chairs of the Portfolio Committees on Foreign Affairs, Finance and Health. The Chairs of the Portfolio Committees on Justice and Constitutional Development, Safety and Security, and Welfare were unavailable for interviewing during the interview period. In addition, a representative from each of the components of the NGM was selected, notably the National Office on the Status of Women, representatives from the Head Office of the CGE and a representative from the Department of Justice Gender Focal Point. The Chair of the Joint Committee on the Improvement of the Quality of

Life and Status of Women was unavailable for interviewing during the interview period.

Representatives from the NGO sector were drawn from organisations that are working in the sectors of governance, GBV and SRHR. In addition, representatives from organisations working with women and law, and men and masculinity were selected.

Academics were selected on the basis of their knowledge and experience of working with the South African legal framework and policies in the key areas under research. They included a lawyer and a political scientist, who were experienced in gender issues in South Africa.

A total of 14 interviews were conducted using the question guideline provided by the lead researcher. Each interview lasted between half an hour and three hours (reference to the interviewees in the report will be indicated as Interview 1–4). The annex in section 13 will provide the details of each person interviewed.

A notable limitation to the selection of interviewees was the time period in which the research was conducted (November–December 2004). This coincided with the Sixteen Days of Activism against Violence Against Women Campaign and the end of year planning, evaluation and report writing. One interview was conducted in January 2005. Parliament was also closed during this time, and many government officials were either travelling and/or unavailable.

Notes

[1] In the South Africa section, the broader concept of GBV was discussed rather than VAW. In this section, sexual rights are included even though Article 14 of the African Women's Protocol is not explicit about them.

12

Literature Review

ANALYSIS OF NATIONAL LEGISLATION, POLICY DOCUMENTS AND COUNTRY POSITION ON EXPERIENCE WITH INTERNATIONAL AND REGIONAL LEGISLATION AND POLICY DOCUMENTS

A BRIEF BACKGROUND will provide a broad description of the events and processes leading up to the adoption of the South African Constitution. Mention will be made of the international, regional and sub-regional instruments agreed to by the South African government. This will be followed by an analysis of how a selection of these has been translated into the national legislative and policy framework. The discussion will focus primarily on gender policies, national machinery and gender mainstreaming.

Background

The un-banning of the ANC in 1990, a result of decades of resistance to the imposition of apartheid rule, heralded the beginnings of the new South Africa and ushered in the process of transformation and the establishment of a democratic state.

South Africa's Constitution is lauded as one of the most progressive and inclusive of all time. The writing of the Constitution included an extensive consultation process. This consultation process, happening at the same time as women were preparing for the 1995 United Nations' Fourth World Conference on Women (FWCW) in Beijing (hereafter referred to as Beijing) meant that women in South Africa were able to discuss human rights in the context of creating a new country, as well as in a world programme of action – giving each process dynamism and added impetus. Women's organisations fed their input into the Constitution from both provincial and national levels (Gender Manual Consortium, date unstated).

The enabling legal framework for women, embedded in the Constitution, was the outcome of organised women's discussions, lobbying, influencing and contesting the political process. Two instances are worth noting: when the Women's National Coalition (WNC) intervened to protest the exclusion of the principle of non-sexism from the Constitutional principles (agreed upon during the Conference for a Democratic South Africa [CODESA][1]) and when it challenged traditional leaders' attempts to exclude customary law from the Bill of Rights, particularly in the Equality Clause (Albertyn et al, 1999).

The preparations for Beijing also provided South African women the forum to call on the new South African government to ratify the CEDAW. Previously opposed by the National Party in 1993, the government of national unity of South Africa ratified the CEDAW (without reservations) in December 1995, legally binding the government to undertake the necessary steps to ensure women's political, civil, economic, social and cultural equality (Foster, 1998).

Women's lobbying and input at a national and provincial level, combined with the preparations for Beijing and the ratification and ensuing domestication of the CEDAW, provided the impetus for South Africa's recognition of gender discrimination, legislative changes and its subsequent formulation of policies to address gender inequalities.

Prior to the 1994 elections, the General Law Fourth Amendment Act (1993) repealed several discriminatory laws regarding citizenship; attendance at trials; the dismissal of female employees on marriage; and the prohibition of women performing dangerous or night shifts (Foster, 1998). Since 1994, South Africa has acceded to a number of sub-regional, regional and international instruments that either promote gender equality or include provisions related to the promotion of gender equality. These include (OSW, 2004):

- ACHPR (1981);
- The Dakar Platform for Action (DPA);
- The International Conference on Population and Development (ICPD, 1994);
- The Beijing Platform for Action, 1995;

- The Convention on the Elimination of all Forms of Discrimination Against Women (1979);
- The SADC GAD (1997), and its Addendum on the Prevention and Eradication of Violence Against Women and Children (1998);
- UN Millennium Declaration adopted at Millennium Summit (2000);
- The New Partnership for Africa's Development (NEPAD);
- The Protocol to the ACHPR on the Rights of Women in Africa (2003)

The creation of an enabling environment for gender transformation can be roughly timelined in the following manner (OSW, 2004):

- **1994–1998**: the establishment of an enabling legislative framework and institutional mechanisms. Adoption of key legislation related to personal autonomy, GBV, SRHR and the development of policies. Beginning attempts at implementation.
- **1999–2003**: consolidation of legislative and policy-making phase. Continued attempts at implementation, beginning of disgruntlement at uneven and slow pace of implementation.
- **2004–present day**: continued attempts at implementation. Growing disgruntlement with lack of progress in improving women's status and conditions. A number of laws pertaining to women still to be adopted.

The government's commitments to gender equality, both in terms of law and policy, and its ability to implement them, need to be read against the backdrop of its GEAR policy framework adopted two years after coming to power. A dramatic change from its previous policy framework, the Reconstruction and Development Programme (RDP), GEAR's key features include "reducing the budget deficit; privatisation; lowering interest rates; lifting exchange controls; export-led growth and labour market reforms" (Albertyn et al, 1999: 17). However, GEAR included many of the principles and intentions of the RDP within an economic policy that prioritised fiscal discipline.

Prioritising fiscal discipline and controlling government spending often leads to reduced social spending and places constraints on policy implementation. Ensuring that the budget responds to women's needs and interests inevitably depends on an organised and coordinated women's lobby and pressure group, on the one hand, and political will on the part of the South African state to ensure that the commitments are put into practice. As will be discussed below, these two conditions have become increasingly absent from the South African political scenario.

The South African Constitution

The South African Constitution has incorporated many of the provisions included in the international commitments and programmes of action, in this way creating an enabling framework for the promotion of women's rights. Gender equality is a fundamental value of the Constitution and the entrenchment of a justifiable Bill of Rights means that the government becomes accountable in relation to several 'gender' rights. Sections of the Constitution have been highlighted to illustrate the gender-enabling framework in the areas of governance, GBV and SRHR. These include the following:

- The Equality Clause, which states that:
  - Everybody is equal before the law and has the right to equal protection and benefit of the law. (9.1).
  - It includes provision for positive measures or affirmative action. It states "legislative and other measures" may be taken to "protect or advance" people who have been disadvantaged (9.2).
  - It protects against unfair discrimination (direct or indirect) on one or more grounds, including race; gender; sex; pregnancy; marital status; ethnic or social origin; colour; sexual orientation; age; disability; religion; conscience; belief; culture; language and birth (9.3).
- The right to security and freedom of the person (Section 12), which specifically incorporates:
  - The right to be free from all forms of violence from either public or private sources (12.1[c]); and
  - The right to bodily integrity and psychological integrity including the right to make decisions concerning reproduction, to security in and control over their bodies (12.2[a] and [b]).
- The constitution requires that legislation recognising marriages concluded under any tradition, or a system of religious, personal or family law must be consistent with other provisions of the Constitution (15.3[a], [i] and [b]). Thus it is argued that if there

is a conflict between customary law and the Constitution, for example, the Constitution will take precedence (Foster, 1998).

- Every citizen is free to make political choices, which includes the right:
  - To form a political party;
  - To participate in the activities of, or recruit members for, a political party; and
  - To campaign for a political party or cause (19.1[a], [b], [c]).

- It goes on to say that "Every adult citizens has the right:
  - To vote in elections for any legislative body [...] in secret; and
  - To stand for public office and, if elected, to hold office" (19.3(a) and [b]).

- The right to freedom of expression specifically excludes the promotion of hatred based on race, ethnicity, gender or religion which incites people to harm (16.2[c]).

Albertyn et al. (1999) argue that the provision for social and economic rights in the Constitution also creates the conditions to promote gender equality and social justice. These include, amongst others, health care, food, water and social security. It states "everyone has the right to have access to health care services, including reproductive health care" (27.1[a]). However, the Bill of Rights may be limited if the limitation is "reasonable and justifiable in an open and democratic society based on human dignity, freedom and equality" (36.1).

The Constitution also allows for the creation of statutory bodies, supporting constitutional democracy. Six bodies, including the CGE and the HRC were formed.

The CGE's mandate includes "promote respect for gender equality and the protection, development and attainment of gender equality. It has the power to monitor, investigate, research, educate, lobby, advise and report on issues concerning gender equality" (9.187[1], [2]). The HRC must "promote respect for human rights and a culture of human rights; promote the protection, development and attainment of human rights; and monitor and assess the observance of human rights in the Republic' (9.184 [1a, b, c]). The statutory bodies, which are directly accountable to parliament and the Ministry of Finance through the Department of Justice, allocate their budgets.

Thus, it is clear that the South African Constitution is an important resource and tool for women's rights activists, along with the commitment of the first democratically elected government, to demonstrate the ability of women's organisations to lobby for gender equality and ensure that their interests are included.

Gender Policies, National Gender Machinery and Gender Mainstreaming

Considering this broad commitment to gender equality, provisions related to the promotion of gender policy, NGM and gender mainstreaming in international agreements will be highlighted. This will be followed by an examination of how this has been translated into practice through laws, policies and their implementation.

International Agreements

Several provisions of the international agreements signed by South Africa pay specific attention to the development of national machinery and gender mainstreaming as a means to promote and achieve gender equality. They call on states to:

- Create national machineries at the "highest level of government for the advancement of women".
- Give these machineries a clearly defined mandate.
- Provide the machineries with adequate resources.
- Ensure the ability and competence of the machineries to influence policy, and to formulate and review legislation (Beijing POA, Strategic Objective H).
- Integrate a gender perspective in legislation, public policies, programmes and projects (Beijing POA, Strategic Objective H2).

Law

- The CGE Act, No 39 of 1996 established the CGE in accordance with the constitutional mandate.

Policy

The Cabinet Memorandum of 1996 (No 3 of 1996, dated 27 June 1996, File No 13/1/1/1) established the Office on the Status of Women, at a national and provincial level (OSW, 2004).

The National Gender Policy on Gender Equality and Women's Empowerment was finalised and adopted by Cabinet in December 2000. It made specific recommendations for the necessary processes and mechanisms for gender mainstreaming to take place at national and provincial level. However, local government was not treated in sufficient depth (OSW, 2004).

Several departments (related to the themes under discussion) have developed gender policies, namely: Justice; Welfare; Social Development; and Health. However, a general critique of these is that the gender policies do not speak to the departmental objectives or priorities, creating a scenario where gender mainstreaming is seen as a parallel process (Interview 9).

Implementation and Monitoring

South Africa has an established, extensive and sophisticated NGM, which is conceptualised to be an integrated package of structures strategically placed within the executive legislature, as a statutory body, and within civil society. The NGM constitutes four pillars that meet in the Coordination Forum of the National Gender Machinery. It includes:

- The OSW located in the Office of the President at a national level and within the Premier's Office at a provincial level, and Gender Focal Points (GFP) located within government departments at national and provincial levels;
- Joint Committee on the Improvement of the Quality of Life and Status of Women (JCIQLSW) located in parliament;
- Commission on Gender Equality, an independent statutory body;
- Civil society organisations, including women's and other NGOs.

Each component ostensibly has clearly designated roles and responsibilities, although in practice, there is a lot of overlap and confusion over powers, roles and responsibilities.

1. The **OSW** is a coordinating structure whose role is to primarily:
   - Develop and maintain a national gender programme;
   - Develop national action plans or frameworks for mainstreaming gender within governmental structures;
   - Support government departments and public bodies to mainstream gender in all policies and programmes and to promote affirmative action within government;

- To monitor the implementation and progress of gender mainstreaming (OSW, 2004; CALS, 2003/2004).

2. The **GFPs** have the main responsibility for:

   - Ensuring the internal transformation of the civil service to ensure gender representation (along the equity guidelines identified by the Department of Public Service Administration).

   - Mainstreaming gender in departmental policy and implementation of programmes (OSW, 2004; Albertyn et al, 1999).

3. The **JCIQLSW's** main responsibilities are to:

   - Monitor progress in the advancement of the status and improvement of the quality of South African women.

   - Monitor and assess whether government policy implements national and international commitments with respect to the Constitution, the National Gender Equality Framework, the CEDAW, Beijing and the Dakar Platforms for Action.

   - Monitor gender mainstreaming in government policies and programmes, including the national budget and fiscal framework (OSW, 2004).

4. According to the Constitution, the **CGE's** main responsibilities are:

   - To monitor and evaluate policies and practices of organs of state, statutory bodies and functionaries, public bodies or private businesses;

   - To develop education strategies and provide information to foster understanding about gender equality;

   - To evaluate Acts of Parliament, of personal and family law, indigenous law, customary practice and any other law and to propose laws;

   - To investigate gender matters, complaints and resolve conflicts by mediation, conciliation and negotiation;

   - To maintain close liaison with the HRC, the Public Protector and other institutions with similar objectives;

   - To monitor government's compliance with international conventions with respect to gender equality;

   - To prepare and submit reports to parliament on aspects relating to gender equality, conduct research; and

- To consider recommendations for the promotion of gender equality from any source.

Mainstreaming Gender in Government – the OSW and GFPs

The National OSW is currently located in the President's Office and the provincial OSW structures are located in the Premier's Office. Currently eight of the nine provinces have provincial OSWs (OSW, 2004).

The OSW mandate is primarily advisory and there is no guarantee that is automatically included in policy-making and priority setting processes (Albertyn et al, 1999; CALS, 2003/2004). They operate with little staff and a minimum budget.

The OSW produced the National Gender Policy Framework on Gender Equality and Women's Empowerment (hereafter referred to as the Gender Policy Framework), providing broad policy guidelines and principles for promoting women's equality and gender mainstreaming in government. This framework has to be implemented by the different national and provincial government structures and departments (not restricted to the NGM).

Several government departments have developed their own specific gender polices, namely: Justice; Water Affairs and Forestry; and Welfare. However, these have been developed both prior and subsequent to the Gender Policy Framework, indicating that they were not developed within its framework and were initially operating within a vacuum (Albertyn et al, 1999). Critiques of the policies include that they are not systematically related to their departmental priorities, resulting in parallel rather than integrated interventions.

The success of South Africa's mainstreaming strategy depends on, to a large extent, the ability of the GFPs to promote gender transformation within the civil service, as well as to influence their departmental policies and programmes. However, an audit conducted by the OSW in 2003[2] revealed that of the 29 departments that responded:

- Only nine departments (31.03 per cent) had GFPs appointed at the level required by the Gender Policy Framework. Eleven departments had GFPs appointed at Deputy Director Level, while six departments had GFPs located at Assistant Director Level. This demonstrates that GFPS have been appointed below the intended level of research required for effective mainstreaming

- Sixteen departments had a GFP staffed by only one person, indicating that it would not have the capacity to undertake the work required.

- Fourteen departments indicated their GFP carried out four or more functions over and above the gender mainstreaming functions, seriously undermining any serious attempt at effective gender mainstreaming (OSW, 2004).

The audits did not assess the skill levels of the GFPs, nor the financial resources allocated for their functioning.

An interviewee outlined some of the obstacles which undermined the GFPs' effectiveness, including:

- Attention to gender in practice translating to specific women's issues, and not to the core work of the department – effectively making gender an added on consideration;
- GFPs were not invited to participate in the business units' planning processes;
- The lack of planning from a gender perspective resulted in a lack of (or limited) gender responsive budgeting;
- Government functionaries were resistant to gender training and had the perception that gender mainstreaming was a complicated and time-consuming process.
- GFPs were often allocated an inadequate budget.[2]

Albertyn et al (1999) point out that a fair proportion of the staff appointed to the GFPs did not have the necessary gender mainstreaming experience or skills, which undermines the ability of the GFPs to assume their functions.

In 2001, South Africa introduced an integrated governance system, grouping the programmes of government departments into clusters according to their sector work[3]. An interviewee stated that the task of the GFPs and the OSW was to integrate gender concerns into the clusters' strategic objectives and priorities. However, there has been an uneven engagement of GFPs with governmental planning processes, resulting, on the whole, in gender priorities and concerns falling outside of these objectives. At the same time, at the coordination and monitoring level, the OSW and the Policy Coordination and Advisory Services (PCAS)[4] have not managed to effectively ensure the integration of gender concerns in monitoring and evaluating government performance.[5]

Gender Mainstreaming in Parliament – The JCIQLSW

This committee consists of members of the National Assembly and the National Council of Provinces. Initially established as an ad hoc committee in 1996 to monitor and oversee government's progress in the implementation of CEDAW and the Beijing POA, the JCIQLSW became a joint standing committee with higher status and more powers in 1997 (Albertyn et al, 1999).

Initially it was a very dynamic and active committee, holding consultations with civil society in relation to key legislation and policy, particularly around gender based violence, HIV/AIDS and poverty. The Women's Budget Initiative was one of its flagship programmes, which aimed to assess the extent to which departments prioritised women's needs and interests, and to examine the differential impact of spending on women and men (CALS, 2003/2004).

Parliament has enacted a number of laws that affected the status of women (see OSW, 2004 for a detailed treatment of these laws), which included:

- Criminal Procedure Act, 1995;
- Labor Relations Act, 1995;
- Choice on Termination of Pregnancy Act, 1996;
- Employment Equity Act 55 of 1998;
- The Electoral Act 73 of 1998;
- Domestic Violence Act 116 of 1998;
- Recognition of Customary Marriages Act 120 of 1998.

The experience and challenges facing women parliamentarians will be discussed under the governance section. As of 2005, the JCIQLSW's profile had been substantially diminished, with no record of the committee having met (or at least minutes of their meetings have not been published on the web site detailing parliamentary portfolio committee meeting minutes, www.pmg.org.za) since November 2003.

Monitoring and Promoting Gender Equality in Government, the Private Sector and Civil Society – The CGE

Established in 1996, the CGE is currently operating with a staff complement below the legally stipulated amount – seven commissioners, four full-time (including the chairperson) and three part-time.[6] The commissioners are assisted by staff to realise their mandate. The CGE offices are located in a head office in Johannesburg, a parliamentary office in Cape Town, and five provincial offices (in Kwa-Zulu Natal [KZN], the Eastern Cape, Free State, Limpopo and the Western Cape).

The CGE has three departments – Public Education, Advocacy and Training, the Legal and Complaints Department and the Policy and Research Department – which implement the CGE's Plan of Action. This is based on five programmatic themes: namely Governance; GBV; Gender and Poverty; Gender, tradition, culture, religion and sexuality and finally Gender and HIV/AIDS (CGE, Annual Report, 2002/2003). This component has arguably the most power, since it has the power (with a warrant) to search premises and seize documents, to call people to appear and produce documents and to hear evidence under oath. The CGE may report to the president on any matter, which must then be tabled in parliament. It can present reports to parliament at any time, and approach the president on any matter pertaining to its work (CGE, Annual Report, 2002/2003).

The CGE has held gender dialogues, public education and training workshops and run campaigns around each of the programmatic themes (notably around witchcraft and virginity testing; GBV and women's political participation). The most complaints from the public have been around maintenance and GBV issues. It has monitored the implementation of a number of laws, including the Domestic Violence Act (DVA) of 1998, the Recognition of Customary Marriages Act (1998) and the Employment Equity Act (1998). It has made submissions on the Electoral System, on matters pertaining to the DVA (1998) and the budget. The CGE has monitored progress in gender mainstreaming through the use of an Annual Report Card and has conducted research on various issues related to women and local government, including the Integrated Development Plans and gender budgeting.

The CGE's effectiveness as a watchdog body has been undermined by an inadequate budget (it is the most under-resourced of the statutory bodies), having to resort to donor funding in order to implement its programmes. Apart from not always having the full staff complement at its disposition, the CGE has also been hampered by internal tensions and rivalries and a high staff turnover. In addition, the staff has not always had the required gender skills and analysis, undermining the CGE's ability to strategically define and prioritise where and how it should focus its work and develop sustainable plans of action (CALS, 2003/2004). There have been difficulties in clarifying roles and responsibilities with the OSW (this has improved lately with the Coordination Meetings), with resultant tensions affecting the overall performance on the NGM. At the same time, the CGE has not always effectively harnessed and promoted a consistent, close working relationship with women's NGOs, decreasing its leverage and ability to mobilise around key issues. Albertyn et al also point out that the CGE has not used its powers effectively to hold government to account for its slow and uneven implementation of its commitments to gender equality (1999).

International Reports and Monitoring

South Africa has only presented two CEDAW reports to the UN Committee on the Status of Women (CSW) by January 2005. It failed to present a third report when it was due and submitted a combined third and fourth report in 2005. However, in the compilation of the combined reports, it appears that consideration of the committee's recommendations had not been taken into account, and it was being revised at the time of conducting this research (personal communication, member of the NGM). On the one hand, this demonstrates that the CEDAW is not used as a primary framework within which to locate strategies to promote gender transformation, and on the other hand, this demonstrates that the recommendations were not used as a reference for future action. This might have been influenced by changes in leadership and staff, which impacts on consistency and follow-through on previous work undertaken. In addition, the first official CEDAW report was not widely circulated, and this contributed to it not being used as a tool to inform future action.

The South African government had written two reports on the Beijing Platform for Action, highlighting the progress it has achieved and the obstacles it has faced during the implementation of its commitments by the beginning of 2005.

It is clear that at the formal level of the legislative framework, policies and statements, South Africa has demonstrated a political will to implement its international and national commitments to promote gender equality. However, it has fallen short of demonstrating this will to ensure that these are effectively implemented, through the provision of an inadequate budget, the lack of skilled human resources assigned to implement its gender programmes, not paying enough attention to ensuring that gender is successfully integrated into its cluster objectives and departmental programmes and ensuring that a strong message of promoting gender equality is heard by government functionaries.

General comments on the Effectiveness of the NGM

The coordination and leadership of each of these structures has changed hands a number of times since their inception. Differing levels of knowledge, expertise and commitment to promoting gender equality of the respective leaderships, as well as changes in political climate and ability to promote a gender agenda, and closeness with civil society organisations, has affected the structure's visibility and effectiveness in promoting its gender agenda.

The lack of an overall gender action plan with measurable targets and indicators, connected to government priorities, have made it difficult to ensure coordinated and effective mobilisation of the little resources that exist. At times, actions take place in a haphazard way, with each component of the gender machinery operating within its own imperatives, which has made it difficult to ensure that government actions effectively address the needs of (poor, black, rural) women. It also lacks the coordinated action and leverage to ensure that government complies with the Gender Policy Framework. Using a number of frameworks, policies, international conventions and actions plans, there is an understandable confusion when it comes time to plan and measure any progress achieved. It would be highly recommended for the NGM to create a single framework based on the priorities and problems faced by South African women, with measurable benchmarks and indicators. In addition, monitoring and evaluation of information could be maintained in a central database and accessed as and when necessary by various members of the NGM.

At the same time, women's research, training and advocacy NGOs work in a piecemeal, isolated fashion with different sections or components of the gender machinery, either conducting capacity building or picking up on the gender work outsourced by the gender machinery. These NGOs have also not taken advantage of the mechanisms that exist to call government to account for the slow and uneven implementation of its commitments to gender equality. NGOs are themselves under-funded and understaffed, working along sector lines without any clear coordination and linkages with other NGOs and CBOs, substantially weakening what was once promising to be a vibrant and active civil society organisation.

SITUATION OF WOMEN WITH REGARD TO GOVERNANCE, VIOLENCE AGAINST WOMEN AND SEXUAL AND REPRODUCTIVE HEALTH AND RIGHTS

Governance[7]

This section will consider women's participation in leadership and decision-making structures. In South Africa, there is no law that makes it mandatory for political parties to have quotas to ensure women's participation. However, the Constitution does contemplate the promotion of affirmative action measures where necessary, and the Employment Equity Act No 55 of 1998 outlaws discrimination on the basis of race, sex, gender, family responsibility, pregnancy and HIV status. In addition, the Electoral Act No 73 of 1998 outlines how registered political parties and candidates must facilitate the full and equal participation of women in political activities.

At a policy level, the ANC is the only political party to have a quota (30 per cent) on women's representation in decision-making positions, as well as in the presidential choices for the Executive (CALS, 2003/2004), and a 50 per cent at local government level. The White Paper on the Transformation of the Public Service (WPTPS, 1995) set a target for women to constitute at least 30 per cent of the new recruits to middle and senior management during 1995–1999 (OSW, 2004). These targets are echoed in the Gender Policy Framework. The lack of mandatory quotas for women's representation is seen as a weakness, as there is no legal means to ensure that all political parties promote women's representation, or to provide legal recourse in the event of the ANC changing their 30 per cent women's quota policy.

South Africa has one of the highest percentages of women's representation in political and decision-making structures in the world. The last 10 years has seen marked progress in this arena, particularly in the national and provincial legislatures. However, the arenas of local government, public service, judiciary, armed forces and private sector continue to demonstrate a marked male dominance in their leadership structures.

Women in National Parliament

The latest national elections in April 2004 saw women constituting almost a third of the National Assembly (32.75 per cent). This has demonstrated an increase from the 27.8 per cent that women occupied in 1997. By April 2004, women occupied 42.8 per cent of ministerial posts and 47.6 per cent of the deputy ministers. Currently, women hold two (out of the five) office bearer positions, namely the speaker and deputy speakers of the National Assembly.

Women in National Council of Provinces (NCOP) and Provincial Legislatures

At the provincial level, a similar 'success story' can be seen where women constitute 19 of the 54 permanent members (35.18 per cent). Four out of the nine Premiers are women, with women heading the provinces of Eastern Cape, Northern Cape, Free State and North West Province. On average, women constitute 32.3 per cent of the provincial legislatures. Gauteng has the highest representation of women (43.2 per cent), while the Western Cape and KZN hold with the lowest, with 28.5 per cent each. Executive posts held by women at the provincial level range from 50 per cent in Gauteng (five out of ten), 27.27 per cent in Free State (three out of eleven, including the Premier) to 10 per cent in KZN.

Women in Local Government

The local government level, arguably the most important for ensuring that service delivery benefits women, has been the most difficult for women to break into. In 2002, women constituted less than 16.9 per cent of the legislature. This improved in 2003 when women's participation increased, with women councillors constituting 23 per cent of the legislature. However, this still falls below the expected 30 per cent quota.

Women in Public Service

Women's representation in management positions within the national and provincial public service is a mere 23.9 per cent. If this figure is disaggregated by race, it is clear that South Africa is still carrying its apartheid legacy, as black women (African, Coloured and Indian) only constitute 6.7 per cent while white women constitute the remaining 17.1 per cent. Ten years of democracy have not demonstrated a notable gain for women's representation, as it has only improved from just over 10 per cent in 1997 to 23.9 per cent in 2003. The administrative management level also paints a bleak scenario, with women constituting only 9.5 per cent of municipality managers and only 13 per cent of officials in Planning and Implementation Support Centres.

Women in the Judiciary, Armed Forces and Police Services

These areas have proved to be traditional bastions of male power and privilege, demonstrating a considerably slower pace of change. Considering women's participation in the senior judiciary, there are only two women judges in the Constitutional Court and only one female High Court judge. Women make up less than 10 per cent of the total staff components of senior officials employed by the government in the judiciary. Women are not represented at all at the highest levels of the Armed Forces. Rather, most women in senior management in the Armed Forces are colonels, which is a rank at the lower end of the senior management system. However, even then, they are a minority, as in 2003 women constituted only 12 per cent of the total number of colonels. The scenario in the police services does not reveal any significant difference to this picture with women never having been appointed national or provincial commissioners. In 2003, one out of five deputy national commissioners was a woman, a small improvement from zero in 1997.

Comments on women's leadership and representation

There have been many debates amongst women's organisations and political parties about the best way to improve women's representation in decision-making structures. There has never been a consensus, with there being supporters of the need to adopt an official quota system (this ranging from 30–50 per cent) while others argue that increasing women's participation does not automatically translate into real gains for women, since what is required are people (men and women) who are sensitive to the needs and interests of women and have strong links to women's organisations. However, the ANC's 30 per cent quota for women's representation has undoubtedly contributed to the marked inroads that women have made at provincial and national level, with a slower uptake in the local government and the public sector.

The marked increase of women's representation did improve the working conditions of women in parliament. This resulted in changes in the working hours of parliament and the increase of facilities for women, such as childcare and toilets. At the same time, it has been argued that the 'sheer presence of numbers' also created a favourable environment for ensuring that many of the women-friendly laws and policies were adopted.

However, enormous barriers continue to be experienced by women politicians (at all levels, but particularly at local government level) and members of the public service. These would include amongst others, negative attitudes and suspicion of a woman's ability to hold public office, traditional practices and norms, including the gender division of labour, and lastly, electoral procedures (at local government level). As Albertyn states (1999), "the problems of representative democracy for women stem from women's inequality in civil society".

At national and provincial level, women parliamentarians have indicated that some of the challenges that they face include:

- The need for capacity development;
- Balancing the dual role of participating in parliamentary committee work, along with participating in parliamentary institutions established to promote gender equality;
- The skills to determine what are adequate resources to enable effective gender mainstreaming, and accessing such funds;
- Lack of funding for their work in the parliamentary committees (the latter is not a specific gender related challenge, but would apply to all committee members) (OSW, 2004).

A study carried out on women and local government by the Women's Development Foundation (WDF) in 2000 revealed that some of the challenges that women councillors have to deal with include:

- "Hostile male and/or white dominated environment that favoured incumbents from the older order;
- Overcoming language barriers, mainly Afrikaans, which was the main language in public service business prior to 1994; and
- An initial ambivalence towards women's participation in local government" (WDF, 2000 cited in CGE, 2001:13).

At the local government level, there are no specific measures that promote women's participation in electoral politics. An interviewee outlined the need for concrete measures to support women's entry into local government politics, including earmarked funding for women[9].

Based on a series of interviews with black women working in the public service, a study[10] found that the four broad obstacles to black women's effective participation include:

- The grip of culture:
- The belief that it is men who should be working in public office, which negatively influences both men and women's perceptions of their 'place' in society.

- Alienation – the 'chilly climate':
  - Gender (and racial) norms and stereotypes that underpin our unconscious and conscious behaviours and belief systems. These impact on power relations between people from different racial and gender groupings, which impacts on how black women are treated and sends a message to black women in management and elected offices that women are "outsiders to politics, governance, senior management and decision-making" (Gender Manual Consortium, date unstated: 190).

- The double-bind of assertiveness:
  - Black women are expected to be docile and deferential towards whites and men in the public service, while, at the same time, having to manage them and be assertive. If black women are assertive and strong, they are labelled as uncontrollable or insubordinate.

- The problems with women's multiple roles:
  - The conflict between work, domestic and community responsibilities have negative consequences for marriages, children, family and friends.

- Devaluation:
  - Black women's intellectual capacities and abilities to make decisions are constantly undermined, as white, male managers are seen to have the voice of wisdom and experience.

It has been argued that when it comes to affirmative action, racial redress is seen as more important than gender. An interviewee explained, "When we talk transformation, it's more about the racial side of things, black people are being empowered, and the side of women is slow to pick up."

Violence Against Women

South Africa has one of the highest incidences of VAW in the world. The different kinds of VAW discussed in this section will include domestic violence, rape, sexual harassment, trafficking and harmful traditional practices (namely FGM, virginity testing[11], dry sex, abduction or forced marriage).

The GBV sector is arguably the sector with the most organised civil society, ranging from local service providers to research, training and advocacy NGOs. Many of these are affiliated/connected to the Network on VAW at provincial levels. The Western Cape on VAW appears to be the most organised and vibrant network in the country.

The South African government has recognised that GBV is a priority issue and it is one of the areas where extensive progress has been made (especially in relation to domestic violence and rape) in terms of the development of laws, policies, plans and institutional mechanisms (CALS, 2003/2004).

Domestic Violence

Domestic violence is rife in South Africa with statistics revealing a systematic pattern of women abuse, both at a physical and economic level. This is invariably accompanied by emotional and psychological abuse as well.

Some of the statistics on DV indicate that:

- One in five currently married women reported economic abuse (SADHS, 1998).
- One in ten women had been physically assaulted in the year prior to the study: 6 per cent by their current or ex-partner and 4 per cent by somebody who was not a partner (SADHS, 1998).
- 28 per cent of women abused by a current or ex-partner needed medical attention. This demonstrates that men are very brutal when they assault their partners, and may point to under-reporting of less substantial abuse, such as slapping or emotional abuse (SADHS, 1998).
- Male relatives (mostly a cousin or an uncle) perpetrated 30 per cent of the cases of assaults by a non-partner, while a female relative (most commonly the mother) perpetrated 11 per cent of such cases (SADHS, 1998).
- Every six hours, a woman is killed by her intimate partner. This is the highest rate (8.8 per 100 000 female population 14 years and more) that has been reported in research throughout the world. Legal guns and alcohol play a significant role in these crimes (MRC, Policy Brief No 5, 2004).

In response to the high levels of DV suffered by women, and working closely with GBV NGOs in its development, the government adopted the DVA No. 116 of 1998. A considerable advance from previous laws, the DVA provides protection from both actual and threatened physical violence, sexual, emotional, verbal, psychological and economic violence as well as intimidation, harassment, stalking, damage to or destruction of property, or entry into a woman's home without her consent (OSW, 2004).

The DVA is structured in such a way that both the police and the courts share responsibilities for its effective implementation. It outlines the responsibilities of the Department of Safety and Security and of the Department of Justice and Social Development, since each of these departments have developed policies in this regard (CALS, 2003/2004). The Justice, Crime Prevention and Security Cluster have also established a process of coordinating government's strategy for eradicating violence against women and children (OSW, 2004).

Department of Justice (DoJ)

Prevention of VAW is a flagship programme of the Department of Justice's Gender Policy and includes ensuring that adequate administrative arrangements are in place for effective implementation of the Act. Other business units in the Department of Justice have also developed plans to implement the DVA, including the establishment of Family Courts to deal with family matters and domestic violence. Domestic violence interdicts are now sought within the Magistrates Courts and the specialised Family Courts. Five pilot family courts have been operating for several years, with additional resources allocated to them in 2003. The decision still has to be taken on whether, and how, to develop additional Family Courts. The National Prosecuting Office has a Sexual Offences and Community Affairs Unit that focuses on prosecuting crimes relevant to family violence issues. About 29 Sexual Offences Courts have been established to deal with cases of sexual violence (CALS, 2003/2004).

Department of Safety and Security

One of the South African Police Services (SAPS) key strategic priorities in 2000 included the reduction of crime against women and children to be implemented across its operational activities (administration; crime prevention; operation and response services; detective services; and crime intelligence and protection services). In 2003, the department identified the improvement of the investigation and prosecution of crimes, especially domestic violence, as a priority. This also included the need to conduct extensive training of police officers in the DVA (CALS, 2003/2004). The department has also restructured its special investigating units to establish 46 Family Violence, Child Protection and Sexual Offences Units, which are expected to increase over the next few years (Estimates of National Expenditure, 2003, 575 cited in CALS, 2003/2004).

Department of Social Development

This is the lead department in the inter-ministerial Victim Empowerment Programme (VEP), which provides victims of domestic violence with counselling, information and shelters. The VEP has begun to establish 'one-stop centres' which provide a combination of services, including support from specially trained police; health care services; courts; counselling services by government social workers; and shelters provided by NGOs.

Continued obstacles to effective redress

A study[12] conducted by a consortium of research NGOs to monitor the implementation of the DVA revealed that despite the national legislation, policies and programmes, there seems to have been no significant improvements in service delivery for victims of domestic violence. Women continue to be the victims of violence and to be subjected to secondary victimisation from the police and justice sectors. Some of the key barriers to implementation of the DVA identified by the study include:

- Fragmented service provision within the criminal justice system.
  - A court clerk indicated that there is a breakdown in the system when "police stations do not want to provide a service to a complainant if the complainant does not reside in the area (which falls under the jurisdiction of the police station), even though the respondent may reside there or work in the area" (Parenzee et al, 2001: 82). A further problem identified was the lack of infrastructure within the police and court systems to track cases or records (across jurisdictions), making it impossible to identify who has applied for an order in another jurisdiction or who is applying for a counter-order.

- Fragmented service provision: the health sector.
  - The DVA does not place obligations on health sector personnel to assist victims of domestic violence. This is a vital omission, considering that health services are often the first (and at times, only) point of contact with public sector service. The study detailed that criminal justice services have little or no interaction with health services. Although the Department of Health's

Strategic Priorities Plan 1999–2004 recognises that in principle, the health sector has an important role to play in addressing GBV, it has been slow on the uptake compared to the other departments.

- Lack of support services outside the criminal justice system:
  - The Act allows magistrates to order that the respondent to a DV charge be evicted from the home. However, the study revealed that magistrates are not all sensitive to the dynamics of gender violence and gender relations in general, and often do not resort to such measures. This often places women in the situation of having to leave their homes and, in most cases, requiring the services of a shelter. However, the demand for shelters far outweighs the supply, and many women are unable to access these services. Even if a woman is able to access a shelter, she is only allowed to stay for three months. Cases normally take longer than that to be heard in court, resulting in many women having to leave the shelter without having had access to legal recourse.

- Lack of resources:
  - Parenzee et al (2001) argue that the failure to budget for this legislation before it was enacted has undermined the ability of courts and police stations trying to undertake their specific (extended) responsibilities, as they all operate with insufficient and limited budgets. Other research has found that inadequate financial resources for domestic violence programmes take three forms. Firstly, there is often no, or insufficient, budgetary allocation to a programme; secondly, the existing allocation is often limited to covering the costs of personnel rather than programme implementation costs; thirdly, funds are sometimes not even being spent, usually in relation to personnel costs (Vetten and Khan, 2003 cited in CALS, 2003/2004). Concrete examples include: Magistrate Courts which were not provided with additional resources to implement their added duties, resulting in staff shortages; the ability of the SAPS to assist in cases of domestic violence is limited by a shortage of vehicles and understaffing; the Department of Social Development is only able to facilitate funding for less than half the shelters for abused women and children run by NGOs (CALS, 2003/2004).

- Attitudes of personnel:
  - Many of those responsible for implementing the legislation do not understand the dynamics of domestic violence and have traditional gender beliefs and behaviours, including stereotypes and myths that blame women for domestic violence. In addition, the study points out that evidence exists of high levels of domestic violence within the police force, indicating that police officers are unlikely to conduct themselves favourably in cases of domestic violence, if they themselves are perpetrators. These negative attitudes are worsened by a degree of ignorance of the additional roles and responsibilities the DVA requires of them. Training has been identified as one of the means to deal with this serious problem. However, considering the problems of budgetary, personnel and time restrictions, this training has often been too little and too piecemeal to effectively address attitudes which undermine the intent of the law.

At the same time, the government has not provided the public and government and public service officials with enough information about the DVA, its approach and strategies. Dissemination is often not widespread enough and is not sufficiently targeted. Exceptions to this can be found during ceremonial occasions and specific times of the year, such as National Women's Day and the Sixteen Days against VAW Campaign (CALS, 2003/2004).

Rape

The available statistics on rape and sexual assault reveal that women being forced or persuaded to have sex when they do not want to, is a common practice in South Africa. The statistics outlined below need to be considered in the context of rape being an under-reported phenomenon. Rape Crisis has argued that only one in twenty women report a rape to the police (www.rapecrisis.org.za).

- Seven per cent of all women who had ever had sex had been either forced or persuaded to have sex at some time when they didn't want to (SADHS, 1998).
- Only 15 per cent of women who were forced to have sex reported the rape to the police (SADHS, 1998).
- A recent Human Rights Watch Report[13] reveals repeated allegations of teachers having engaged in sexual relations with underage girls.

Teachers often pay students or offer them good grades in exchange for their silence. The report revealed that school officials have often swept these issues under the carpet, often delaying disciplinary action against perpetrators (if they happen at all).

- 33 per cent of women who reported being raped under the age of 15 stated that the perpetrator had been their schoolteacher (SADHS, 1998).

- Considering how few rapes are actually reported and the high rates of sexual violence, what is most concerning of all is that only seven per cent of reported rapes were convicted in 2003.[14]

- Examining the relationship between HIV/AIDS and VAW, it is frightening to note that women who have experienced physical or sexual violence in their lifetime are one and a half times more likely to be HIV positive than women who have never been abused (Steinberg et al, 2002).

The DVA outlaws marital rape, a step that few countries in the world have taken. The current legal definition of rape is limited (both in terms of understanding what constitutes a rape, and who can be raped). The South African Law Commission (SALC) has reviewed the substantive and procedural law of rape and sexual assault, and revised legislation, in the guise of the Sexual Offences Bill, was approved by parliament. It had not yet been signed by the president as of September 2007. Once signed, it will become law.

The South African government has committed itself to reducing GBV and the Departments of Justice (through the National Prosecuting Office), Safety and Security (through the SAPS), Health and Social Development have all made policy commitments to this effect.

Cabinet has approved an inter-departmental Anti-Rape Strategic Framework. However, the government is still developing detailed plans for all government departments in order to have an integrated inter-departmental approach that focuses on prevention, response and support of rape survivors (CALS, 2003/2004).

Department of Justice

The National Prosecuting Office has a Sexual Offences and Community Affairs Unit that focuses on prosecuting crimes relevant to family violence issues. Sexual Offences Courts (about 29) have been established to deal with cases of sexual violence (CALS, 2003/2004).

Department of Safety and Security

The SAPS plans are outlined in the domestic violence section above. The SAPS will also play a central role in the national anti-rape strategy, improving the detection and disposal rate of rape crimes. In addition, the SAPS, together with the Departments of Education and Social Development, has developed integrated programmes to address rape and domestic violence.

Department of Health

The Directorate on Maternal, Child and Women's Health is developing detailed policies to train health workers to effectively address sexual violence in their work. Training is carried out at a provincial level. Norms and Standards for dealing with rape survivors have been introduced within the Primary Health Care Package.

The Department of Social Development is implementing its plan through the Victim Empowerment Programme (see domestic violence section above). Social workers provide counselling in the Sexual Offences Courts.

Programmes to address rape and sexual assault across all departments are hindered by insufficient funding and the lack of trained and sensitive personnel. This has negatively affected the delivery of the Sexual Offences Courts and the ability of the SAPS to implement its plans fully (lack of vehicles and trained officers, etc). A study of the Sexual Offences Courts in the Western Cape evidenced staff shortages and the need for training of personnel in order for them to respond sensitively and appropriately to rape survivors (IDASA, 2001 cited in CALS, 2003/2004). Considering the need to transform patriarchal gender norms and beliefs generally, and the myths relating to rape particularly, training is an important component of any governmental strategy to improve service delivery. However, there is an inadequate government training budget, and departments have had to raise funds from international donors in order to train their staff.

The government maintains basic statistical records and monitors prosecutions and convictions reports to the SAPS. The Department of Justice monitors the prosecution and conviction rate in courts, especially the Sexual Offences Courts. On a positive note, these have shown an increase from 50 per cent in 1997/8 to an average of 67 per cent in 2003 (CALS, 2003/2004).

Sexual Harassment

Sexual harassment is understood as any unwanted attention of a sexual nature that takes place in the workplace, in schools and in public places. Sexual harassment in the workplace is one of the most prevalent forms of GBV in South Africa and is rife in schools (SHEP, 2003; HRW, 2000).

Statistics reveal that:

- 77 per cent of women and 20 per cent of men have experienced sexual harassment sometime during their working lives (SHEP, 2003).
- 83 per cent of perpetrators are men with 66 per cent of the perpetrators occupying positions of office either as supervisors or senior management (SHEP, 2003).
- Sexual harassment is most prevalent in the security services, construction, mining, the entertainment industry and the informal sectors (SHEP, 2003).
- Only 17 per cent of sexual harassment incidents have been reported (SHEP, 2003).
- Only 44.2 per cent of reported cases are resolved in favour of the complainant.

There are several laws that protect people from sexual harassment, including:

- Labour Relations Act, No. 66 of 1995, which is the main act that deals with sexual harassment in the workplace. Sexual harassment at the workplace constitutes an unfair labour practice (AIDS Law Project and Aids Legal Network, 2003).
- Employment Equity Act, No. 55 of 1998 stipulates that harassment of an employee is a form of unfair discrimination.
- Promotion of Equality and Prevention of Unfair Discrimination Act, No. 4 of 2000 provides general protection against sexual harassment.
- The Employment of Educators Act, No. 53 of 1998, amended in 2000 explicitly makes sexual harassment a form of serious misconduct for educators (Section 17), becoming grounds for dismissal.
- The South African Schools Act, No. 84 of 1996 outlines how sexual harassment constitutes misconduct by learners.

At the same time, the South African government has a Code of Good Practice on Sexual Harassment, providing policy guidelines to employees on how to address the issue of sexual harassment. General complaints of sexual harassment fall within the Equality Courts under the Department of Justice. Sexual harassment in schools falls under the Department of Education. There are general policy commitments to reducing sexual harassment in schools outlined in the Department of Education's Strategic Plan 2002–2004. However, there is no comprehensive national policy on the prevention and eradication of sexual harassment in schools. By early 2005, there was a process in place by the GFP in the Department of Education to consolidate the national policy on the prevention and eradication of sexual harassment in schools.

Implementation and Monitoring

Sexual harassment in the workplace falls under the Department of Labour's Employment Equity Directorate and the Commission for Conciliation, Mediation and Arbitration (CCMA) and the Department of Justice's Labour Court. Unfortunately, the CCMA does not have an operations budget. Commissioners who hear CCMA cases, however, have been trained on sexual harassment and related issues. The number of complaints and cases brought before the CCMA or the courts are monitored. To date, there has been no systematic evaluation of the existing mechanisms to address sexual harassment (CALS, 2003/2004).

The SHEP (School Health Education Programme) study reveals that formal workplaces on the whole did have a sexual harassment policy. However, only 20.7 per cent of the respondents knew that their companies had a sexual harassment policy while 43.6 per cent of the respondents believed that their companies did not have a policy. Informal sector workplaces, like domestic workers and street vendors, will not be protected by such measures, and are extremely vulnerable to exploitation and harassment.

By 2005, the Department of Justice was in the process of establishing Equality Courts, and has developed a plan for their rollout. The Equality Courts are able to hear cases of sexual harassment, save for employer–employee relationships. A now familiar story, budgetary constraints have resulted in a limited rollout. Presiding officers and clerks have been trained on general issues pertaining to the Promotion of Equality and Prevention of Unfair Discrimination Act, No. 4 of 2000 (using donor funding). The Department of Justice records all sexual harassment cases that find their way to the Labour Courts, and will also record cases in the Equality Courts (CALS, 2003/2004).

The Department of Education handles complaints within the schools via Life Skills educators and the District Office. However, as described above in the situational analysis, school boards are loath to take any meaningful disciplinary action against staff members and the issue is more often than not swept under the carpet. The Department of Education is beginning to monitor complaints and disciplinary cases related to incidents of sexual harassment and violence in schools on a monthly basis. However, the lack of a comprehensive plan to combat sexual harassment means that there is no fully elaborated budget. In addition, schools facing resource constraints often do not have the required trained Life Skills educators. The department has, however, developed training modules on Managing Sexual Harassment and Gender Based Violence for both teachers and learners (CALS, 2003/2004).

Trafficking of Women (and Children)

Trafficking of women (and children) is a severely under-reported and under researched area in South Africa. A recent stakeholders conference revealed that trafficking was more pervasive than previously thought, and reveals that South Africa is both a transit and destination point for trafficking women. Intra-country trafficking of women takes place, mostly from rural to urban areas. Issues that still need further research include the extent to which South Africa is a source of trafficked women, the actual extent to which women are trafficked into and through South Africa, and for what purposes (National Stakeholders Consultative Conference Report, 2003, cited in OSW, 2004).

South Africa does not have legislation specifically dealing with trafficking of women and children. The South African Law Commission (SALC) is considering trafficking in its current review of the Sexual Offences Act, developing a Comprehensive Issue Paper on trafficking (OSW, 2004). To date, the SALC has recommended the formulation of specialised legislation to address trafficking for prostitution and other purposes. Trafficking in children will be dealt with in the Sexual Offences Bill and the Children's Bill (CALS, 2003/2004). The Sexual Offences Bill was approved by parliament in 2007 and was awaiting consent by the president before it became law.

There are a number of policy commitments from several departments. These include the Department of Justice's Gender Policy, which aims to create a legal environment conducive to eliminating all forms of trafficking of women and children; and the Department of Labour's draft White Paper on a National Child Labour Action Programme for South Africa, which deals with the issue of trafficking of children and recommends specific actions to be adopted by several government departments (CALS, 2003/2004).

However, both of the above are not policies yet. Currently, South Africa policies trafficking under the current Sexual Offences Bill, which deals with alien control and refugees. People who are trafficked are most often treated as illegal immigrants and deported. Other laws which can be used to prosecute traffickers and protect women who are trafficked, include:

- The Prevention of Organised Crime Act, No. 121 of 1998;
- The Refugees Act, No. 130 of 1998;
- The Domestic Violence Act, No. 116 of 1998;
- The Basic Conditions of Employment Act, No. 75 of 1997;
- The Child Care Amendment Act, No. 96 of 1996.

However, it is clear that the absence of specific legislation on trafficking undermines both efforts to protect women and children who are being trafficked and the capture and prosecution of offenders (OSW, 2004).

The lack of specific trafficking legislation is not a new concern for South Africa, and was already highlighted in South Africa's first CEDAW Report, 1998. In fact, the committee, in its concluding comments on South Africa's report, requested that the legal situation and the situation of trafficked women be addressed and reported on in South Africa's next report (Report, para 125 and 126 cited in CALS, 2003/2004). This is something that South Africa has been slow to address.

Harmful Traditional Practices

Harmful traditional practices in the South African context include FGM; virginity testing; dry sex; abduction or forced marriage; ukungena; and the burning and victimisation of women called 'witches'.

There is disagreement as to whether FGM is currently practised in South Africa. However, Klugman et al (1998) argue that it may be present as a result of increasing immigration to South Africa of people from communities who practise it. At the same time, with changing approaches to Islam, it was argued that the practice is present in some sections of the Muslim community. Considering this uncertainty, the

Department of Health has been called upon to conduct research to establish the prevalence of FGM in South Africa (CALS, 2003/2004).

Testing to determine whether a girl has lost her virginity ('virginity testing') is still performed in some provinces, including the Eastern Cape and Limpopo, and has recently been revived in KZN. Considering the current context of HIV/AIDS, this practice has taken on new proportions, as it is popularly seen as a means to 'protect' young girls from potential HIV infection. However, women's and human rights organisations have argued that the practice denies young girls their right to autonomy and dignity (especially considering no similar practices of promoting young boys' virginity exist). In the context of the 'virgin myth' (the belief that having sex with a virgin will cure you of HIV/AIDS), it is argued that this practice might place young girls who are 'proven' virgins at an increased risk of sexual violence or exploitation, and possible infection (Klugman et al, 1999; Centre for Reproductive Law and Policy, 2001).

'Dry sex' is a common practice in South Africa.[15] Some of the substances used are harmful to the vaginal mucosa and cause ulceration (Boikanyo, 1992 cited in Klugman et al, 1998). Apart from making sexual relations painful for women, it has been associated with higher HIV and other STI transmission rates as it is more likely to result in the vaginal wall tearing during sexual relations (Centre for Reproductive Law and Policy, 2001).

Abduction, or forced marriage, still exists in some areas of the country (CALS, 2003/2004). The North West Provincial CGE has reported that some young girls are still being forced into arranged marriages, often to older men, for the sake of the family's survival (CGE, Annual Report, April 2001–March 2002).

Burning and victimisation of women accused of being 'witches' in the community and ukengena were also named as traditional practices that are harmful to women (OSW, 2003). In the early 1990s, there was a dramatic escalation of witchcraft related violence in South Africa, particularly in Limpopo. In March 1995, the Executive Council of the then Northern Province (currently Limpopo) appointed a Commission into Witchcraft Violence and Ritual Murders. Police statistics revealed that between 1990 and April 1995, 445 cases of witchcraft were reported, with most of the cases (54 per cent) occurring between April 1994 and April 1995.[16] During the period of 1 April 1994 to 16 February 1995, 97 women and 46 men were killed as a result of witch accusations between the period of April 1994 to 16 February 1995 (CGE, 1998).

South Africa's legal framework contemplates harmful traditional practices in terms of the following:

- The Promotion of Equality and Prevention of Unfair Discrimination Act protects women from discrimination. Possible cases of unfair discrimination include FGM, GBV and 'any practice, including any traditional, customary or religious practice, which impairs the dignity of women and undermines equality between women and men, including undermining the dignity and well being of the girl-child (Section 8 a, b, d).
- The Customary Marriages Act, No. 120 of 1998 outlaws forced marriages, as it requires the consent of both parties.

Policy commitments exist at a fairly abstract level. The Constitution protects women from violence and harm, and protects their rights to life, dignity and health. However, no detailed policies exist on specific harmful practices, such as virginity testing or other harmful practices outlined in the situational analysis above (CALS, 2003/2004).

Both the CGE (virginity testing and witch burning) and the OSW (traditional leaders) have held public hearings on harmful practices. However, the government has not conducted research on these issues, nor has it conducted information or education campaigns.

Considering the extent of harmful traditional practices in South Africa, and its resultant loss of life and/or abuse of women's human rights, this is an area that urgently needs exploring.

Sexual and Reproductive Health Rights

In South Africa, there is a contradiction between women's sexual and reproductive health rights (SRHR) on paper, and their ability to exercise them in practice. On the one hand, there is a positive legislative and policy framework, counter faced with women experiencing difficulties to exercise their SRHR, both within the family, the community and in relation to the government. On the other, negative traditional gender norms and practices, along with the unequal status of women, result in women being seen to be primarily responsible for contraception and childcare, with little power to negotiate when, with whom and why to have sex. Women also bear the brunt of the HIV/AIDS pandemic – both in terms of levels of infection, as well as shouldering the burden of caring for those living with HIV/AIDS.

The range of issues considered includes maternal health (including termination of pregnancy); access to and use of contraception; the situation of adolescent sexual and reproductive health; STIs; and HIV/AIDS.

Maternal Health

Antenatal care, delivery and postnatal services are offered free of charge in the public health sector, greatly improving women's access to health services. The SADHS (1998) reveals that 95.1 per cent of women attend antenatal care at least once in their pregnancy and 83.7 per cent of women give birth in an institution. However, women who are less educated and those that have more babies are less likely to attend antenatal services.

African women account for 92 per cent of maternal deaths (DOH, 1999), mostly occurring during the postpartum period. First time pregnancies, women with more than five children and those who are older than 30 years of age are at greater risk of dying during childbirth. The maternal mortality ratio is estimated to be between 175 and 200 deaths per 100 000 women (DOH, 2000 a).

In terms of the legislative framework, the Promotion of Equality and Prevention of Unfair Discrimination Act (No. 4 of 2000) prohibits the denial of access to services. It also mentions women's right of access to social services or benefits, including health. In addition, the National Policy Health Act, No. 116 of 1990 made deaths during pregnancy, childbirth and puerperium notifiable deaths. The National Committee on Confidential Enquiries into Maternal Deaths (NCCEMD) was established in 1997 to collect data, monitor and report on maternal deaths and to make recommendations to the Department of Health (DOH) on how to reduce the maternal mortality ratio.

Overall policy development lies with the Maternal, Child and Women's Health (MCWH) Directorate in the National Department. The Directorate also coordinates and facilitates the reorganisation of maternal health services and develops standardised case management protocols for the care of women and children. Similar units exist at provincial level to oversee the planning, implementation, supervision, monitoring and evaluation of integrated MCWH services. District health teams, in the process of being established, should perform similar functions at district level (CALS, 2003/2004). The National Department of Health has developed a range of policies to monitor and reduce cases of maternal mortality.[17] However, there has been an uneven development of plans at provincial level (CALS, 2003/2004).

The Safe Motherhood Programme includes five areas of work, including choice on contraception, antenatal care, clean and safe delivery, essential obstetric care and choice on termination of pregnancy.

Some of the challenges to ensuring that the guidelines and policies are implemented include:

- A shortage in the provision of accessible public clinics and functioning hospitals that can carry out comprehensive, emergency obstetric care (CALS, 2003/2004).

- A shortage of facilities in some rural areas, resulting in some women being more than an hour away from a facility providing essential obstetric care (CALS, 2003/2004).

- Poor health care worker performance, which occurred in more than half the cases of maternal deaths. The majority of these deaths occurred at primary health care level, with failure to follow standard protocols being the key problem (Smit et al, 2004). Haemorrhage remains an important cause of maternal death, associated with substandard care and poor referral systems in outlying areas (DOH, 2000 a).

- Staff shortages contribute to poor technical and human quality of care. Skilled staff leaving to work overseas exacerbates the staff shortage and that the vast majority of obstetricians and gynecologists are in private practice and unevenly spread in the provincial public sector (Smit et al, 2004 and CALS, 2003/2004).

The Choice on Termination of Pregnancy Act No. 92 of 1996 (CTOP) opened the door for women and girls to opt for safe abortions in the case of unwanted pregnancies. CTOP makes provision for adolescent girls to access abortion on demand within the first 12 weeks of pregnancy, without the need for parental or medical consent.

Between 1997 and February 2004 (RRA, 2004):

- 344 477 women and girls have undergone termination of pregnancies (TOP) at public health facilities, 89 per cent of them above the age of 18.

- 62 per cent of designated facilities are online (193 facilities), 76 per cent in the public sector.

- Out of the public health facilities providing TOP, 90 per cent are hospitals with the rest being community health centres or primary health care clinics.

However, women and girls continue to experience a range of problems accessing good quality TOP services, which has been unevenly spread amongst the provinces. Gauteng has performed the most number of TOPs, followed by the Western Cape and Free State. Some designated health facilities still do not offer this service.

Ignorance of the right to a legal abortion, living far away from designated facilities and stigma are fundamental obstacles to women's access to TOP. Ignorance of the law accounted for the main reason why 55 per cent of women in Gauteng did not use a designated facility (DOH, 2000 b). This lack of knowledge will probably be considerably greater in the rural areas. For their part, health care workers report lack of managerial support and negative attitudes from colleagues, clients and the broader community contributing to hindering good quality services. Nurses have the right to conscientious objection, and some do exercise it.

CTOP has faced a number of legal attacks from pro-life organisations; however, the government has been successfully able defend the constitutionality of the law, thereby protecting women's right to access TOP.[18]

Contraception

One of the core priorities of the DOH's Health Sector Strategic Framework 1999–2004 includes improving women's health and reducing teenage pregnancy. In 2002, the National DOH published its National Contraceptive Policy Guidelines, which aimed to remove barriers that restrict access to contraceptive services, increase public knowledge of client's rights, contraceptive methods and services and to provide high quality contraceptive services. The policy highlights the need to integrate contraception services into reproductive health services, within the primary health care system (CALS, 2003/2004).

The MCWH directorates are directly responsible for managing contraceptive services at provincial level and for overseeing delivery through the district health system within their respective provinces. These delivery points range from clinics and community health centres and mobile units at community level to district hospitals, tertiary hospitals and academic centres (National Contraceptive Guidelines, pg 12 cited in CALS, 2003/2004).

The SADHS (1998) reveals that the current contraceptive prevalence for women is high (61.2 per cent). However, this scenario varies according to provincial and urban/rural location, age, education, marital status and race. Young women between the ages of 20–24 and educated women have a higher level of contraceptive use. The public sector is the main source of free contraceptives for women, with an injectable contraceptive being the most widely used.

Female sterilisation services are not easily accessible to women, especially in the rural areas and vasectomy services are almost non-existent in the public sector. The male condom, although widely available, has not been actively promoted for contraceptive use, but rather for STIs and HIV prevention. The availability of the female condom, on the other hand, is very limited. The diaphragm is unavailable at public sector services. Although emergency contraception was down scheduled in November 2000 and is now available over the counter in pharmacies, it is seldom accessed from the public sector (Smit et al, 2004).

Service delivery guidelines to implement the National Contraceptive Policy Guidelines have been developed, and training is ongoing. Although vertical family planning services still remain in the large urban clinics, these services have been integrated into primary health care services in an ongoing fashion since 1991 (Smit et al, 2004).

However, challenges remain including staff shortages, high turnover and poor quality of care. A particular challenge is the need to promote the ethos that the client needs to choose the contraceptive method that suits them best. Poor working conditions of primary health care workers, including the expectation to provide an increasing number of services with the primary care package offered without a concomitant increase in staff, undoubtedly contribute to this. The government is aware of these issues, and is attempting to address them through improved management and training of health care workers (CALS, 2003/2004). Training is taking place at district level to strengthen the capacity of health workers in capturing information for the purpose of monitoring and evaluation (DOH Annual Report cited in CALS, 2003/2004).

Adolescent Sexual and Reproductive Health

Most young South Africans begin having sexual relations in their mid-teens. The national average age of first intercourse is 15 for girls, and 14 for boys (DOH, 2001).

The teenage pregnancy rate is high, which indicates a low level of contraceptive use, at least before the conception of the first child. The latest demographic health survey revealed that 16.4 per cent of women aged 15–19 had been pregnant at least once, and that by the age of 19, 35.1 per cent of teenagers surveyed had been pregnant. There is, however, a relatively high contraceptive prevalence, of 64.4 per cent among 15–19-year-old sexually active young women, thereafter.

Factors contributing to the high teenage pregnancy rate are high levels of sexual coercion faced by young girls; their limited ability to negotiate safe sex and their socialisation, which makes them see men as the sexual decision makers.

In 1991, maternal mortality was almost double for women under 20 years of age compared to that of women older than 20 years (DOH, 2001).

Amongst South Africans that are sexually active, those in the youngest age groups are most at risk of contracting STIs and HIV/AIDS; in fact, 60 per cent of all HIV infections occur in the 15–24-year-old age group (DOH, 2001). However, young women are particularly vulnerable to HIV infection, and 77 per cent of those living with HIV/AIDS in the 15–24-year-old age group are young women (UNAIDS, 2002).

The 2001 Adolescent and Youth Health Policy Guidelines marked the government's commitment to provide accessible and youth friendly services to young women and men, including the integration of SRH services (including TOP). The National Adolescent Friendly Clinic Initiative aims to make primary health care clinics more accessible to youth.

However, barriers to access to services continue to be experienced. These including the fact that:

- Health services continue to be relatively inaccessible to young people, especially the poor and those living in rural areas. Young people often do not have the money for transport to clinics or health care facilities.

- Issues of confidentiality remain a concern – either as a result of moralistic attitudes on the part of the health care worker, or structurally because the clinics do not provide adequate spaces to ensure privacy.

- Negative attitudes on the part of health care workers, who treat adolescents rudely and ask intrusive questions, often reinforcing gender stereotypes.

- Ignorance of existing youth friendly initiatives (DOH, 2001).

An important approach of the Policy Guidelines is to identify a range of intervention sites that extend beyond the health facility. These include, the home, the school, the workplace, community based organisations and residential centres.

Apart from services provided in the public health sector, several NGOs have established adolescent or youth centres which offer sexual and reproductive health services. These include LoveLife (heavily financed by the SA government) and the Planned Parenthood Association of South Africa (PPASA). NGOs also offer training and conduct educational campaigns, along with advocacy campaigns to promote youth's access to services.

STIs and HIV/AIDS[19]

South Africa is experiencing a generalised pandemic whose mode of transmission is predominantly heterosexual. Owing to the extent of the pandemic, funding and vertical programmatic services have removed HIV/AIDS from being considered an area of sexual and reproductive health. Women and girls experience a higher vulnerability to HIV transmission than men and boys, for a number of reasons. Apart from biological reasons, social, cultural and economic inequalities create the conditions whereby the HIV prevalence rate is higher for women and girls. The following statistics reveal the extent of the HIV/AIDS pandemic in South Africa (UNAIDS, 2004a and c):

- 5,300,000 adults and children are living with HIV/AIDS in South Africa.
- Women make up 57 per cent of the 5.1 million adults, between the ages of 15 and 49, who are HIV positive.
- There is a 21.5 per cent HIV prevalence for adults, one of the highest in the world.

HIV/AIDS Policies and Plans

The Department of Health developed the HIV/AIDS/STI Strategic Plan for South Africa: 2000–2005. The plan, which recognises the vulnerable position of women, attempts to ensure that women do no suffer discrimination nor remain unable to take effective measures to prevent infection (para 4 cited in CALS, 2003/2004). However, since the plan encourages the women's sector to develop their own policies, it seemingly marginalised women's concerns from the plan. On the whole, the gendered dimensions of the epidemic are not considered sufficiently; unequal power relations between women and men, for example, are not taken into account in the section on prevention. Women are regularly treated as vulnerable groups that require special measures (mothers, survivors of violence, sex workers).

The policy covers the dimensions of prevention, treatment and mitigation of the effects of HIV/AIDS. It provides for HIV/AIDS services to be located within the primary health care system. In 2003, Cabinet committed itself to the provision of ARV therapy in the public sector, and has since developed an implementation plan. Cabinet committed itself to assist families affected by HIV/AIDS and to improve the system of home-based and community-based care. The provision of economic resources, through the Department of Social Development, is mainly targeted at women as caregivers (through the child support grant) and at old people (through pensions).

In October 2000, the Department of Health released a series of HIV/AIDS Policy Guidelines, including guidelines for managing and treating patients with HIV/AIDS. Some of these include the Prevention of Mother to Child Transmission and Management of HIV Positive Pregnant Women and the National Policy on Testing for HIV (2000).

Implementation and Monitoring

The Department of Health has a National Directorate on HIV/AIDS, which is mirrored with Provincial Directorates on HIV/AIDS in all provincial health departments. Inter-departmental Provincial Committees are being established, which are replicated at the district level. However, major restructuring has affected provincial departments and some district structures are still in the process of being established. The integration of gender-based violence and HIV/AIDS into primary health care institutions is still an ongoing process.

The Department of Social Development has programmes to mitigate the socio-economic impact of HIV/AIDS carried out by the HIV/AIDS Directorate, located within the Development Implementation Support Directorate. The National Integrated Plan is located in the Departments of Health, Education and Social Development, with structures that exist down to district level.

Planning for the implementation of the policy takes place at a national and provincial level, with provinces and local levels developing detailed plans. Progress has been made in some provinces to formulate policies to integrate HIV/AIDS activities into primary health care; however, this has taken place in the context of major restructuring of the health services (Adar and Stevens cited in CALS, 2003/2004).

Prevention of HIV/AIDS

The emphasis of prevention messages is on lifestyle changes. However, the governmental (and NGO) promotion of 'Abstain, Be faithful and Condomise (ABC)' prevention messages do not take into account the high levels of sexual coercion and rape experienced by women and girls. In addition, it is common for young girls and older men to have sex in South Africa. Older men's resistance to using condoms[20], and the fact that it is more likely for older men to be HIV positive than younger men, contribute to a young girl's risk of HIV transmission. Sex in exchange for groceries, school fees, clothes and/or luxury goods contributes to the dangers of these relationships. The likelihood of young girls having the power to negotiate safe sex is poor (UNAIDS, 2004 b).

Men's multiple sexual partners, in the context of their resistance to condom use, worsen the situation. Women have indicated that it is more difficult to negotiate condom usage with stable or permanent partners than it is in casual sexual relationships.

Access to treatment

Voluntary Counselling and Testing (VCT) has become a routine part of antenatal care. However, clients that attend primary health care clinics or hospitals for other services have to actively request to be tested. The largest provision of VCT services is in the most urbanised provinces where there is better infrastructure, more staff and fewer social and cultural constraints. The STI baseline survey reveals that 53 per cent of Primary Health Care (PHC) facilities are designated VCT sites, however, only 67 per cent of all PHC facilities were offering HIV counselling and 69 per cent were offering HIV testing in July 2002 (Doherty et al, 2004).

Prevention of Mother to Child Transmission (PMTCT) pilot programmes have been extended to include a more universal rollout in several provinces. This was adopted after a high profile court battle, where the Treatment Action Campaign (TAC) successfully litigated to ensure government extended the provision of these programmes. A baseline survey of STI and HIV services in July 2002 estimated that 29 per cent of PHC facilities were providing PMTCT services (Doherty et al, 2004). South Africa is one of the few countries with PMTCT+ services. In the PMTCT+ model, women's access to care and treatment continues after their baby has been born.

The AIDS Directorate has rolled out post-exposure services, but planning and implementation is uneven across provinces.

The DOH's treatment policy focuses on support through positive living; effective, prompt treatment of opportunistic infections; and care for those living with HIV/AIDS. A national plan for the provision of ARVs has been developed; however, this has been slow in rolling out and access to ARVs is not at optimum levels. Of the approximately 500 000 South Africans who could immediately benefit from Highly Active Anti-Retroviral Treatment (HAART), only between 20 000–40 000 are currently receiving this treatment. The majority of these are accessing treatment through the private sector (Doherty et al, 2004).

The Department of Social Development's Strategic Plan 2002/3–2004/5 lays out a plan for addressing the mitigation of "the social and economic impacts of HIV/AIDS on vulnerable groups". These include community and home-based care and information programmes for women.

Overall, the budget for HIV/AIDS has increased over the years, and is set to increase further. Most of the money will go to the provinces for them to allocate where they consider necessary. There has been an increased allocation to PMTCT services and community and home-based care from R5 million in 2001 to R138 million in 2004/5.

In general, health care workers are not fully equipped to deal with HIV/AIDS, in particular the situation of women. High staff turnover, burnout and negative attitudes continue to be obstacles in providing an effective service. HIV also affects the health services itself, including loss of staff owing to illness; absenteeism; low staff morale; and increased burden of patient load (Doherty et al, 2004).

Government monitors the prevalence of HIV, providing a gendered breakdown. The development of effective and gendered monitoring systems and systematic evaluation is still in progress.

AU Women's Protocol
Country Position and Process Followed in South Africa
The Process of Adopting Protocols in South Africa

Protocols adopted under Section 231 (3) of the Constitution (technical, executive and administrative protocols) are adopted by the Executive Cabinet and tabled in parliament. Parliament merely takes note of such a Protocol and approval is not required.

Protocols adopted under Section 231 (2) of the Constitution require parliamentary approval. They bind South Africa's National Executive office vis-à-vis other state parties (i.e. it applies only to that part of the state that can enter into international relations; excluding provincial and local governments).

These protocols are first discussed at Executive Cabinet level, after which it is tabled before the National Assembly, where it is immediately referred for further discussion and investigation to the relevant parliamentary committee. The department responsible for the protocol would seek legal counsel from the state legal advisors to determine South Africa's obligations under international law and its effect on South Africa's domestic law (as the country is still held accountable to other state parties for its domestic legal framework).

The relevant parliamentary committee would present their

recommendations in a report (approval or not) on the Protocol to the National Assembly. The National Assembly would then discuss it and either approve it or not. If its approved, the protocol is then sent to be discussed and approved (or not) at the National Council of Provinces (NCOP). If the NCOP approves it, the protocol is considered to have been approved by parliament. The instrument for ratification is then drafted and deposited with the relevant structure or body.

If there is an intention to domesticate the protocol (i.e. for the protocol to form part of South Africa's domestic law) it needs to be incorporated by means of a legislative act, and to be adopted under 231 (4) of the Constitution. Laws (based on the provisions of the protocol) that are consistent with the Constitution would then be enacted, if necessary. It is only then that the protocol will become legally enforceable in South African courts.

The Process followed by the Women's Protocol
Internal Discussions

In preparation for the March 2003 Ministerial Meeting to be held in Addis Ababa to discuss the Draft Protocol on Women's Rights in Africa, the Department of Foreign Affairs, members of civil society and academics began discussing South Africa's position vis-à-vis the Draft Protocol. The CGE held a consultative seminar on the South Africa. In the summary, the general perception was that the South African legislative and policy framework superceded the provisions contained in the Draft Protocol.

- March 2003, Ministerial Meeting in Addis Ababa
  - The Draft Protocol was tabled for discussion. The South African delegation, led by the then Deputy Minister of Justice and Constitutional Development, included representatives of the Departments of Foreign Affairs and Justice, the NGM, academics and civil society. South Africa noted a series of verbal reservations during the meeting and attempted to influence the content of the instrument. The Draft Protocol was then referred for further discussion during the AU Summit to be held in Maputo in July 2003.
- June 2003, Cabinet Meeting
  - The Department of Foreign Affairs (with substantial input from the then Deputy Minister of Justice) reported on the Addis

Ababa meeting to Cabinet. It was recommended that the Draft Protocol (with South Africa's reservations) be used as the basis of South Africa's position during the forthcoming AU Summit.

- In order to gauge South Africa's legal standing vis-à-vis the Draft Protocol, the Department of Foreign Affairs sought legal counsel from the state legal advisors to the Department of Foreign Affairs (international law) and the Department of Justice (domestic law). Domestic law was also considered, as South Africa could be held accountable to another state party if the domestic system acted in contravention of certain principles. On the whole, no major contradictions were found between the Draft Protocol and South Africa's national and international law.

- July 2003, AU Assembly in Maputo
  - The Draft Protocol is adopted. The Assembly then opened the Women's Protocol for signature by member states.

- October 2003, Cabinet Meeting
  - Cabinet approved the recommendations of the June Cabinet Memorandum and also approved that the Women's Protocol be submitted to parliament.

- March 2004
  - Presidential Minute 181 (10 March 2004) pressurised the Minister of Foreign Affairs to sign the Women's Protocol, which she duly did on 16 March 2004.

- August–October 2004
  - The Draft Protocol was referred for discussion to the Parliamentary Committee on Justice and Constitutional Development (to confer with the Department of Foreign Affairs). Ambassador JNK Mambolo from the Department of Foreign Affairs briefed the committee providing background to the process, and outlining South Africa's country position to date. The Women's Protocol was discussed during three committee meetings in August and October 2004.[21]

  - In October, the Parliamentary Committee on Justice and Constitutional Development drew up a report on the Women's Protocol, recommending that parliament ratify the Women's Protocol, subject to reservations expressed on Articles 4(j), 6(d) and 6(h) and interpretative declarations.

- The Department of Foreign Affairs sought legal counsel again to ensure that no contradictions existed between the Women's Protocol and South African international and national law in preparation for tabling of its report in parliament.[22]

- November 2004
  - On 11 November, the National Assembly adopted the report of the Portfolio Committee on Justice and Constitutional Development and approved the Women's Protocol in terms of Section 231 (2) of the Constitution (Announcements, Tablings and Committee Reports, 11 November 2004: 1275) subject to the reservations and interpretations described below. It was then sent for discussion to the National Council of Provinces where it was conceded and adopted on the 17 November.
  - Official AU records note that South Africa acceded/ratified the Protocol on the 17 December, and the instrument for ratification was deposited with the Chairperson of the Commission of the Commission of the AU on the 14 January 2005.

South Africa's Reservations and Interpretative Declarations[23]

Reservations:

The following reservations were outlined:

- **Reservation 1:**
  - *Article 4: The Rights to Life, Integrity and Security of the Person*
  Article 4:2 (j) State parties will take appropriate and effective measures to "ensure that, in those countries where the death penalty still exists, not to carry out death sentences on pregnant or nursing women."
- The South African government in its reservations stated:
  - "Article 4(j) does not find application in the Republic of South Africa as the death penalty has been abolished. Inasmuch as the existence of Article 4(j) may be construed to be an inadvertent sanctioning of the death penalty in other State parties, this may conflict with section 2 of the Constitution of the Republic of South Africa, 1996 (Act No. 108 of 1996). South Africa is in principle opposed to the application of the death penalty and no adverse legal consequences, including any conflict with section 2

of the Constitution of Republic of South Africa, may be visited upon the Parliament and the Government of the Republic of South Africa pertaining to its ratification of the Protocol."

- **Reservation 2:**
  - *Article 6: Marriage*
    State parties shall ensure that women and men enjoy equal rights and are regarded as equal partners in marriage. They shall enact appropriate national legislative measures to guarantee that: *Article 6 (d)* Every marriage shall be recorded in writing and registered in accordance with national laws, in order to be legally recognised.

- The South African government in its reservations stated:
  - "The Republic of South Africa makes a reservation and will consequently not consider itself bound to the requirements contained in Article 6 (d) that a marriage shall be recorded in writing and registered in accordance with national laws in order to be legally recognised. This reservation is made in view of the provision in section 4(9) of the Recognition of Customary Marriages Act, 1998 (Act No. 120 of 1998), which stipulates that failure to register a customary marriage does not affect the validity of that marriage, and is considered to be a protection for women married under customary law."

- **Reservation 3:**
  - *Article 6 (h)*
    A woman and a man shall have equal rights, with respect to the nationality of their children except where this is contrary to a provision in national legislation or is contrary to national security interests.

- The South African government in its reservations stated:
  - "The South African Government makes a reservation to Article 6(h), which subjugates the equal rights of men and women with respect to the nationality of their children to national legislation and national security interests, on the basis that it may remove inherent rights of citizenship and nationality from children."

Interpretative Declarations:

The following interpretative declarations were outlined:

- *Article 1: Definitions*
  - Article 1 (f) 'Discrimination against women' means any distinction, exclusion or restriction or any differential treatment based on sex whose objectives or effects compromise or destroy the recognition, enjoyment or exercise by women, regardless of their marital status, of human rights and fundamental freedoms in all spheres of life.

- The South African government presented their interpretation of this article as follows:
  - "It is understood that the definition of 'discrimination against women' in the Protocol has the same meaning and scope as provided for in section 9 of the Constitution of the Republic of South Africa, 1996 (Act No. 108 of 1996); as interpreted by the Constitutional Court of the Republic of South Africa from time to time."

- *Article 31: Status of the Present Protocol*
  - None of the provisions of the present Protocol shall affect more favourable provisions for the realisation of the rights of women contained in the national legislation of state parties or in any other regional, continental or international conventions, treaties or agreements applicable in these state parties.

- The South African government presented their interpretation of this article as follows:
  - "It is understood that the provisions contained in Article 31 may result in an interpretation that the level of protection afforded by the South Africa Bill of Rights is less favourable than the level of protection offered by the Protocol, as the Protocol contains no express limitations to the rights contained therein, while the South Africa Bill of Rights does inherently provide for the potential limitation of rights under certain circumstances. The South African Bill of Rights should not be interpreted to offer less favourable protection of human rights than the Protocol which does not expressly provide for such limitations."

Status of the Women's Protocol in Terms of South African Law

The Women's Protocol shall only enter into force 30 days after the deposit of the 15ᵗʰ instrument of ratification. Once it enters into force, the ratification of the Women's Protocol binds the South African state vis-à-vis other member states but does not bind individuals. In this case, state refers only to the National Executive office and applies only to that part of the state that can enter into international relations. This, therefore, excludes provincial and local governments. The judgment of the African Court of Human and Peoples' Rights does not have any legal effect domestically and only has persuasive force.[24] For the Protocol to have effect in South African domestic law it must be enacted into law by national legislation (Section 231 (4) of the Constitution), in this way becoming directly applicable to South Africans. However, only laws that are consistent with the Constitution will be enacted. It is only then that the provisions of the Protocol will be legally enforceable in South African courts.[25]

Gaps, Ambiguities, Controversies that Could Hinder the Women's Protocol's Use as a Tool for Promotion of Gender Equality

During the interviews, several general criticisms were levelled at the Women's Protocol, highlighting some of the shortcomings that would hinder its use as a tool for the promotion of gender equality. Most of them are related to the actual application or implementation of the Protocol and include the following:

Matters of Interpretation and Accountability

Until such time as the African Court of Human and Peoples' Rights is established, the African Commission on Human and Peoples' Rights will be responsible for matters of interpretation which arise from the application or implementation of the Protocol. However, as was presented to the Portfolio Committee on Justice and Constitutional Development:

> "... neither judgments by the African Court or findings by the African Commission have any legal status in terms of South African law. These instruments have not been incorporated into South African domestic law. In terms of international law, their provisions require states to give effect to judgments/findings, but that does not translate into domestic law where South African courts enjoy supremacy. At most in legal terms, such judgments or findings will have persuasive value in South African courts, while a conflicting situation may of course also be politically embarrassing."[26]

Any complaint relating to the protection of human rights has to first be adjudicated in the South African court systems in terms of South African law, as all local remedies have to be exhausted before it can be considered before the African Commission on Human and People's Rights, or the African Court on Human and People's Rights.[27] However, it was pointed out that considering South Africa's legal framework, in the event of a case being considered by either of these bodies, the possibility of conflicting judgments between domestic courts and supranational African institutions is limited.

In addition, the system is structured in such a way that "individuals or NGOs may not, without parliament having proved their competence, approach any of the courts having jurisdiction for relief under the Protocol".[28] What becomes apparent is that the implications of the Women's Protocol for domestic legislation is fairly limited and that avenues to call government to account for non-compliance, such as direct access to the courts, are to a large extent controlled by the government of the day. This gives them the potential power to screen and obstruct demands for compliance or calls for accountability. As one interviewee stated, "it is like the police policing the police."[29]

Monitoring, Reporting and Sanctions

Article 26 of the Women's Protocol states that state parties shall ensure the implementation of this Protocol at a national level. In accordance with Article 62 of the African Charter on Human and People's Rights, State parties are required to report every two years on the legislative and other measures adopted in order to give effect to the rights and freedoms recognised and guaranteed by the charter. Such reports on the Women's Protocol will also be required to be submitted. This will provide the forum for both monitoring the compliance and implementation of the Protocol on Women, as well as the monitoring the forum's capacity to call for any amendments should the need arise.[30]

However, several interviewees pointed out that the Women's Protocol does not include a provision that lays out sanctions that could be applied to a state if it does not comply. Thus, it is argued that the Women's Protocol does not go far enough as it does not include enforcement mechanisms.[31] Another interviewee also pointed out that, "there is no mention of who is going to be responsible for effective sanctioning of Member States who do not comply with the provisions. The African Commission on Human Rights does not have any sanctioning rights, and in fact there is no overarching office that is going to force a country to do anything." [32] In this scenario where there are no sanctions or enforcement mechanisms, nor an indication of which body will be able to provide effective sanctioning, the possibility of the Women's Protocol being an effective tool for the promotion of gender equality is limited.

Domestication

An interviewee argued that, "until such time as the Protocol is domesticated, it will not be a source of rights for women" and its ability to be a useful tool for the promotion of gender equality will be undermined. Outlining two consequences of not domesticating the Women's Protocol, she argued that, firstly, the national Constitution in many countries in the region does not apply to family law. This means that international human rights standards are not applied to personal law, arising in a potential conflict between what is understood to be customary law and traditions and women's constitutional human rights. [33] Secondly, as it is not domesticated, states cannot be held responsible for the programmatic duties ensuring that the creation of conditions for the implementation of the Women's Protocol. Considering the case of VAW as an example, there is no obligation of states to provide the institutional framework to ensure that women are protected from violence in real terms, such as ensuring that there are enough police stations with the necessary facilities, sufficient police cars, sufficient suitably trained gender sensitive personnel, etc. [34]

Importance of the Women's Protocol for South Africa

Notwithstanding the criticisms levelled above, several interviewees noted the value of the Women's Protocol for South Africa. It was argued that the Women's Protocol provides South Africa with the added value of a regionally negotiated and agreed upon document to back and support its efforts to promote gender equality on the continent and in the AU. Additionally, at a national level, the Women's Protocol contemplates issues not dealt with in sufficient depth in the South African legislative framework, such as the trafficking of women, harmful traditional practice and the protection certain vulnerable groupings are afforded.

In a similar vein, the Women's Protocol was also thought to be useful in the South African context for its "potential to inform processes around gender transformation, which are still incomplete, to inform ongoing policy and guidelines development, and to be a tool for discussion and debate around issues which we have not dealt with at an in-depth level in the country. [...] These would include issues, such as harmful practices and the right to live a positive cultural life. In the latter, this could be unpacked in the context of what it means to harmonise customary and religious law with the values of the Constitution."[35]

On the whole, the African Women's Protocol strengthens the legal framework promoting gender equality; it contributes to harmonising culture and tradition with international human rights law; it highlights the specific challenges facing African women; and it provides tools to help bridge the gap between policy and practice (personal communication, Rosemary Mukasa).

Notes

[1] The Conference for a Democratic South Africa, a multiparty negotiation forum, which lasted from December 1991 to mid 1992. The other main negotiation forum was the Multi-Party Negotiating Process during 1993.

[2] Twenty-nine national departments out of a total of 36 responded to the 2003 Audit.

[3] Interview One.

[4] The clusters are: Social Sector; Economy and Employment; International Relations, Peace and Security; Justice, Crime Prevention and Security; Governance and Administration. There are corresponding clusters of Director-Generals who work closely with the Policy Coordinating and Advisory Services Unit in the Presidency (OSW, 2004).

[5] The PCAS, located within the President's Office, is tasked with monitoring and evaluating government performance.

[6] Interview Three.

[7] The Commission on Gender Equality Act No. 39 of 1996 stipulates that the CGE should comprise 8–12 commissioners, of whom no fewer than two may be part-time.

[8] Unless otherwise specified, all statistics and information presented in this section is drawn from OSW, 2004.

[9] Interview Four.

[10] Gender Manual Consortium, date unstated, Chapter 9: Government and Politics.

[11] There is recognition that proponents of virginity testing do so in the context of promoting moral regeneration, African renaissance and/or controlling the spread of HIV/AIDS. However, the researcher contends this practice becomes a harmful traditional practice when there is forced virginity testing, or virginity testing directed solely at girls. This then makes it a discriminatory practice against girls, as they bear the burden and responsibility of promoting and demonstrating their 'morality', in a context where unequal power relations between young girls and young boys and men often result in young girls being the victims of incest, sexual abuse or rape. There is hardly ever an investigation as to why a girl is not a virgin (thereby ignoring possible rape or abuse). Apart from considering the unequal and double standards applied to girls and boys, this discussion needs to be held within the context of the need to harmonise the right to participate in the cultural life of his or her choice with a young girl's right to gender equality, dignity and privacy as enshrined in the South African Constitution.

[12] Parenzee, P., Artz, L. and Moult, K with contributions from Fedler, J., Carter, R. and Jacobs, T. 2001. Monitoring the Implementation of the Domestic Violence Act: First Research Report 2000–2001. Institute of Criminology, University of Cape Town, Cape Town.

[13] Human Rights Watch. 2001. Scared at School: Sexual violence against girls in South African schools. New York.

[14] Government of South Africa. 2003. South African Police Annual Report 2003.

[15] Preparation of the vagina with astringents or douches prior to sex in order to make it dry, reportedly to increase male sexual pleasure.

[16] SAPS, National Crime Information Management Centre in Northern Province (currently Limpopo).

[17] Some of these policies include Guidelines for Maternity Care in South Africa: A manual for

clinics, community health centres and district hospitals (DOH, 2000); Saving Mothers: Policy and Management Guidelines for Common Causes of Maternal Deaths (DOH, 2001); National Maternity Case Record and Guidelines for Completing the National Maternity Case Record.

[18] The first case was heard in the Constitutional Court where pro-lifers attempted to disbar the law in its entirety; the second case was an attempt to overturn a minor's right to decide for herself without the need for parental consent. The most recent attempt to undermine the law comes from a nurse who is currently claiming workplace discrimination after she exercised her right to conscientious objection to performing a TOP.

[19] Unless otherwise stated, this section is drawn from CALS, 2003/2004.

[20] The Nelson Mandela/HSRC survey (2002) indicated that 47.9 per cent of respondents, aged 15–19, used a condom at last intercourse, compared to only 28 per cent of 30–34 year olds.

[21] See Portfolio Committee Minutes for 5 August 2004 at *www.pmg.org.za/2004/viewminute. php?id=4259; www.pmg.org.za/docs/2004/appendices/040805briefing.htm; www.pmg.org. za/docs/2004/appendices/040805notes.htm.* See Portfolio Committee Minutes for 12 August at *www.pmg.org.za/docs/2004/viewminute.php?id=4306.* See Portfolio Committee Minutes for 27th October at *www.pmg.org.za/docs/2004/viewminute.php?id=4769 and www.pmg.org.za/docs/2004/ appendices/041027woman.htm.*

[22] For an in-depth consideration of the existing differences between the Protocol and the South African law, please refer to Report of the Portfolio Committee on Justice and Constitutional Development on the Protocol to the African Charter on Human and Peoples' Rights on the Rights of Women in Africa. 27th October 2004, pp 1282–1287. Announcements, Tablings, and Committee Reports No. 104 – 2004.

[23] This section is drawn from the Report of the Portfolio Committee on Justice and Constitutional Development on the Protocol to the African Charter on Human and Peoples' Rights on the Rights of Women in Africa. 27th October 2004, pp 1279. Announcements, Tablings and Committee Reports No. 104 – 2004.

[24] Notes on the Protocol to the African Charter on Human and People's Rights on the Rights of Women in Africa, document discussed at Portfolio Committee on Justice and Constitutional Development meeting, 5 August 2004. *www.pmg.org.za/docs/2004/appendices/040805notes.htm.*

[25] Ibid.

[26] Notes on the Protocol to the African Charter on Human and People's rights on the Rights of Women in Africa. *www.pmg.org.za/docs/2004/appendices/040805notes.htm.*

[27] Report of the Portfolio Committee on Justice and Constitutional Development on the Protocol to the African Charter on Human and People's Rights on the Rights of Women in Africa, 27 October 2004 pg 1276. Announcements, Tablings and Committee Reports No. 104–2004.

[28] Report of the Portfolio Committee on Justice and Constitutional Development on the Protocol to the African Charter on Human and People's Rights on the Rights of Women in Africa, 27 October 2004 pg 1279. Announcements, Tablings and Committee Reports No. 104–2004.

[29] Interview Seven.

[30] Foreign Affairs Briefing to the Portfolio Committee on Justice and Constitutional Development, 5 August 2004. *www.pmg.org.za/docs/2004/appendices/040805briefing.htm.*

[31] Interviews Seven, Ten and Twelve.

[32] Interview Twelve.

[33] Interview Ten.

[34] Interview Ten.

[35] Interview Thirteen.

13

Implications of the Protocol for the Thematic Areas under Examination

EACH OF THE INTERVIEWEES was asked what they considered the implications of the Women's Protocol to be in relation to the key thematic areas under examination. These implications included analysis in terms of gaps/advances in content and political perspective, implications for the South African legislative and policy framework and finally in terms of implementation or application, either of the Women's Protocol or the South African legislation/policy framework.

IMPLICATIONS OF THE PROTOCOL FOR GOVERNANCE

Article 9: of the African Women's Protocol Right to Participation in the Political and Decision-Making Process

1. State parties shall take specific positive action to promote participative governance and the equal participation of women in the political life of their countries through affirmative action, enabling national legislation and other measures to ensure that:

   a) Women participate without any discrimination in all elections;

   b) Women are represented equally at all levels with men in all electoral processes;

   c) Women are equal partners with men at all levels of development and implementation of state policies and development programmes.

2. State parties shall ensure increased and effective representation and participation of women at all levels of decision-making.

SA Legal and Policy Framework

South Africa's legal and policy framework demonstrates a fair degree of compliance with the provisions outlined in the Protocol. A detailed discussion is provided in Chapter 13.

Implementation

Resistance

In spite of the high representation of women at national and provincial levels, most interviewees were in agreement that there is still a degree of resistance and obstacles (negative attitudes; gender norms and roles; sexual harassment; electoral procedures) that would make it difficult to implement the provisions called for in the Protocol. One interviewee argued that these provisions would also meet with resistance from other African countries; however, he saw the Protocol as providing a moral framework that will provide South Africa with a useful resource in promoting women's representation in regional bodies and structures. [1]

Popularisation

Faced with this scenario, an interviewee saw the popularisation of the Protocol as being in line with the civil society initiated and driven campaign for women's 50 per cent representation in all three spheres of government.[2] The CGE also saw the Women's Protocol as an added incentive to continue its lobbying of political parties to improve their representation of women and to ensure their manifestos speak to women's needs and interests.[3]

Many of the interviewees pointed out that a particular difficulty would be experienced at the level of local government. This is a result of a combination of the electoral system at local government level; women not being perceived to be apt councillors and the hostile environment towards women at local government level. Speaking about the local Government electoral system, an interviewee argued, "The problem lies in constituency representation, the wards are (mostly) subscribed by me, [...] people really don't want to vote for women representatives at local Government."[4]

Lessons to be Learnt

Considering the lessons that can be learnt from women's participation in electoral processes and in high level office positions, several interviewees argued that the mere presence of women makes a positive difference, and can even result in some practical changes in how business is done. However, aiming just to increase the number of women in the different spheres of Government, will not necessarily translate into women benefiting from policies and programmes.

On the 'politics of presence', one interviewee stated, "They [women] make a difference. It does promote much more women-centred and sensitive policies."[5] In addition, another interviewee pointed out that, "it's good that there are women there, even though not all the women that are there are gender sensitive, there is a greater chance of women's issues being raised."[6]

In order for there to be effective leadership on the part of women, interviewees went on to explore some of the conditions that need to be put in place. One interviewee stated, "Unless you have champions driving a women's agenda, you won't get change [...] champions have to form alliances with sympathetic, male leaders (with vision and analysis) in order to get legitimacy and advance their causes. You need to have a civil society that is organised, mobilised, and able to engage with the state, which has a level of expertise and understanding about politics, a sophisticated and in-depth understanding of the law and governance."[7] Several interviewees also argued for the need to ensure that women's capacity is built and that support is provided to them.[8]

Elaborating on the need to ensure women leadership's link with civil society organisations, an interviewee stated, "When we first had a democratic government there was a strong link and open relationship between civil society and women (political) representatives. Over the years, this relationship has become more distant. It also has got to do with NGOs and CBOs negotiating their relationships with government, of not wanting to tread on the toes of those who might give money, or loyalty to old comrades."[9]

On the whole, governance and women's representation in South Africa has mainly focused on increasing the number of women in public office, without the same attention being paid to ensuring that government fulfills and meets women's practical needs and interests.

IMPLICATIONS OF THE PROTOCOL FOR VIOLENCE AGAINST WOMEN

Article 4: The Right to Life, Integrity and Security of the Person

1. Every woman shall be entitled to respect for her life and the integrity and security of her person. All forms of exploitation, cruel, inhuman or degrading punishment and treatment shall be prohibited.

2. State parties shall take appropriate and effective measures to:

   a) Enact and enforce laws to prohibit all forms of violence against women including unwanted or forced sex whether the violence takes place in private or public;

   b) Adopt such other legislative, administrative, social and economic measures as may be necessary to ensure the prevention, punishment and eradication of all forms of violence against women;

   c) Identify the cause and consequences of violence against women and take appropriate measures to prevent and eliminate such violence;

   d) Actively promote peace education through curricula and social communication in order to eradicate elements in traditional and cultural beliefs, practices and stereotypes which legitimise and exacerbate the persistence and tolerance of violence against women;

   e) Punish the perpetrators of violence against women and implement programmes for the rehabilitation of women victims;

   f) Establish mechanisms and accessible services for effective information, rehabilitation and reparation for victims of violence against women;

   g) Prevent and condemn trafficking of women, prosecute perpetrators of such trafficking and protect those women most at risk;

   h) Prohibit all medical or scientific experiments on women without their informed consent;

   i) Provide adequate budgetary and other resources for the implementation and monitoring of actions aimed at preventing and eradicating violence against women;

j) Ensure that, in those countries where the death penalty still exists the state cannot carry out death sentences on pregnant or nursing women;

k) Ensure that women and men enjoy equal rights in terms of access to refugee status, determination procedures and that women refugees are accorded the full protection and benefits guaranteed under international refugee law, including their own identity and other documents.

Article 4: Elimination of Harmful Practices

1) State parties shall prohibit and condemn all forms of harmful practices which negatively affect the human rights of women and which are contrary to recognised international standards.

2) State parties shall take all necessary legislative and other measures to eliminate such practices, including:

a) The creation of public awareness in all sectors of society regarding harmful practices through information, formal and informal education and outreach programmes;

b) Prohibition, through legislative measures backed by sanctions, of all forms of FGM, scarification, medicalisation and para-medicalisation of FGM and all other practices in order to eradicate them.

Content

Several interviewees noted that provisions contained a very limited definition of GBV. One interviewee noted, "You need to have very specific and detailed references to the range of violence which women are exposed to; to the notion that its all about power and it should stipulate actors, including the existence of marital rape."[10] In support of this viewpoint, interviewees noted that issues of economic violence should have been highlighted[11] and that "the section on marital rape could be more strongly worded".[12]

On the other hand, interviewees remarked that recognising that violence takes place in both public and private was a positive step, along with addressing elements in traditional and cultural beliefs, practices and stereotypes which promote or condone VAW.[13] Considering that the lack of a sufficient budget and resources has been a serious obstacle to implementing South Africa's legislation and policy framework and guidelines, the call for adequate budgetary and other resources for implementation was lauded.[14]

South African Legislative and Policy Framework

Most interviewees felt that the Protocol did not posit any significant advances to the South African legislative and policy framework. However, one interviewee believed that the call on states to actively promote peace education and to raise issues of how culture and tradition and gender stereotypes promote and condone VAW was an advance on the South African Constitution.[15] In addition, there is clearly room for improvement in South Africa's policy and treatment of harmful traditional practices.

Implementation

Many problems were raised in terms of the South African government's ability to implement the Protocol and to decrease the high incidence of GBV in South Africa. Societal attitudes and practices were highlighted as a severe obstacle to implementation, along with South Africa's poor track record of implementing its existing legislation and policy guidelines around GBV.

One interviewee stated that, "Real transformation will be a problem. Culture, tradition and religion are all very highly andocentric. We have all these nice policies and legislations, but we haven't managed to get society to change. Here we are talking about changing mindsets, changing cultural beliefs and practices, deep seated beliefs about the role and position of women and men."[16]

Considering South Africa's poor track record of implementing existing legislation, an interviewee argued that she did not believe the Women's Protocol would carry any weight. She noted, "It might be a support for campaigns and advocacy at a high up level in order to increase the budget allocated to gender-based violence, but we should consider how long that process is and how long we have been fighting about getting adequate service provision. These types of protocols might not play a significant role in terms of getting an adequate budget."[17]

Echoing similar frustrations and noting shortcomings in the Women's Protocol, an interviewee stated that, "The problem lies with the institutional framework, the actual practices of institutions in society. This is where the Protocol stops [it does not address] what happens when the state doesn't fulfill its obligations? There are no enforcement mechanisms to make the state accountable. If the police don't have a car, if the police do not respond (to complaints of domestic violence), then what happens when you are not 'continually free from violence'? They have programmatic duties as a state, to ensure that the institutional framework is there – budgeting, minimum number of police officers, minimum number of police cars, etc."[18]

However, another interviewee was not so pessimistic and posited that "It [the Protocol] will help and support the fact that the government needs to make it a priority; we need to promote the political will of the Government to keep up work on gender-based violence."[19]

The researcher believes that the provision relating to the need for effective budgeting might be an additional tool for women's organisations to lobby for more money to address VAW, especially considering that the DVA is silent on this issue. However, considering that there are no clear provisions for sanctions for governments who do not comply with the Protocol, any advocacy strategy to increase budgets would have to rely on a government not wanting to tarnish its image internationally and regionally.

IMPLICATIONS OF THE PROTOCOL FOR SEXUAL AND REPRODUCTIVE RIGHTS

Article 14: Health and Reproductive Rights

1. State parties shall ensure that the right to health of women, including sexual and reproductive health, is respected and promoted. This includes:

   a) The right to control their fertility;

   b) The right to decide whether to have children, the number of children and the spacing of children;

   c) The right to choose any method of contraception;

   d) The right to self protection and to be protected against STIs, including HIV/AIDS, in accordance with internationally recognised standards and best practices;

   e) The right to have family planning education.

2. State parties shall take all appropriate measures to:

   a) Provide adequate, affordable and accessible health services, including information, education and communication programmes to women especially those in rural areas;

   b) Establish and strengthen existing pre-natal, delivery and post-natal health and nutritional services for women during pregnancy and while they are breastfeeding;

    c) Protect the reproductive rights of women by researching medical abortion in cases of sexual assault, rape, incest, and where the continued pregnancy endangers the mental and physical health of the mother or the life of the mother or the foetus.

Content

When commenting on this provision, interviewees were quick to pick up on the subtext of the underlying notions of womanhood and concerns, a view that is shared by the researcher. It was argued that the provisions reinforce traditional gender stereotypes and expectations of women, notably equating being a woman with reproduction. The emphasis is on reproductive health concerns, with a limited understanding of reproductive rights. Where sexuality is mentioned, it is linked to the issue of public health and protection from and control of STIs, including HIV/AIDS.

As a few interviewees note, "There is a very limited depiction of reproductive rights."[20] In fact, the Protocol outlines "the lowest denominators of reproductive rights".[21] A presenter at an Oxfam Public Dialogue on the Protocol points out "the language is weak" and that "there is a need to go beyond the language of family planning" to speak more clearly about SRHR. She goes on to criticise the limited conditions in which women's rights to abortion is promoted and argues for the need to recognise and promote women's rights to choose when to terminate her pregnancy, as it exists in South African legislation.[22] At another Oxfam Public Dialogue, the lack of recognition of a woman's right to choose her childbearing method was also highlighted.[23]

A number of interviewees argued that women's rights to choose when to have sex, with whom they want, and why they want is completely absent from the provisions, with issues of sexuality being restricted to public health concerns, notably those surrounding STIs and HIV/AIDS.[24] Groups of people who are socially marginalised and those thought to engage in taboo sexual relations, notably lesbians, sex workers and young girls, are also not mentioned.[25] The researcher believes that in this context, the Protocol would have to be used as a lobbying tool in conjunction with more strongly worded international agreements like Beijing and Cairo.

South African Legislative and Policy Framework

Interviewees commented that the Women's Protocol did not represent significant advances for South Africa, considering the exceptional breadth and recognition of a wide range of sexual and reproductive health and rights in the South African legislative and policy framework.[26]

Implementation

Interviewees argued that in spite of South Africa's enabling legislative and policy framework, culture, tradition and religion presented major obstacles to women enjoying their SRHR. One interviewee pointed out that religion, culture and tradition shapes and informs women and men's notions of identity and expected behavior. Women are "constructed subject to men (father, brother etc.) and have very little choice about their own (sexual and) reproductive lives. Religion instructs you to have as many children as possible, culture sees you as a mother/nurturer and tradition sees men as the head of the family."[27]

It is these attitudes and practices that undermine women's ability to exercise their rights and is that which disempowers them. As one interviewee states, "Legislation gives women the right to determine her reproductive health and life, however, the reality out there is that patriarchy is a big influence. Women are not able to negotiate condom use and sexual practices."[28]

Religion, culture and tradition also influence "health seeking behavior and affect how nurses treat women"[29] creating yet another layer of obstacles for women enjoying their SRHR.

In the face of such a monumental negative social and cultural environment, an interviewee argued that a "fundamental attitudinal change is needed".[30] At the same time, there is an argument to promote a culture of human rights over and above the dictates of religion, culture and tradition. This should be reinforced by "approaching (religion, tradition and) culture as dynamic and should be used to get rid of the backward elements".[31] This would require change not only at an individual level, but also within the very structures in society, which promote and reproduce such belief systems and practices, something that is not an easy task.

One interviewee argued that there is a rising international and national conservatism, which is threatening to undermine the gains made by women over the last few decades. She argued, "There is a huge swing back to religious fundamentalism at an international level in terms of [President] Bush and [the policies promoted by] US AID. Moral regeneration is being misinterpreted and misapplied [promoting] the need for abstinence, and going back to family values. We see the deputy president and the churches promoting virginity testing, putting the onus on women [to prevent HIV] and controlling women's sexuality."[32]

The researcher believes that the current context provides many challenges for sexual and reproductive health and rights activists, requiring us to review the strategies that we have embarked upon. There should be a multi-pronged approach, which emphasises changes at the individual level, promoting women's individual empowerment (in the private sphere) and a constructive dialogue with the tensions between harmonising women's human rights with patriarchal cultures and traditions. This should be combined with a concerted effort to build and consolidate women's organisation to promote women's access to services and ensure implementation of policies and programmes in the public sphere.

Notes

[1] Interview Four.
[2] Interview Fourteen.
[3] Interview Two.
[4] Interview Twelve.
[5] Interview Twelve.
[6] Interview Nine.
[7] Interview Twelve.
[8] Interview Fourteen.
[9] Interview Nine.
[10] Interview Twelve.
[11] Interview One.
[12] Interview Fourteen.
[13] Interviews Twelve and Fourteen.
[14] Interview Twelve.
[15] Interview Four.
[16] Interview Twelve.
[17] Interview Nine.
[18] Interview Ten.
[19] Interview Fourteen.
[20] Interviews Three and Twelve.
[21] Interview Thirteen.
[22] Emelda Boikanyo, presentation at World AIDS Day Public Dialogue on the African Union Protocol to the African Charter on Human and Peoples' Rights on the Rights of Women in Africa organised by Oxfam GB, Pretoria. 30 November 2004.
[23] Gawaya, R. 2004. Report on the Public Dialogue on the AU Women's Protocol, 20 September. Oxfam GB, Johannesburg.
[24] Interviews Three and Thirteen and Sisonke Msimang, presentation at World AIDS Day Public Dialogue on the African Union Protocol to the African Charter on Human and Peoples' Rights on the Rights of Women in Africa organised by Oxfam GB, Pretoria. 30 November 2004.
[25] Interviews Seven, Eight, Twelve, Thirteen and Fourteen.

[26] Interviews Two, Ten and Thirteen.
[27] Interview Twelve.
[28] Interview One.
[29] Interview Thirteen.
[30] Interview Ten.
[31] Interview Six.
[32] Interview Seven.

|4

Awareness about the Protocol

THIS SECTION DISCUSSES levels of knowledge and ability to use the Protocol by policy makers and civil society organisations. Considering a range of variables aimed at measuring this[1], each of the interviewees was asked to grade themselves in relation to the Protocol. The interviewees have been sub-divided into Policy Makers (gender machinery; relevant sector ministries; parliamentarians) and Civil Society (CBOs; human rights NGOs; academia; the media).

Prior to each interview, most of the interviewees were sent both the question guide and a copy of the Protocol. This would undoubtedly have influenced their knowledge and ability to answer these questions, as they would have had the opportunity to read the Protocol prior to the interview and so the responses have to be read with this in mind.

POLICY MAKERS

Six policy makers were interviewed – three from the NGM (OSW, CGE and the Gender Focal Point [GFP]) and three from relevant sector ministries/parliamentarians. All three of the NGM representatives rated themselves with a grade of 5, indicating that they were able to use the Protocol to promote women's rights. However, one of the interviewees remarked that she would not necessarily consider the Protocol an immediate reference point noting, "I still only think about the Constitution."[2] One of the three relevant sector ministry interviewees rated himself a five, while the other two knew of its existence but could not speak to its relevance for their particular sectors.

CIVIL SOCIETY ORGANISATIONS

All eight of the civil society representatives could use the Protocol to promote women's rights. However, one of the interviewees provided her own perceived rating of the different sectors, rating human rights NGOs and academics in general as a 2, denoting that she believed that CSO might (at best) know of its existence, but were ignorant of its content. This level of knowledge and awareness decreased to a 1, in reference to CBOs and the media, denoting that she believed that they had never even heard of it.[3]

The researcher would tend to agree with the above interviewee's analysis, and would argue that the discussions held within the country, around the Protocol, have counted on the participation of a limited number of NGOs in relation to the number of NGOs that exist in the country. In addition, the researcher would argue that government functionaries in general are equally ignorant of the existence and content of the Protocol. This would be less so for members of marliament who participated in discussions on the Protocol during parliamentary sessions. However, the researcher would contend that it is mainly the members of the Portfolio Committees on Justice and Constitutional Development and the Portfolio of Foreign Affairs, and members of the governmental delegation who participated in the actual negotiation process who would have any degree of in-depth knowledge of the Protocol and its applicability.

MASS MEDIA

All interviewees remarked that the mass media has not covered the Protocol, and none of them had read or heard anything about it via these means. There has been information circulating via emails and list servers, but on the whole, the South African public is ignorant of the Protocol's existence, never mind its content.

This would confirm that one of the major thrusts of any work around the Protocol is to popularise and promote the usefulness of the Protocol to the South African public, community based organisations and civil society in general, along with members of the South African state.

Notes
[1] Graded in the following manner:
   1 – Never heard of it;
   2 – Aware it exists, but ignorant of content;
   3 – Can describe at least two provisions;
   4 – Have read it;
   5 – Can use it to promote women's rights.
[2] Interview One.
[3] Interview Eight.

15

Challenges

THE CHALLENGES TO PROMOTING and achieving gender equality in South Africa have been referred to throughout this paper; however, a short summary will be presented here, dealing first with efforts to achieve gender equality within South Africa generally, and second, by looking at specific challenges in relation to working with the Protocol at country level.

A decade after having had a democratically elected government in South Africa, efforts to promote gender equality have resulted in an enabling legislative and policy framework, which promote women's autonomy and rights in the areas of GBV, SRHR and governance. However, there have been serious obstacles to their implementation, as has been highlighted in Chapter 3. Generally, the challenges can be summarised to include the following:

- Insufficient budget allocated to the NGM as a whole, and to the implementation of polices relating to the key themes under discussion (governance, GBV and SRHR).
  - Two issues have influenced this. Firstly, the adoption of GEAR, whose underlying principles and values have created severe structural limitations to prioritising government spending that is pro-poor and pro-women. Secondly, the decision to move away from a gender budget (which provided the government with a means to allocate monies in a consciously gender disaggregated manner) to gender responsive budgeting has undermined the government's ability to ensure that budget is being spent on women's needs and interests. In addition, the absence of a governmental plan of action, which has integrated

gender concerns with clear objectives; programmes; indicators and monitoring mechanisms in the context of limited resources to respond to multiple interests and needs, has created the conditions for gender to slip off the (budget) agenda.

- The lack of skilled and gender sensitive personnel, within the gender machinery as a whole, as well as within the departments tasked with the responsibility of implementing governmental policies.

- Traditional gender norms and beliefs, and resistance to working with gender on the part of government functionaries and personnel within the departments and structures tasked with implementing policies within the three areas under examination.

  - Arguably the most important level where work must be done in order to transform commitments from paper to reality. This challenge has, more often than not, been met with gender training or training in the specific laws and policies. However, undoing a mindset and transforming approaches takes time, and training programmes are generally under-funded and short. Training, in and of itself, is of limited value if the system and 'way of doing business' is not transformed as well. At the same time, we have not seen a fundamental change in the mindset of South African society at large, with generations of deeply rooted traditional beliefs, knowledge and practices in relation to women and gender relations almost untouched by the Constitution, laws and policies.

- Equating working with gender as working on 'women's issues', which are subsequently marginalised to specific issues such as GBV, TOP and quotas for women, and not wanting to understand how integrating gender considerations relates to the core functions and responsibilities of every aspect of government performance and delivery.

- Related to the above, the low value assigned to working on what are considered to be 'women's issues'.

- The lack of effective integration or mainstreaming of gender considerations in government's objectives, plans and monitoring and evaluation systems.

- The lack of an overall gender action plan, with specific short, medium and long-term objectives.
  - Related to this, is the absence of a clearly articulated policy framework that makes it difficult, if not impossible, to effectively monitor the impact of government's policies (both internally as well as externally in terms of governmental performance and service delivery). This would require the development of a unified policy framework that integrates the many international conventions and programmes of action to which South Africa is a signatory.

- The specific challenges of mainstreaming gender and women's participation at the level of local government (in chapter four).

- The tensions and confusions related to roles, responsibilities and loyalties between the different components of the gender machinery which have undercut its effectiveness, as well as the shared weaknesses such as those outlined in the situational analysis – insufficient budget; lack of skilled personnel; low level of authority and legitimacy to effectively promote gender equality; ineffective use of existing mechanisms to call government to account for its poor performance.

- The disintegration of a 'women's movement' in South Africa, resulting in the lack of a coordinated and cohesive response and challenge to government's poor performance (calling for accountability to its commitments made to women).
  - This is influenced by a negative funding environment; the dependence on fundraisers' priorities and flavours of the day; and a lack of policy and advocacy skills to promote effective change for women. In addition, not enough attention has been paid to building cross-sector alliances, nor have solid alliances been built between CBOs, trade unions, women's NGOs and other social movements. The effectiveness to hold government to account and to promote gender equality has been worsened by the weak, fragmented relationship between civil society (especially women's organisations) and the national gender machinery.

Considering the specific challenges related to using the Women's Protocol in the context of South Africa, one must acknowledge that it is, first and foremost, a perception that the Protocol does not offer any significant gains or advances to the current legislative and policy framework. Considered to include the bare minimum requirements necessary to promote gender equality, which are fewer than what the South African legislative and policy framework offers. However, there is (a limited) recognition that the Women's Protocol offers South Africa clarity and a more detailed treatment of harmful traditional practices, an issue that has not, to date, been taken up in any meaningful way in the country.

At the same time, there is not a general practice of referring to or using international agreements as benchmarks in creating a programme of action, or as a lens to measure the extent of the problems experienced by women in the country. At the same time, there is an inadequate tradition for using international agreements as leverage in support of calls to improve the legislative or policy framework and/or their implementation.

Evidence of this can be found in the fact that the South African government did not submit its second CEDAW report to the committee, and is currently combining its second and third report. Women's organisations did not protest this inaction, so not even they are monitoring government's duties nor seeing its importance in relation to the UN. At the same time, the recommendations from the UN Committee to the South African government were not used as a strategic entry points to build a programme of action, and on the whole, women's organisations do not even know what these recommendations were. A similar pattern can be found in terms of the International Conference on Population and Development (ICPD) and the Beijing processes.

A related issue is the relatively low level of importance given to the AU by women's organisations in South Africa. It is not seen as a strategic arena with which to engage the South African government and the region as a whole. This could be attributed partially to the fact that it is relatively new, and that the African Parliament has only been recently established. However, the fact that it is in South Africa and does not feature in women's organisations' organisational agenda indicates that its strategic value has not been appreciated.

16

Achievements and Best Practices

DEMOCRATIC SOUTH AFRICA'S TEN-YEAR HISTORY provides us with a range of best practices in relation to the promotion of gender equality, combating GBV and promoting women's SRHR pertinent issues. These practices include:

- The victory of women's organisations to ensure the inclusion of non-sexism in the founding principles of the Constitution; the Bill of Rights, especially the Equality Clause; and the fact that the Constitution takes precedence if there is a conflict between customary law and the Constitution.

- The progressive laws and policies adopted which promote women's autonomy in the areas of governance, GBV and SRHR, including the:
  - National Policy Health Act, No. 116 of 1990;
  - Labour Relations Act, No. 66 of 1995;
  - Choice on Termination of Pregnancy Act, No. 92 0f 1996; The South African Schools Act, No. 84 of 1996;
  - The Employment Equity Act of 1997;
  - Domestic Violence Act, No. 116 of 1998;
  - Recognition of Customary Marriages Act, No. 120 of 1998;
  - Electoral Act, No. 73 of 1998;
  - The Promotion of Equality and Prevention of Unfair Discrimination Act, No. 4 of 2000;

- The Employment of Educators Act, No. 53 of 1998, amended in 2000.

- Cabinet has adopted the National Policy Framework for Women's Empowerment and Gender Equality, and a considerable number of government departments have developed gender policies, addressing the gender concerns of their particular sector.

- The South African government has adopted policies and institutional mechanisms in order to address the concerns of every one of the themes under consideration by this research. It has also established inter-sector structures and strategies to address GBV and HIV/AIDS. The quota system, adopted by the ANC to promote women's representation in political and public life, has undoubtedly contributed to the high representation of women within national and provincial parliaments.

- The policy process, which allows for public participation and input particularly through the work of parliamentary portfolio committees, has paved the way for community participation and accountability.

- The public pledge to gender equality made by high-ranking government officials, combined with the public condemnation of GBV and the space dedicated to the issue in the mass media during the 16 Days of Action against VAW and other ceremonial days, including National Women's Day.

- The establishment of specialised Sexual Offences Courts, Family Courts, Equality Courts and one-stop centres to respond to the needs of women and children suffering from domestic violence, rape and sexual assault. Although these are in effect too few to meet the demand, are under-funded and staffed by personnel who require more training, they are the beginning of an attempt to turn the tide on VAW.

- Several government departments, the NGM (particularly the OSW) and women's organisations have promoted the participation of men in their efforts to transform unequal gender relations. These have mainly concentrated on supporting organisations of men who are confronting other men to stop exercising and supporting GBV, promoting safer sex and responsible sexuality and creating alternative visions and constructions of masculinity in support of gender equality.

- The effective mobilisation by CBOS and NGOs, spearheaded by the Treatment Action Campaign (TAC) to ensure access to ARV treatment. Through a number of court cases and community mobilisation, the Department of Health and the South African government was compelled to rollout PMTCT services beyond the initial pilot programmes, and to implement the cabinet decision to provide ARVs through the public health system.

- In the Western Cape, the incipient development of a gender network, including the CGE and the OSW; the City of Cape Town and the Department of Local Government together with women's NGOs and organisational networks, such as the network on VAW, are attempting to address the bottlenecks and obstacles to the effective implementation of public policies.[1]

Notes

[1] Interview Eight.

17

Conclusions

SOUTH AFRICA HAS BEEN HAILED, by the African continent and in the world, as a showcase for its formal promotion of gender equality and its enabling legislative and policy framework. However, successive South African governments' financial and political commitment to gender equality has increasingly changed over the years. There is stagnation in the impetus to push for gender transformation. At a public discourse level, the South African government is to be commended for its public support of gender equality and its commitment to the eradication of GBV, its support of SRHR and its promotion of women's political participation and representation. However, in practice this commitment has increasingly diminished. The lack of (both financial and human) resources destined to implement its policies, combined with the public functionaries resistance to change, the view that gender is a women's issue to be dealt with by the gender machinery combined with ignorance on how to ensure that programs and projects effectively respond to women's needs and interests, have all contributed to government's commitment to women not being effectively transformed into practice.

This situation is worsened by largely unmanageable and ineffective gender machinery. As a whole, the NGM has demonstrated a lack of strategic planning and analysis, displaying itself in a lack of coordination, piecemeal actions and piecemeal monitoring and evaluation, and a duplication and confusion over roles and responsibilities. The lack of a gender action plan, and the lack of a concerted push from all the components of the gender machinery to ensure the governmental priorities and programmes include women's interests and needs, is evidence of the need for rethinking the role of the NGM and its relationship to civil society and other structures in government.

The loss of many skilled gender activists, in both civil society and government, left an increasingly smaller pool of civil society organisations to ensure that government implemented its policy commitments. The initial plan to work side by side with government in order to assist in the development of laws and policies has become less a feature of the political scenery and, over time, there has been an increasingly narrow political space to influence and inform governmental processes. To date, there still has not been a consolidation of civil society organisations, even less so in the context of women's organisations. There is also a lack of clarity on the role of NGOs and their relationship to the state. This, together with the lack of coordination and common agendas between NGOs, has severely impacted on the ability of women's organisations to see their role as that of a pressure point for mobilising and ensuring government's accountability to its constituency and its citizens.

The past decade has demonstrated that efforts to promote gender equality have been focused primarily in the public arena – transforming the state in terms of increasing women's numerical representation, building gender machinery and developing a positive legislative and policy framework. Although these are important first steps, much more needs to done to ensure implementation. However, the focus on the public sphere has resulted in change and transformation lagging behind in the private spheres. Gender relations defined by patriarchal cultures, traditions and religions continue unabated. Thus, it is clear that this area of work requires more public discussion, debate and community organisation.[1]

In spite of the perception that the Protocol does not significantly advance South Africa's legislative and policy framework on the whole, work around the Protocol was seen as an opportunity to revive/strengthen discussion, debate and organisational actions in response to: the uneven and poor implementation of governmental policies and programmes; the slow pace in service delivery; and the resulting lack of concrete gains in improving the quality of women's lives. At the same time, it was hoped that through this process it would be possible to 'rescue' the NGM, revive the organisational strength of women's organisations, promote a more coordinated and common vision and agenda, as well as strengthen/promote their relationship with other civil society organisations in order to increase their political clout.

At governmental level, it was hoped that a focus on the Protocol would provide a much-needed impetus to considering the condition and status of women, and to ensuring that its efforts to be responsive to the concerns of women are strengthened. Notably, the fact that the Protocol is a document written and adopted by African heads of state will provide gender activists and proponents of gender equality with a useful tool to counteract the argument that gender equality is a foreign concept. In addition, it raises issues that are pertinent to the African context, highlighting issues and concerns, which have not been prioritised by other international instruments and programmes of action.

The Protocol can provide a lens through which to analyse the particular problems experienced by women in South Africa, providing benchmarks and indicators for the definition of national plans. Popularising the Protocol will provide the opportunity for government and civil society to see international conventions, Protocols and plans of action as tools to be used to support calls for accountability in the context of the uneven and slow implementation of existing government policies. An important consideration is the emphasis placed in the Women's Protocol for ensuring an adequate budget and mechanisms for addressing concerns such as good governance, GBV and SRHR.

The Protocol provides the opportunity to, once again, promote the belief that the responsibility for promoting gender equality, improving the conditions for women's participation in politics and public life, eradicating VAW and improving women's SRHR, is the responsibility of everybody. It is the responsibility of all levels of government; all departments; all members and organisations of civil society (organisations working around land rights, workers' rights, right to health and other socio-economic rights, etc); and is not just that of women's organisations or the gender machinery.

At the same time, popularising the Protocol could provide the opportunity for women's organisations and government to begin/consolidate efforts to promote gender equality at a regional level. It lends itself to promote and consolidate networks and alliances, sharing strategies and actions, best practices, and the development of a common regional agenda. It provides South African civil society with the opportunity to see the AU as an important arena and resource in their efforts to promote gender equality, both in South Africa and the region.

Notes

[1] Sisonke Msimang, Presentation during World AIDS Day Public Dialogue on the African Union Protocol to the African Charter on Human and Peoples' Rights on the Rights of Women in Africa organised by Oxfam GB, Pretoria. 30 November 2004.

18

Recommendations

WHAT FOLLOWS IS A DESCRIPTION of the recommendations made by the interviewees on how to take the work around the Protocol forward at both national and regional levels. Recommendations are laid out on who should be the actors to drive the process of ratification, popularisation and implementation of the Protocol; along with a brief description of their main roles, responsibilities and areas of competence. Key activities are outlined, with their respective target audiences, including both regional and national approaches.

KEY DRIVERS/ACTORS IN THE PROCESS OF RATIFICATION, POPULARISATION AND IMPLEMENTATION

The organisations outlined below are recommended drivers of ratification, popularisation and implementation of the Protocol. There is an urgent need for public representatives (both men and women) of the Protocol.[1] These 'public faces' could be emblematic examples for each of the key actors driving the process of ratification, popularisation and implementation.

NGOs

Regionally, the role of South African NGOs is to work in solidarity with NGOs in other African countries to promote ratification of the Protocol. Nationally, they should be at the forefront of spreading the existence, content and usefulness of the Protocol to the goals and aspirations of social movements, worker organisations, CBOs and other NGOs. They should also monitor government's compliance with the Protocol, drive litigation and law reform where appropriate, do capacity building and training and finally, ensure that there is community mobilisation and alliance building with strategic partners in order to call the state to account in the case of non-compliance with the Protocol.[2]

Commission on Gender Equality (CGE)

The CGE should have a driving role in promoting the existence and relevance of the Protocol within civil society, government and private sector. It should both monitor the South African government and private sector's compliance with the Protocol, and report to government and civil society on the Protocol.[3]

Office on the Status of Women (OSW) and Gender Focal Points (GFPs)

The role of the OSW should be to ensure that the provisions in the Protocol are fed into and become incorporated into policy-making and evaluation processes, and to monitor governmental compliance.[4] The OSW should also promote the existence, usefulness and relevance of the Protocol to the provincial OSWs, the departmental GFPs and within government clusters in order for them to integrate the Protocol in their programmatic objectives and projects. The GFPs, on the other hand, should promote the existence, usefulness and relevance of the Protocol within their departments, and jointly examine the concrete applications of the Protocol in their particular sectors and programmes.

Joint Monitoring Committee on Improvement on the Quality of Life and Status of Women (JMCIQLSW)

The JMCIQLSW should ensure that the South African parliament complies with the provisions of the Protocol (in terms of discussions on legislation and policies). It should also promote discussion and debate of the Protocol within parliament and parliamentary committees.

The Coordination Forum of the National Gender Machinery

This forum could be a space to formulate common actions and evaluate strategies and activities undertaken by the different components of the NGM.[5]

Government Departments

Two government departments were highlighted as having specific roles to play in the promotion of the ratification and popularisation of the Protocol. These were the Department of Communications, which could promote the existence and central arguments of the Protocol within the mass media and via the government communication service.[6] As well as the Department of Foreign Affairs, which could play a key role in promoting the ratification of the Protocol by other AU member states. The Minister of Foreign Affairs could consistently raise the issue with other heads of state and promote discussion of the Protocol in the Pan African parliament.[7]

Academia

Departments, such as Legal Studies, Public Policy, Political Science, Gender Studies and African Studies, could include the study of the Protocol in their curricula, as well as research the implementation of the Protocol in South Africa and other African countries (once it comes into effect).[8]

CONCRETE ACTIVITIES TO PROMOTE RATIFICATION AND POPULARISATION OF THE PROTOCOL

The methods and activities to be undertaken to promote the ratification and popularisation of the Protocol, at both a regional and a national level, can be broadly classified as:

- Promotion of ratification;
- Popularisation of the existence of the Protocol and unpacking its implications for the promotion of gender equality as a whole, as well as for specific sectors;
- Specific actions based on and for the Protocol;
- Integration of the Protocol into existing campaigns and activities.

Promotion of Ratification

Actor	Proposed Strategies and Activities	Target Group
NGOs (Gender links, Women's Legal Centre, Network on VaWomen, WC)	Intensify ratification campaigns currently being promoted by FEMNET, Kenya. Draw in additional NGOs and networks to campaign to widen the coverage and increase the social base of the campaign. Invitations to join ratification campaign need to be accompanied by information on the Protocol, and by the Information, Education and Communication (IEC) material discussed below. National NGOs in African countries; regional gender structures; regional thematic networks, such as Amanitare; VAW networks and right to health networks, are examples of organisations to be included.	• AU Parliament • AU gender structures • Individual Member States: Ministers of Foreign Affairs
NGOs	Develop cross-country caucuses and alliances between NGOs at a regional level, as well as with AU and sub-regional gender structures, in order to support efforts to ratify the Protocol.	
CGE	Encourage the South African government to promote ratification of the Protocol with other African member states. It should also liaise with its counterparts in other African countries in support of their efforts to ratify and implement the Protocol.	
Department of Foreign Affairs	Promote the ratification of the Protocol with other African member states. Form alliances to develop a ratification promotion strategy with existing signatories, ensuring a wider representation, greater legitimacy and credibility.	• AU parliament • African heads of state

Popularisation of the Protocol/Unpacking Implications of Provisions

ACTOR	PROPOSED STRATEGIES AND ACTIVITIES	TARGET GROUP
All political parties	Inform their constituencies of the existence of the Protocol. Make links between local and regional issues. Use the upcoming local government elections to promote the provisions in the Protocol, especially as they relate to the promotion of women's right to participate in elections and to represent their constituencies, on the one hand, and the need for government policies and program, to respond and cater to women's interests, on the other.	• Political parties' constituencies • Local government wards
OSW (national and provincial)	Develop conceptual document, which draws the link between the Protocol and the Gender Policy Framework, and discuss it in the Coordination Forum of the NGM, distribute IEC material for popularisation campaigns. Discuss the Protocol and the implications for their particular sectors with the GFPs.	• Coordination Forum of the National Gender Machinery • National and provincial GFPs
OSW jointly with the Dept of Communications	Inform all organs of state and government departments about the existence of the Protocol and the implications of the provisions for their particular sector.	• The presidency, commissions involved with rights of children and people with disabilities • All government departments

Actor	Proposed Strategies and Activities	Target Group
OSW Departmental GFPs	Promote the existence of the Protocol and unpack the implications for each sector during government cluster meetings and Director General (DG) forums; holding forums disseminating information on the implications of the Protocol for their particular sector and to raise it during planning and evaluation of government department projects.	• Government clusters especially Justice, Social Development • DG forums • All government departments
JMCIQLSW (with Foreign Affairs)	Promote discussion of Protocol and disseminate IEC material in parliament and parliamentary committees.	• Parliament • Portfolio committees
JMCIQLSW	Hold meetings with relevant sector ministers to promote the existence of the Protocol and to work through the implications of the Protocol for their particular sectors. Provincial legislatures and local councils should also receive information. The speakers should be approached and convinced of the importance of the Protocol.	• Ministers • Provincial legislature

Actor	Proposed Strategies and Activities	Target Group
NGOs and CGE	Hold meetings with chief whips from each political party. Hold roundtables, dialogues with representatives of the different political parties to inform, educate and get buy in. Hold meetings to discuss existence and relevance of Protocol with mayors and local councillors. Hold gender dialogues and public hearings to popularise Protocol and discuss implications of Protocol for promoting gender equality in SA.	• Chief whips • Representatives of different political parties • Mayors • Local councillors • Local councils • NGOs, CBOs • Communities, private sector, government
CGE	Inform the other Chapter Nine bodies on the relevance of the Protocol for their work, as well as explore the possibility of joint campaigns.	Chapter Nine bodies, especially human rights and electoral commissions
NGOs	Develop a 'commentated publication' that highlights general provisions and principles of the Protocol, its importance for promoting gender equality in the context of South Africa and the region. This should be followed by a detailed exploration of the implications of the Protocol for different sectors and for people's daily lives. Case studies of concrete issues in people's lives and how it relates to the provisions should be used. Accessible and user friendly.	• CBOs • NGOs • Trade unions • Social movements • Government Departments • Policy makers • Media

Actor	Proposed Strategies and Activities	Target Group
	Develop position papers on the different provisions in the Protocol that examine the implications of the provision for each sector and analyse how it's being implemented in the current South African context. These would be useful materials on which to base advocacy campaigns, as well as on which to base discussions with policy makers.	
	Develop fact sheets, pamphlets and posters to popularise the Protocol and its application/relevance for NGOs, government departments and private sector. These could also be distributed to the media.	
	Develop educational material directed at people with a lower level of education, such as photo comics.	
NGOS; CGE and Dept of Communications	Conduct media campaigns promoting the Protocol and the relevance of its provisions for different sectors and the person on the street. This could include publishing the above material in one's own publications; the Womensnet web page; Gender Stats; the government and CGE web page. Participate in radio talk shows; community radio; posting radio adverts; and inserting the material in a popular form in local television soaps.	• General public • CBOs • NGOs • Government • Private sector

Actor	Proposed Strategies and Activities	Target Group
Training NGOs and CGE	Develop training material/guides on the Protocol and its relevance. This could be both an informational training manual, as well as a guide on how to use the Protocol for advocacy purposes. It could include basis information on the AU and its structures and processes; the different provisions of the Protocol and its relevance to each sector (including case studies); guidelines on how to use it as an advocacy tool, including the monitoring procedures, and avenues available for accountability. The above-mentioned educational material, such as fact sheets, position papers, commentated publications, could be included as informational resources. It would need to be developed for a number of audiences, notably community organisations, NGOs and government departments.	• CBOs • NGOs • Trade unions • Social movements • Media • Government departments
NGOs and Dept of Education	Promote that formal educational institutions include the Protocol in the curricula, as well as consider it in its research projects. These could include the Departments of Legal Studies; Public Policy; Political Science; Gender Studies and African Studies. Schools.	• University students • Academics • Schools
NGOs	Promote that the Protocol be included in winter and summer schools that run short courses.	• CBOs • NGOs • Social movements
OSW	Include Protocol in the curricula of the South African Management Development Institute, which trains all managers within the public service.	• Public service managers

Integration of the Protocol into existing Ongoing Activities

Actor	Proposed Strategies and Activities	Target Group
SA parliamentarians who participate in regional AU committees	Ensure that Protocol is used as a reference point and framework for work of regional AU committees in order to develop common strategies to combat common problems (e.g. equity and access to services).	Relevant sector AU Regional Committees
Parliamentarians	Integrate the Protocol, provisions and specific implications for their particular sector in their political party's existing programmes of action.	• General public • Political party constituencies
NGOs, OSW, GFPs, CGE	Use the Protocol as a resource and a strategic, political tool – a standard or checklist. Use Protocol as a tool to promote discussion and debate, to refine understanding and analysis (e.g. a woman's right to the free development of her personality). A useful notion as it refers to issues of personal empowerment, of fulfilling human potential. Use Protocol to inform our political demands and organisational strategies, to lobby for advances in the normative framework, to refine and close the gaps around incomplete law reforms and to promote the actual implementation of existing policies.	• NGOs • Government

Actor	Proposed Strategies and Activities	Target Group
Sector specific NGOs (SRHR, VAW; HIV/AIDS; Land Rights; Men's training networks/forums)	Integrate Protocol in existing campaigns. Sector specific NGOs should popularise the Protocol and use the pertinent provisions in support of current campaigns. A few examples include the 50/50 campaign, the 16 Days of Activism against VAW and inclusion in the Women's Dialogues.	• CBOs • NGOs • Government departments • Private sector
NGOs, CGE and OSW	Integrate the provisions in the Protocol into monitoring and evaluation frameworks that are used to measure government's compliance with international conventions (CEDAW); international programmes of action (for example Beijing Platform for Action and ICPD Programme of Action and MDG)	• NGOs • CGE • OSW • Coordinating Forum of the National Gender Machinery

Specific Actions Based on and for the Protocol

Actor	Proposed Strategies and Activities	Target Group
NGOs	Develop and promote common legal strategies and arguments to address common problems/barriers to gender equality. Examples of these are the inclusion of marital rape in domestic violence or sexual assault legislation, denial of women's access to land rights, and the primacy of customary law over constitutional law. Developing a database where successful judgments are posted to act as a resource for similar litigation in other countries. Conduct strategic litigation training at a regional level on how to advance women's rights in the region by using regional and international human rights standards.	• Regional NGO legal networks • Regional NGO networks • Feminist/women's legal rights NGOs
Women's legal rights sector specific NGOs; sector specific NGOs and the CGE	Lobby and litigate to domesticate particular sections of the Protocol that are not included in South Africa's current legislative framework.	SA legal system
NGOs; trade unions; social movements	Take up specific campaigns on key problems in South Africa, around issues highlighted in the Protocol. Focus on improving service delivery and compliance with existing legislation and policies. Issues could include the slow distribution of ARVs; the lack of funding for family courts; poor service provision and poorly equipped facilities for survivors of domestic and sexual abuse; lack of funding for NGM.	• CBOs • NGOs • Local, provincial and national government
NGOs, Dept of Foreign Affairs	Lobbying to improve the provisions in the Protocol.	• AU parliament

203

Notes

[1] Interview Seven

[2] Interviews One, Two, Three, Seven, Eight, Nine, Ten, Eleven, Twelve, Thirteen and Fourteen.

[3] Interviews Two, Three, Seven, Nine, Ten and Twelve.

[4] Interviews Seven and Ten.

[5] Interview Twelve.

[6] Interview Twelve.

[7] Interview Four.

[8] Interviews Ten, Twelve and Fourteen.

Section Three

Zambian Country Report
Stephen L. Muyakwa
Revised and edited by Matrine Bbuku Chuulu,
2007, WILSA

Foreword

A FEW YEARS BEFORE THE WORLD entered into the twenty-first century, the drive by African countries to advance and realise women's rights was accelerated. This drive also took on a powerful and global momentum in 1995, twenty years after the United Nations Conference on Women was held in Mexico. With the 1995 Beijing Conference on Women, the campaign for equality between women and men witnessed momentous changes and undeniable advances. The conference offered a platform for governments to acknowledge their support for the advancement of women's rights and equality and an opportunity for women to demand accountability from their governments.

The Beijing Conference was backed by the 1979 United Nations, the CEDAW and the International Bill of Rights for Women. In 1994, the Fifth African Regional Conference on Women decided to include the vital role that women play in the family, culture and socialisation among the twelve critical areas of concern in the Dakar Platform for Action and to work to strengthen it. The Dakar Conference acknowledged that women's responsibilities are disproportionately more than those of other members of the family and, therefore, decided to take measures to strengthen their central role in maintaining family unity and such basic functions as social integration, national cohesion, peace and stability.

These processes were followed by the adoption by the African heads of state and government at their annual summit in the year 2003 in Maputo Mozambique of the Protocol to the ACHPR on the Rights of Women in Africa. Further, the African heads of state and government through this Protocol committed themselves to taking concrete steps to give greater attention to the human rights of women in order to eliminate all forms of discrimination and gender based VAW. Recalling that in March 2003, Amnesty International urged the AU Ministerial meeting convened in Addis Ababa, Ethiopia to agree on the measures to be included in the Protocol to include provisions that would ensure greater accountability of states to eliminate prejudices and practices that impede African women's right to equality and freedom from discrimination. The organisations also reiterated the need for African governments to send a clear message that the human rights of women are inalienable, integral and indivisible part of human rights.

The 32] articled Protocol addresses many sensitive and important issues, which are deeply anchored in African societies and are not being sufficiently tacked at national levels. This aspect can be noted in many African countries whose constitutional equality also permits exceptions in private law areas of customary, personal and family law. It is particularly noteworthy that the Protocol affirms the principles of life equality and non-discrimination, while guaranteeing the rights to life, integrity, security, elimination of all harmful practices, and access to justice and equal protection before the law. Consequently, the importance of the place of rights of women in the socio-political priorities of Africa has been stressed and re-enforced through the challenge to move from words to actions in order to ensure visibility and access by women of their human rights.

– Matrine Bbuku Chuulu, Ag. Regional Coordinator, WILSA

Summary

THIS SECTION PROVIDES Zambia's situation in relation to Women's Rights.

Chapter 19 contains the introduction, which provides the purpose of the research, the justification for the study and the study limitations.

Chapter 20 provides the literature review. This discusses the general situation of Zambia i.e. the geographical and population features, socialisation and personal empowerment, the legal and policy framework i.e. the Constitution as it relates to women's rights, marriage laws and practices, inheritance rights and property grabbing and access to land.

Chapter 21 examines Zambia's policy framework in relation to the thematic areas for this study.

Chapter 22 analyses Zambia's national policy framework in relation to international instruments as it relates to women's rights. Some of the international women's human rights instruments are discussed and how these have impacted on Zambia's gender machinery and policy framework.

Chapter 23 discusses the African Women's Protocol as it relates to VAW, governance and sexual and reproductive rights. It assesses the benefits and gaps in the Protocol to these areas in the Zambian context. The research indicates that the African Women's Protocol strengthens Zambia's policy framework in relation to women's rights.

Chapter 24 discusses the challenges relating to gender mainstreaming in Zambia. Most of these relate to political will, budgetary resources, negative attitudes and beliefs and budgetary resources.

Chapter 25 discusses the achievements and best practices in relation to gender and women's rights in Zambia. Some progress has been attained in strengthening its policy framework and mechanisms for addressing gender and women's rights, and addressing women's sexual and reproductive health.

Chapter 26 contains the conclusions and recommendations. The research concludes by saying that although there is a fair policy framework in relation to gender equality and women's rights, there is a discrepancy between the policy framework and its impact on the daily lives of women. Patriarchy affects issues of gender equality and women's empowerment. At the time of conducting the research, the African Women's Protocol was less known among policy makers. The situation has since changed owing to popularisation of the Protocol by women's rights organisations. Women's rights organisations have been instrumental in advocating for the establishment of the gender machinery.

19

Introduction

In July 2003, African heads of state adopted the Protocol to the ACHPR on the Rights of Women in Africa (hereby referred to as African Women's Protocol) at the Maputo Summit in Mozambique. It has 32 articles, embracing various social, cultural, economic, legal and political issues in the area of women rights.

The African Women's Protocol commits states to adopt all measures necessary for women to be able to enjoy their rights, as well as ensuring that they provide budgetary and other resources for the full and effective implementation of the rights contained in the Protocol. The Protocol is significant in three ways. Firstly, it reinforces attention on women's rights that other international and regional instruments have elaborated. Secondly, it is the first instrument in international law to officially state, with regards to women's sexual and reproductive rights, that women have the right to undergo abortions when pregnancy has resulted from rape or incest or when the continuation of pregnancy endangers the health of a mother. It also prohibits the practice of FGM. Thirdly, it is the first time in Africa that there is an instrument developed by Africans for African women.

The July 2004 Heads of State Summit Declaration on gender equality noted specific gender issues women face. These include: HIV and AIDS; conflict; poverty; harmful traditional practices; high population of refugee women and internally displaced women; VAW; women's exclusion from politics and decision-making; illiteracy and limited access of girls to education.

RESEARCH JUSTIFICATION

As part of the efforts to enhance gender equality, Oxfam conducted a policy research on the African Women's Protocol that will be used to inform policy makers and implementers about the Protocol. This research forms part of the Oxfam GB Southern Africa regional strategy on the African Women's Protocol. It seeks to raise awareness and assess the implications of the Protocol to the ACHPR on the Protocol of Women in Africa. The research has been used to strengthen the popularisation and mobilisation campaign in at least three countries (Mozambique, Zambia and South Africa). The policy research examined women's rights in relation to VAW, governance, SRHR (including HIV and AIDS). The purpose of the policy research is to inform Oxfam, its partners, members of the civil society organisations and parliamentarians at national and AU level about the implications of the African Women's Protocol at various levels.

METHODOLOGY

The research applied two types of research tools. Namely:

- Key informant interviews with Pan African members of parliament; leading national CSOs on gender/women rights; regional women's organisations; academicians and representatives from the Ministries/Departments of Gender, Foreign Affairs and Parliamentary Affairs. The researcher was only able to interview those available and willing to participate in the research effort.
- A review of literature, such as national legislation relating to gender and any other policy documents, to find information on the national position on CEDAW and the SADC Gender Policy (i.e. ratification and domestication); lessons that can be learnt; areas of best practice and challenges women rights face in areas addressing VAW, SRHR, marriage, governance and widow's rights.

This research was followed by a half day seminar/dialogue for policy makers, CSOs and parliamentarians at national and AU level in order to debate the results of the research and give input into the research findings.

STUDY LIMITATIONS

In interpreting the findings of this study, the reader is drawn to some limitations of the research process. The main limitation was that the study took place during the festive period (over Christmas and New Year). For this reason, many potential respondents were not available for interviews.

The second limitation is that the period for the study was rather short. It was, therefore, not possible to meet some potential respondents within the scheduled time. The Ministry of Foreign Affairs, for example, was only ready to give an interview on 4 April 2005. After several attempts to meet the Permanent Secretary and his Director of Human Resources, a telephone interview with the Gender Focal Point Person, who handles gender issues in the ministry, was eventually arranged.

20

Literature Review

THERE ARE A NUMBER OF KEY FEATURES and characteristics relating to the Zambian environment, which can be broadly defined to include economic; socio-cultural values and practices; legal and policy frameworks; and political systems. These are areas that are particularly relevant to an examination, assessment and understanding of the impact (actual and potential) of developmental programmes and the empowerment of women. These key features are briefly discussed in this section[1].

GEOGRAPHICAL AND POPULATION FEATURES

Zambia is a landlocked country, covering an area of about 753 000 square kilometres. Located on the plateau of Central Africa, Zambia shares borders with eight countries: the Democratic Republic of Congo and Tanzania in the north; Malawi and Mozambique in the east; Botswana and Zimbabwe in the south; Namibia in the southwest and Angola in the west. The country is landlocked, which gives rise to high transportation costs and, consequently, high prices for imported goods and services. The country has abundant natural resources, including land suitable for agricultural production, minerals, particularly copper and cobalt, and semi-precious stones.

Zambia's population in 2006 was estimated at 11.7 million, out of which 5.9 million were females and 5.8 million were males. Despite this, the status of many women means that they effectively constitute an underprivileged group in the country. Gender-based inequalities exist in all aspects of life, such as: education and literacy levels; skills;

employment; politics and decision-making; health; poverty; etc. (BIWZ, 2005 (SARDC)). The country's population is also exceptionally young (for example in 2000, 45 per cent of the total population was estimated to be below 15-years-old, 24 per cent were between 15 and 24 years, 29 per cent were between 25 and 59 years, and 3 per cent were 60 years and over). It has to be stated that a high ratio of financial dependency has negative implications for the economic and social development of a country.

Nearly 58 per cent of the population lives in urban and peri-urban areas, making Zambia the most urbanised country in sub-Saharan Africa, after South Africa. The urban population increased rapidly after independence when restrictions on the movement of people to urban areas were removed. However, although there are no longer legal restrictions regarding migration to towns for employment, women's mobility and movement continues to be constrained by socio-cultural norms, some of which tend to associate women's freedom of movement with loose morals.

HEADS OF HOUSEHOLDS

Available population statistics indicate that the number of households headed by women has increased from 17 per cent in 1985 to 19 per cent in 2000 (CSO, 2000). Poverty among female-headed households stood at 58 percent in 2003, compared to that of male-headed households, which stood at 43 per cent (CSO, Living Conditions Monitoring Survey, 2003). The incidence of female-headed households (FHH) is higher in rural areas than it is in urban areas. However, despite this development, Zambian government policy continues to be based on the assumption that the prevalent family type in Zambia is a male-headed household. The perception of a woman's primary role as that of a housewife/mother, who is economically dependent on her husband, does not coincide with either the situation in the traditional socio-economic system or with the present day social reality.

It is assumed that being the head of a household is an important role, not only because it entails major responsibilities for family maintenance, but also because the head is the link between domestic economy and market economy. However, this is not always the case. In Zambia today, even though women are not considered heads of households (if she is married or has a partner) many of them are the breadwinners. Many Zambian men have lost their jobs and are unable to support their families and assume the traditional role of 'male house-hold head'. In addition, owing to the HIV and AIDS pandemic, the family has had to cope with the effects of this situation which has entailed new family norms especially child and female headed households.

LEGAL AND POLICY FRAMEWORK

Gender issues and concerns arising from the co-existence of conflicting laws and socio-cultural values and norms relate to the following areas:

- Constitutional provisions on the human rights of women and men;
- Family and marriage relationships;
- Inheritance and property rights, and property grabbing;
- Fertility values and the female/male status;
- Socialisation practices and the empowerment of women and men;
- Land tenure; and
- The general economic situation.

The discussion will briefly examine each of these issues in turn.

The Zambian Constitution

The Constitution is the supreme law, which is supposed to reflect national values (including gender values) and norms, and is the law from which all other laws and sector policies derive their legitimacy. It is supposed to guide and aspire the people to national and individual development. From a gender perspective, however, the Zambian Constitution contains contradictions reflected in the fact that, while it protects women against discrimination under Article 11, Article 23 (4) negates this guarantee by allowing discrimination in matters of personal law.

The Constitution permits discrimination in the areas of law that most affect women. Clause 4 of Article 23 of the Constitution states that Clause 1, which provides that a law shall not make any provision that is discriminatory either of itself or in its effect, shall not apply to any law in so far as that law makes provision:

a. For the appropriation of the general revenues of the Republic;
b. With respect to adoption, marriage, divorce, burial, devolution of property on death or other matters of personal law;

c. For the application in the case of members of a particular race or tribe, of customary law with respect to any matter.

This effectively means that public resources may be administered in a discriminatory fashion. Personal and customary laws may legally discriminate. It is well documented that all Zambians are to a lesser or greater extent governed by fundamentally gendered customary law in their personal lives, especially marital relationships.

While discrimination remains unconstitutional, the government cannot be said to have effectively repealed discriminatory laws. A duality in the system of law engenders and legally perpetuates all manner of discrimination against women. Without the repeal of Article 23(4), the guarantee against discrimination is empty. As the following comments relating to various articles of the CEDAW demonstrate, "this Constitutional provision is the source of most *de jure* and *de facto* discrimination against women in Zambia."

Law reforms are slow and piecemeal in coming. They are also left to NGOs to negotiate making them difficult to enact and later enforce because they are seen to be partial and undesirable to the mainstream. This in turn affects such laws' legitimacy and general understanding as well as their mandatory application.

The government does not follow up its enactment of such laws with sustained and long term public education campaigns to ensure understanding and acceptance of these laws. It is also left up to NGOs to translate and publicise as well as pursue the enforcement of the laws.

In August 2003, the Government set up a Constitution Review Commission to:

a. collect views on what type of Constitution Zambia should enact, considering that the Constitution should exalt and effectively entrench and promote the legal and institutional protection of fundamental human rights;

b. recommend appropriate ways and means of entrenching and protecting human rights, the rule of law and good governance in the Constitution;

c. examine and recommend the elimination of provisions which are perceived to be discriminatory in the Constitution;

d. recommend provisions to ensure the competence, impartiality and independence of the Judiciary and access of the public to justice; and

e. examine and recommend to what extent issues of gender equality should be addressed in the Zambian Constitution.

In 2005, the Constitution Review Commission submitted its findings and a draft Constitution to Government. One of the major findings of the process demanded that the Constitution should be adopted by a Constituent Assembly. The National Constitution Conference is currently sitting and considering the draft Constitution.

Marriage Laws and Practices

Zambia has a plurality of laws that govern the institution of marriage, consisting of customary law, statutory law, religious law and norms and practices. Customary law is mostly unwritten and varied. The system of law applicable to a given case is dependent on whether the parties have contracted a customary, statutory or religious marriage.

Under statutory law, marriage is supposed to be between the contracting parties while a customary law marriage is between two families. A customary marriage is potentially polygamous, and the rules governing the formation of this marriage are more inclined to the perpetuation of a lineage over the attainment of personal goals and autonomy that would benefit the individual.

Marriage payments, which are fulfilled under both forms of marriage, still remain a factor in the marriage process for all forms of marriages, although not a requirement under the Marriage Act. For statutory marriages, neither lobola nor parental consent is necessary in contracting a marriage.

However, it is very rare to find a purely statutory marriage since most parties that purport to marry under statutory law first fulfill the traditional requirements including involving their families and paying lobola (WLSA-Inheritance in Zambia Law and Practice). The marriage payment gives husbands considerable control over their wives and absolute rights over children and reproductive choices in the marriage. In addition, a man who has paid lobola technically owns and controls his wife's rights to access resources. A husband therefore can own his wife's income or earnings.

The Marriage Act (Chapter 50 of the Laws of Zambia) provides for a minimum age of marriage, which is 21 years for both males and females. There is however, no minimum age of marriage under customary law. In some instances, as soon as a girl reaches puberty she becomes eligible for marriage even though she is still too young for this role. On 17 January 2007, the *Post* newspaper carried a press statement issued by the Minister of Gender and Women in Development on early marriages of girl children. The government noted with great concern the increased number of cases of early marriages of children, especially girls, as reported in the press in the recent past and is wary of its long term effect on the girl child. Government is also cognisant of the fact that early marriages are one form of gender violence, which mostly affects the girl child who is forced to withdraw from school in preference for marriage. Government also recognises that forcing children into marriage, especially girl children, is a violation of human rights as they relate to the rights of the child.

Under both customary and statutory law, women are entitled to maintenance after dissolution of marriage, although the Local Courts Act provides for maintenance of a divorced woman under customary law for only three years after the dissolution of the marriage. This is owed to the fact that most people live their lives according to customary law. Traditionally, customary law denies women any rights to family property or maintenance on dissolution of the marriage. Further kinship systems, marriage and access to children favour males over females. It is also a fact that the contribution women make towards acquiring family property during the subsistence of the marriage is never taken into account. The government is currently in the process of coming up with an indigenous Matrimonial Causes Act that will take into account all the above issues and will greatly improve the situation of women after divorce. In recent times, there have been progressive judgments by the judiciary where 50/50 per cent share of the matrimonial property has been ordered although enforcement of these judgments is still a big problem.

With regards to property ownership in the home, both women and men have the right to own property. Under customary law however, only the man has the power to dispose of property, though his spouse and children may have access to it. In addition, in the Supreme Court case of Chibwe V Chibwe (2000) it was ruled that all couples are entitled to an equal share of property after divorce.

Inheritance Rights and Property Grabbing

Issues of succession are governed by the Intestate Succession Act of 1989, which provides for the protection of widows when one dies without making a will. The Wills and Administration of Testate Estates Act (Chapter 64 of the Laws of Zambia) provides for the protection of widows where a deceased person makes a will. The WLSA study on inheritance law and practice reveals that many Zambians die without making wills. As already indicated most people live according to customary law, which is understood by the majority of the people. Under customary law, spouses are not expected to inherit from each other or to own property jointly. Bonds of kinship are more emphasised than bonds of marriage.

In general, household property is regarded as belonging to the husband, which contributes to the practice of property grabbing from widows by the husband's relatives in the event of his death. Property grabbing is still widely practised in spite of the Intestate Succession Act having been passed. This is owed to a number of reasons, for instance lack of knowledge of the law by women, especially in rural areas, the fear of witchcraft and the general difficulty of enforcing the provisions of the Intestate Succession Act. Further the Intestate Succession Act only provides for a 20 per cent share of a deceased spouse's estate to the surviving spouse. Biological parents of the deceased also get 20 per cent, dependants of the deceased get 10 per cent while 50 per cent goes to the children. A surviving spouse also has a life interest in the matrimonial home, which expires upon one remarrying.

However, the introduction of the Victim Support Unit in the Zambia Police Service and the sensitisation by women's human rights organisations that property grabbing is a form of VAW has greatly improved the situation. Victims of property grabbing now are assisted by women's organisations to claim their rights.

Fertility Values and Female Reproductive Health

Many factors combine to negatively affect women's fertility and reproductive health status in contemporary Zambian context. Firstly, society encourages having children and links fertility to social status. However, the deterioration in health services provision owing to Zambia's impaired economic situation, has resulted in reduced access to antenatal, maternity, post-natal and under-five clinics. Consequently, Zambia has high infant, child and maternal mortality rates.

The persistence of this 'motherhood' ideology, directly related to the cultural value of fertility, tends to be more pronounced among women and men with little or no formal education. Often such women also have an increased sense of insecurity within a marriage if they are unable to bear children. Indeed, under customary law, barrenness is a viable reason for men to take additional wives or get a divorce. However, the presence of many children means increased responsibilities for women in terms of childcare, which reduces their time to engage fully in other activities.

Socialisation and Personal Empowerment

Most gender-based biases and imbalances can be traced to socialisation, arising from different expectations about the roles of women and men in society. For any society, there are activities and forms of behaviour that are deemed as appropriate for women and for men. Awareness and understanding of gender role expectations in a specific community/ country context is important because it can influence policy formulation and the design of development programmes for supportive interventions. In the Zambian society, females are socialised to acquire characteristics that promote their dependence on males – submissiveness and general subordination to men – which places them in a disadvantaged position in the context of a free market system. Men, on the other hand, are socialised to acquire characteristics of authority (e.g. of leadership and decision-making) that help them operate in the competitive sphere of life.

Culture is also a critical factor in the development of any society and a strong cultural framework is a prerequisite to institutional, economic and social development. Culture and tradition, however, have been used to justify discriminatory practices against women.

Land Tenure Systems

Land is a major factor of production. From 1995, all land in Zambia is vested in the president in perpetuity, on behalf of the Zambian people. By virtue of the Lands Act, land is categorised into state land and customary land, which constitutes about 90 per cent of all available land and is controlled by traditional rulers.

In theory, neither system discriminates against women. However, in practice, women are disadvantaged by many factors. Under customary land tenure, traditional rulers follow patriarchal principles when allocating land as a result women have no direct access to land. Although a chief can allocate land to a woman in certain circumstances, women only have usufructuary rights derived from their male relations i.e. a husband, father, uncle or brother. Traditional leaders are also opposed to the idea of giving land to married women and young women of marriageable age. With regard to state land, the high costs involved in the acquisition of titled land and conditions for developing such land and women's lack of information, knowledge about their rights and resources with which to develop the land, prohibits women from accessing state land.

221

However, the government is in the process of revising the Lands Act, chapter 104 of the laws of Zambia, with specific objectives to recognise and promote people's rights of access to land, provide information and improve land delivery for socio-economic development. In addition, a policy has been put in place which requires that 30 per cent of titled land be reserved specifically for women including those in rural areas.

There is also need to simplify the land administration system and to shorten the process of land acquisition so as to lessen costs so that disadvantaged groups like women access titled land.

The General Economic Situation

Since independence in 1964, Zambia has moved from being one of the richest countries in sub-Saharan Africa to being one of the poorest. This is owing to a combination of factors. These include external factors, such as the rapid decline in the terms of the copper trade, and internal factors associated with financial and economic mismanagement. In 1964, economic growth rates were high and Zambia was placed at the upper end of the scale of middle-income countries. The per capita income was US Dollars $1 200. High economic growth facilitated the rapid expansion of economic and social infrastructure (education; employment; health transportation; manufacturing), all of which led to increased income levels, improved school enrolments and greater life expectancy.

Since the 1980s, however, Zambia's economic and social situation has been deteriorating. The country is now rated as one of the poorest; ranked 153 out of the 174 poorest nations identified by the United Nations Development Program (UNDP) (Human Development Report, 2006). With the change of government in 1991, the implementation of measures under the Structural Adjustment Program (SAP) was accelerated. These measures have worsened, rather than improved, the living situation of the majority of Zambians.

Until 2005, Zambia's debt burden had been a major problem. This implied that much of the resources went for debt servicing and consequently resulted in limited expenditure on social services such as health and education. Having reached the Highly Indebted Poor Country (HIPC) Completion point, expenditure on social sectors is likely to improve. In fact, the CSO National Account Statistics showed that Zambia recorded growth in real Gross Domestic Product (GDP) at 5.2 per cent in 2005. However, this development aid has, at times, been withheld owing to the Zambian government's failure to fulfil the necessary conditions relating to good governance issues. The current administration is trying to revive the economy through the provision of government subsidies to the small-scale farmers. These efforts are instrumental in reviving the country's agricultural sector.

Notes

[1] See ILO/Ireland Aid and JUDIA Consultants (2002): Women Entrepreneurs in Zambia: A Preliminary Report, Lusaka, page 3.

21

Thematic Situation of Women in Zambia

IN THIS SECTION, the discussion will examine the situation of women with regard to the three main themes for this research. These are a) VAW; b) governance and c) sexual and reproductive rights[1].

VIOLENCE AGAINST WOMEN

VAW is a worldwide phenomenon and is located and manifested at three levels: the family, the community and the state. The family socialises its members to accept hierarchical relations between the sexes and power over the allocation of resources. The community (social, economic, cultural and religious institutions) provides the mechanisms for perpetuating male control over women's sexuality, mobility and labour. The state legitimises the proprietary rights of men and women, by providing a legal basis for the family and community to perpetuate these relations through the enactment of discriminatory laws and policies or through discriminatory application of the law. These three constitute not only a persuasive and interactive system for legitimising violence, but the locus of acts of violence as well.

Gender violence is not just an episodic problem affecting two or more individuals, but is instead a structural, strategic problem rooted in wider social, economic, organisational and cultural factors. It is a social phenomenon that bears social costs. Both men and women are subject to specific risks. VAW is a gender problem anchored in attitudes and structures that demean women and confine them to a subordinate position in society. Gender violence has shown that there is a considerable imbalance in the power relations between men and women. VAW is therefore an obstacle to the ongoing development towards equality between men and women.

The issue of violence against women and children in Zambia is experienced in acts that are physical, sexual, psychological, emotional and economic/financial. Violence against women and children is also closely related to their age. Although it can be argued that there are cultural and other social violence in Zambia, culture and other social factors do not amount to violence in themselves; instead it is the attitudes based on culture that provoke or perpetuate situations and beliefs that may lead to physical, sexual, economic and psychological violence.

In the fifth and sixth country report to the CEDAW Committee, the Zambian government recognises that GBV, especially against women and children, continues to be a source of concern that requires immediate attention. In recent years there has been an increase in the number of cases reported, although under reporting is the norm since culture and tradition have socialised women to keep quiet about domestic violence. VAW is also a health issue given the social and economic impact it has on women's health. VAW impacts negatively on the general empowerment of women as it undermines their dignity. The WLSA Phase Five Studies on Gender, HIV and the Law have proven that there is an intersection between gender based violence and HIV. This is owing to the fears and inability of women to protect themselves from contracting HIV.

As indicated above, VAW does not just affect the direct and immediate victim, but the wider community as well. The visible consequences are physical injuries that vary from death to maiming and fractures to bruises. In addition to physical injuries, victims may be infected with sexually transmitted infections (STIs) including HIV. The social and economic impact of violence against women and children on national development is yet to be fully measured, especially in terms of health, lost work hours and failure by women and children to realise their full potential.

Figure 21.1

The number of police reported cases over a period of five years

Offence	2001	2002	2003	2004	2005
Child neglect	1551	1495	1420	1571	628
Depriving beneficiaries	909	641	1233	544	169
Defilement	366	865	734	1374	1511
Rape	198	198	308	289	216
Child desertion	74	121	219	149	10
Indecent assault on females	65	139	196	145	159
Incest	16	21	36	22	67
Sodomy	5	8	26	12	9
Infanticide	5	10	11	6	8
Indecent assault on boys below 14 years	3	21	8	2	3
Abortion		16	8	12	10

Figure 21.1 shows that the incidence of defilement of children is very high. The numbers of cases reported is significantly higher than that of convictions. This indicates that there is a flaw in the system, especially where the violation of children's rights is concerned, particularly with regards to the girl child. What is more serious is that in some cases, the parents of the victim opt for compensation at the expense of their children's health. This is a serious infringement of children's rights, more so with the advent of HIV and AIDS.

A comparative analysis of the cases of violence against women and children shows that there is an increase in the number of reported cases of defilement from 366 to 865 from 2001 to 2002 respectively. This represents an increase of 136 per cent in a period of one year alone indicating the gravity of the situation. The reported cases of rape remained more or less similar during this period.

It has been observed that some cultural beliefs and practices, such as initiation ceremonies and payment of bride price, have perpetuated VAW. This is compounded by the women's limited awareness of their legal rights, poor enforcement of the law and their low economic status.

In order to address the issues related to violence against women and children, the government, in collaboration with civil society, is undertaking or has put in place the following measures:

- The establishment of the Sex Crimes Unit in the Zambia Police Services to deal specifically with cases of sexual violence. The establishment of the Sex Crimes Unit is intended to supplement the efforts of the Victim Support Unit (VSU), which was created in 1994. Cases dealt with by the VSU include femicide, property grabbing, spouse battering and sexual abuse.

- The introduction of the drop-in centre and shelters for battered women and abused children and counselling services for victims and perpetrators of violence by various NGOs.

- The review of the Republican Constitution, which provides a unique opportunity for issues of gender to be mainstreamed into the supreme law of the land.

- The adoption of the National Gender Policy (NGP) by the government and its Strategic Plan of Action in 2000 and 2004 respectively.

- The initiation of a process of strengthening law enforcement mechanisms by government that is intended to lead towards putting in place an integrated approach on combating VAW through an institutional framework comprising all stakeholders at community, district, provincial and national levels.

- The restatement of customary laws, which will eventually be harmonised with statutory laws so that the application of the two sets of laws is not contradictory. This initiative will address gender issues of gender-based violence under customary law.

- In the Penal Code (Amendment) Act No. 15 of 2005 stiffer penalties for sexual offences were introduced. The amendment also introduced human trafficking as a new offence.

The predominant mechanisms for enforcement of sanctions against GBV are found in bodies such as courts, traditional structures (chiefs), the Director of Public Prosecutions, prisons and police. The mechanisms for enforcement of sanctions have been constrained by factors such as the:

- Lack of a comprehensive Domestic Violence Act. Government, through the Zambia Law Development Commission, is in the process of coming up with a Domestic Violence Act.

- Lack of privacy and confidentiality in court proceedings that cause embarrassment to the victims of violence. This is compounded by the financial expenses associated with litigation that are prohibitive.
- Limited sentencing power among magistrates who handle the bulk of these cases. The maximum sentences that a magistrate class I can impose for rape is seven years. In most cases, the convicts receive lesser sentences. Consequently, this has not deterred perpetrators of these crimes.
- Court's gender insensitive magistrates and court environment influence the decisions of the magistrates negatively.
- Procedures set out in the juveniles Act are rarely followed (i.e. juveniles right to be heard in camera, right to bail, the right to be represented by a guardian, juvenile inspector or legal counsel throughout the proceedings and the right to be incarcerated in an exclusively juvenile institution) are among those rights frequently disregarded.
- Lack of a comprehensive Sexual Offences Act.

The African Women's Protocol and Violence Against Women

The Protocol reinforces the issues surrounding VAW and further adds value to the enactment and enforcement of law to prohibit all forms of VAW. Article 4 (1): The Rights to Life, Integrity and Security of the Person, stipulates that "State parties shall take appropriate and effective measures to enact and enforce laws to prohibit all forms of VAW including unwanted or forced sex whether the violence takes place in private or public."

The Zambian legal system is very weak in addressing issues of the 'private' sphere. Law enforcement agents are often reluctant to deal with marital rape and wife battery, referring to them as domestic issues that should be resolved with the domestic domain. The law does not address issues of marital rape and battery. While acts of violence between human beings are considered assault, the same does not apply or is used indiscriminately in situations where a wife and husband or two intimate partners are concerned. Reference to the 'private sector' in the Women's Protocol will assist in addressing domestic gender violence in Zambia.

Article 4 (d) of the Protocol introduces a new phenomenon where it urges state parties to "actively promote peace education through curricula and social communication in order to eradicate elements in traditional and cultural beliefs, practices and stereotypes which legitimise and exacerbate the persistence and tolerance of VAW".

Peace education through curricula and social communication is not common practice in Zambia today. It is, however, critical in trying to address VAW. Furthermore, peace education will act as a preventative strategy in the event of political or civil turmoil and strife in which VAW is used as a weapon.

Article 4 (j) urges state parties, in those countries where the death penalty still exists, not to carry out death sentences on pregnant or nursing women. The death penalty has not been abolished in Zambia, although no executions have taken place for some time now. This article acts as a reminder to law enforcement agents not to carry out death sentences on pregnant or nursing mothers. There have been reports of women imprisoned or held in custody with their children. This constitutes a gross violation of the children's rights.

Article 5 (a), on the elimination of harmful practices, impresses upon State parties on "creation of public awareness in all sectors of society regarding harmful practices through information, formal and informal education and outreach programmes". This article will encourage the Zambian Government to carry out research on what constitutes harmful practices: the extent, the gravity, as well as the geographic and demographic patterns of such practices. A national consensus involving all women, men and relevant institutions will have to be built in order to agree on what constitutes 'harmful practices'. This will act as the basis upon which public awareness campaigns and legislation will be done and enacted respectively.

Article 22 of the Protocol on Special Protection of Elderly Women brings in the issue of special provisions for elderly women. If domesticated, this will assist government to re-examine the social welfare scheme to target elderly women. Elderly women, in most cases, do not have a pension or means of livelihood. Elderly women, once labelled as witches, have been the targets of violence. Elderly women, in most cases, do not have a pension or means of livelihood. Violence against women policies will give special attention to considering the aggression against elderly women, who are often victims of rape and murder. Cases of elderly women being murdered as a result of being accused of engaging in witchcraft have been reported in the Zambian media and have, in some cases, not been dealt with. In the concluding remarks of the third and fourth CEDAW Reports, the Committee urged the government to do something about the situation of elderly women in communities.

Gaps in the African Women's Protocol

On its own, legal reform is not sufficient to address issues concerning violence against women. A change in attitude amongst all individuals is vital if the application of legal reform is to succeed. Law enforcement agents are prejudiced by stereotypes and as are the perpetrators and victims. The high value society places on marriage, for example, forces women to not report violence by their spouses or partners. Fear of societal reprimand and loss of security, owing to their dependence on their husbands, also forces women to withdraw cases of violence against them. Generally, cultural and societal values and norms discourage this and, therefore, make it difficult for the provisions in the AU Women's Protocol to be enforced.

Proving rape is very difficult. In Zambia, the stigma that is associated with it makes it difficult to report. Proof of bodily harm may not always be evident in an event where the perpetrator has not been aggressive enough to cause bruises. Unless these issues are dealt with, it is very difficult to enforce the provisions in the AU Women's Protocol. The act of knowingly transmitting HIV/AIDS is not adequately addressed in legal provisions at national level and needs to be articulated in the AU Women's Protocol.

GOVERNANCE

Zambian women have equal opportunities to vote and be voted into public office. Politically the fledgling democracy has yet to take hold and strengthen women's roles as public leaders. In addition, there is no quota system in terms of representation. During the 2001 tripartite elections, two women joined the race for Republican president out of 11 presidential candidates but they performed very badly in all parts of the country. The precedent was however, set for women to contest the presidency. In the 1996 presidential and parliamentary elections, 59 women were adopted by various political parties as candidates, out of which only 13 were elected to parliament. On the other hand, 106 women were adopted by various political parties to stand as parliamentary candidates in the 2006 presidential and parliamentary elections. Of the 106 women adopted, only 22 were elected as members of parliament. This represents an increase of 9 percentage points in the number of women elected in parliament.

At Cabinet level, there were a total of 20 ministers out of which six were females, which represented 25 per cent prior to the September

2006 presidential, parliamentary and local government elections. As of 30 October, 2006 out of 24 members of Cabinet only five (five were women, indicating 20.8 per cent women representation. This shows a reduction from the previous Cabinet, which stood at 25 per cent. At deputy minister level, current statistics show that only 10 per cent were women, while at provincial minster level all were males.

In the civil service sector, female representation is similar to that observed in the political arena. At permanent secretary level, female representation stands at 19 per cent. At director level, women only account for 23 per cent, while at deputy director level the female representation equivalent is 43.66 per cent. Female representation at assistant director level is 20.91 per cent.

Zambia's population now stands at 9.9 million people, out of which 50.1 per cent are women. Despite government's efforts to facilitate increased women's representation in decision-making areas and civil society, women have not effectively participated in the decision-making processes. Statistics indicate that women have been under represented at all levels of decision-making in government, parliament, the private sector, special committees, religious groupings, boards and other institutions in the community. Although there has been a steady increase in the number of female members of parliament (MPs) from 1988 the number still remains low.

In order to enhance the participation of women in power and decision-making areas, such as government, NGOs and other stakeholders, the following measures should be undertaken:

- The implementation of the Strategic Plan of Action for the National Gender Policy, which emphasises the need to promote equitable gender representation at all levels of decision-making, especially through affirmative action.
- The implementation of the electoral reforms recommended by the technical committee that reviewed the Electoral Act with a view of putting in place a more robust electoral system. The process was open to the public and efforts were made to ensure that the Act incorporates the various provisions of the CEDAW and SADC Declaration on Gender and Development of 1997 to ensure 30 per cent representation of women in politics. A quota system was also recommended.
- The implementation of the recommendations of the Parliamentary Committee on Legal Affairs, Governance, Human Rights and

Gender. The committee subjects the activities of government administration to detailed scrutiny to ensure that gender issues are given priority and prominence.

- The implementation of the special bursary scheme at the University of Zambia to ensure that more women have access to tertiary education in order to enhance their chances of holding decision-making positions.
- The sensitisation programs by civil society targeting women politicians and political parties to ensure increased women's participation in decision-making.
- The intensification of capacity building and awareness creation activities on the importance of women's participation in power and decision-making through, among other programs, the NGOs' Movement of 2000.
- Enhancing partnership among public, NGOs and the private sector as well as concerned individuals to address inequality in politics and decision-making positions.

Despite some progress achieved in increasing the number of women in power and decision-making positions, a number of constraints have been encountered. These include:

- High illiteracy among women, which is currently at 75 per cent (FNDP, 2007).
- Gender biased cultural beliefs, myths, negative traditional practices and stereotyping, which discourage and prevent women from actively participating in public life.
- Women's poor resource base, in terms of financial resources, information and other tangible assets.
- The structures of political parties and their electoral processes that do not support the effective participation of women.
- Poor media coverage of women role models in power and decision-making.

The African Women's Protocol and Decision-making

Article 9, which states that women have "the rights to participation in the political life of their countries through affirmative action, enabling national legislation and other measures," is stipulated in the CEDAW and the SADC Gender Declaration on Gender and Development to which Zambia is a signatory. Despite the provisions of the AU Women's Protocol, the attitudes and social orientation of people involved in decision-making will continue to affect the enforcement of such provisions. Affirmative action is a phenomenon that is not yet fully embraced and political will is very weak in Zambia. The commitment to this provision is only alluded to, and does not always match up with actions. For example, the number of women ministers is less than 30 per cent.

SEXUAL AND REPRODUCTIVE RIGHTS

SRHR are based on the basic principles of dignity and equality. This class of rights is a composite of larger and broader basic human rights. The framework of this class of rights is set out in the United Nations International Conference of Population and Development Document of 1994 and the United Nations Fourth World Conference on Women, which state that:

> Reproductive rights embrace certain Human Rights that are already recognised in national laws, international laws and International Human Rights documents and other Consensus documents. These rights rest on the recognition of the basic rights to all couples and individuals to decide freely the number, spacing and timing of their children and to have the information and means to do so, and the right to attain the highest standard of sexual and reproductive health. It also includes their rights to make decisions concerning reproduction free of discrimination, coercion and violence as expressed in Human Rights documents.

This class of rights, therefore, includes the right of every individual to decide freely whether or not to have children, as well as how many, when to have them and with whom. This is composite (or part of) of the right to liberty – people are free not just to move around but also free to make choices suitable for them.

The Beijing Platform for Action states: "The human rights of women include their right to have control over and decide freely and responsibly on matters related to their sexuality including sexual and reproductive health, free of coercion, discrimination and violence."

The Protocol on the ACHPR on the Rights of Women in Africa says women have the following sexual and reproductive rights:

1. The right to control their fertility.
2. The right to decide whether to have children.

3. The right to space their children.
4. The right to choose methods of contraception.
5. The right to protect themselves against STIs, including HIV/AIDS.
6. The right to be informed on one's health status and on the health status of their partner.

Sexual and reproductive rights also extend to the right to marry, privacy, freedom from sexual exploitation, right to health, right to modify customs that discriminate against women, the right to not be subjected to torture or other cruel, inhuman or degrading treatment or punishment, the right to enjoy scientific progress and to consent to experimentation, as well as the right to freedom of thought, right to information, education and security of person.

These assertions and definitions raise issues of autonomy and self-determination – (i.e. that women as human beings should be able to make sexual reproductive decisions freely, without interference or coercion).

Women are, however, not fully enjoying these basic rights for a variety of reasons, which include legal, social, cultural and economic challenges. These reasons pose a challenge to women's sexual and reproductive rights and women's right to life. These challenges are all linked to the failure of the law to provide an enabling legal environment for the enjoyment of this class of rights.

The African Women's Protocol and Sexual and Reproductive Rights

Article 14 of the African Women's Protocol on Health and Reproductive Rights reinforces what already exists in the National Framework of Sexual and Reproductive Rights.

However, neither the Protocol nor the National Framework articulates the issue of accidental pregnancy resulting from the failure of contraceptive methods. Contentious as it may be, this is an issue that requires attention.

Dangers to the mental health of women are often ignored in the authorisation of medical abortions. The AU Women's Protocol must articulate provisions for safe abortions for all women who wish to undergo this procedure. This is critical considering the fact that the Protocol states that a woman has the right to determine the number of children she would like to have. The AU Women's Protocol, however, has not addressed this issue.

Notes

[1] See GIDD (2004): Zambia's Progress Report on the Implementation of the Beijing Platform for Action, Lusaka.

22

Analysis of National and International Policy Documents

IN THIS SECTION, the discussion will examine Zambia's participation in regional and international gender and development frameworks. It will also examine Zambia's National Gender Policy, which is a result of national and international pressure from gender advocates. They argued that women's rights must be extended so that women are fully informed about their reproductive and family planning rights, so that they can make informed choices. They argued not only for the recognition of women's sexuality and reproductive autonomy, but also sought an overhaul of the gender system and legal frameworks at all levels, including international state customary church and family levels. The following chronological list of international events and documents illustrates how gender activists' arguments have been incorporated into the policies and laws and will indicate what Zambia's reactions to these incorporations were.

RELEVANT INTERNATIONAL POLICY FRAMEWORKS[1]

Universal Declaration of Human Rights (1948)

Article 1 of the Declaration affirms that all human beings are born equal, in terms of dignity, rights and the endowment of reason and conscience. Clearly, this article recognises individual autonomy, which, according to Article 2, should be enjoyed regardless of sex or other characteristics. Under Article 16, any adult has the right to marry and start a family. Marital status does not affect a person's rights, since this article states that both parties are entitled to equal rights during marriage and after divorce. Marriage must be freely contracted and must have the full consent of both spouses. The concept of autonomy is supported in Article 25, which safeguards access to basic social services; the right to an adequate standard of living for the health and well being of a person and his/her family, including food, clothing, housing and medical care, as well as access to necessary social services and the right to security in the event of unemployment, sickness, disability, widowhood, old age or the lack of livelihood owing to circumstances beyond his/her control. Mothers and children are given special care and assistance under this article, which serves to emphasise women's reproductive functions over her right to individual choice. This, however, conflates a woman's rights with those of her children. Finally, this article enshrines the equality of all children, whether born in or out of wedlock.

United Nations Convention on the Political Rights of Women (1952)

This Convention was ratified by Zambia on 4 February 1972. Under this Convention, women are allowed the to vote, stand for election and hold public office on equal terms with men without discrimination. This Convention is in line with the provisions set out by the African Women's Protocol.

The United Nations Convention on the Elimination of All Forms of Discrimination Against Women (CEDAW) (1981).

The Convention was ratified by Zambia on 21 June 1985. This Convention encompasses all the piecemeal provisions contained in previous documents. It applies the basic principle of non-discrimination. It provides for a committee to monitor its implementation under domestic legislation through regular reporting and individual complaints. Zambia is currently in the process of domesticating the CEDAW[2]. This situation prompted a committee of experts to scrutinise the CEDAW Zambian reports in 2002. This resulted in raised alarm over the continuation of practices that discriminate against women in Zambia.

The results were as follows[3]. Serious concern was expressed about the stereotypes and prejudices that still prevailed in the country, and discriminatory provisions of both public and customary law. There were many violations of women's constitutionally mandated rights in Zambia covering a wide range of issues, including education, health, marriage, divorce and economic situation. The provisions of the Convention had not been incorporated into domestic law, and that question required instant attention.

The experts wondered whether the government had attempted to address, through legislation or other programmes, the modification of customs and practices that resulted in discrimination against women and perpetuated such discrimination. Questions were also raised about the time frame within which the government intended to take action in this regard. The experts concluded that, "Legal reforms should not be connected to the issue of the lack of resources, but should be set in motion immediately." In their defence, the Zambian delegates submitting the reports stated, "One of the constraints in prohibiting customary law was the fact that some ethnic groups associated their identity with those customs and traditions."

The Third Women's Conference (1985)

This conference was held to review and appraise the achievements of the United Nations Decade for Women. It produced the Nairobi Forward-Looking Strategies for the Advancement of Women. The Zambian government and civil society organisations participated in this conference.

United Nations Declaration on the Elimination of Violence Against Women (1993)

The United Nations Declaration on the Elimination of Violence Against Women (1993) condemns any act causing physical, sexual or psychological harm or suffering to women in the family, community or state. It urges states not to invoke custom, tradition or religious consideration in order to avoid their obligations to provide protection from violence perpetuated within the family. Although Zambia is party to this declaration, it is experiencing difficulties fulfilling its obligations because of the constitutional clause that authorises the use of customary law in 'private' spheres, such as marriage.

African Women's Forum in Preparation for the Fourth Global Women's Conference (1994), Dakar

This regional conference enabled African women to come together and consolidate their own concerns prior to the Fourth UN Women's Conference. Zambia fully participated in this conference.

238

The Cairo International Conference on Population and Development (September 1994)

The Cairo International Conference on Population and Development was convened to adopt a strategy to stabilise world population growth and achieve sustainable development. Their plan of action emphasised the importance of empowering women and guaranteeing their ability to exercise choice with regard to family planning. The conference affirmed that there are four requirements necessary for any population and development programme (namely, gender equality; the empowerment of women; the ability of women to control their own fertility; and the elimination of VAW). The 'Women's Declaration of Population Policies', which preceded the conference, agreed that development, rather than the fertility control programmes which have dominated population policies and programmes, was the key to solving population problems, since gender-based power inequities are largely ignored or entrenched by population policies and control programmes. According to the Cairo Conference, equitable development necessitates the enhancement of government policies, with respect to education, public health, housing, employment and social security from their current secondary status, by placing them on an equal footing with policies directed at achieving economic growth. Zambia fully participated in this conference.

World Summit for Social Development (1995), Copenhagen

The summit proclaimed that women must play a central role in fighting poverty, creating productive employment and strengthening the social fabric. The basic thrust of the conference was a people-centered approach to sustainable development, eradication of poverty, expansion of productive employment/reduction of unemployment, social integration and social justice. The equality and equity of women was considered to be a priority. Zambia fully participated in this conference.

THE NATIONAL GENDER POLICY AND MACHINERY

Arising from international exposure and local pressure, Zambia developed a National Gender Policy. The policy is being executed by the Gender in Development Division, Office of the President, Cabinet Office. The policy was drafted in September 1996 and was adopted by the government in March 2000.

The overall goal of the National Gender Policy is to attain equality and equity in all aspects of life in the context of sustainable national development and redressing gender imbalances and disadvantages. The policy is concerned with the following key areas: poverty, culture, the family and socialisation, legal and human rights, education and training, health and nutrition, water and sanitation, labour and employment, agriculture and food security, science and technology, commerce, trade and industry, environment and energy, information and media, housing, the girl child and land.

The policy gives a situational analysis for each key area, objectives and strategies. The objectives, which are mainly framed in general terms, are without verifiable indicators. The task of assigning verifiable indicators is left to the Strategic Plan for the Advancement of Women in Zambia (SPAW) and the implementation plan. Under Labour and Employment, however, the NGP calls for a quota system of 40 per cent by which the government and political parties must reserve a proportion of positions/ seats on Cabinet, Boards, Commissions and management of private institutions, including those controlled by government, to women.

The NGP also suggests appropriate institutional mechanisms at national, provincial and district levels to oversee the implementation of the policy. There is also a monitoring and evaluation mechanism in the plan. In addition, the NGP calls for an unspecified percentage of the national budget to be put aside as part of affirmative action for financing the policy. In the same vein, the policy calls on development partners to set aside a certain percentage of their assistance to gender programmes.

The thrust behind this policy is the recognition of the need for full participation of women and men at all levels of the development process to ensure the attainment of equality and equity between the sexes.

As earlier stated, the realisation of this goal rests with the national gender machinery. The GIDD is supported by an array of civil society organisations and donor agencies in carrying out the mandate. A synopsis of some of the civil society organisations is presented in Figure 22.1.

In terms of budgetary allocations to the GIDD, the picture for 2004 is presented below. In 2004, the national budget stood at ZK 8 328 594 433 065 (equivalent to US $ 1 665 718 886). The allocation to GIDD was ZK 5 754 155 128 (equivalent to US $ 1 150 831) (0.7 per cent). In 2004, about 60 per cent of the budgeted funds were actually disbursed. Donors contributed 36.5 per cent of the national budget in 2004.[4] From 2004 to 2007 the budgetary allocations remained the same, but in 2008 an additional US $ 1 billion was allocated.

Figure 22.1

Gender-based organisations and their profiles

Name of Organisation	Organisational Profile
Non-Governmental Organisations' Coordinating Council (NGOCC)	The thrust is to service member organisations by strengthening their capacities through training, donor linkages, networking, publications and lobbying.
Zambia National Women's Lobby Group (ZNWLG)	Promotion of women's equal representation and participation in decision-making at all levels through lobbying, advocacy and capacity building.
Zambia Alliance of Women (ZAW)	Improvement of the welfare of women and children in Zambia through advocacy.
National Legal Aid Clinic for Women (NLACW)	Offers legal aid to women and children.
Women for Change (WFC)	Their vision is to contribute to the creation of sustainable economic and social systems controlled by, and for the benefit, of rural people through networking, training and advocacy.
Young Women's Christian Association (YWCA)	The mission is to empower women in order to achieve a better community.
Zambia Media Women's Association (ZAMWA)	To promote professionalism among female member media practitioners.

Name of Organisation	Organisational Profile
Women in Law and Development in Africa (WILDAF)	To promote the effective use of various strategies, including law, achieve development.
Women and Law in Southern Africa (WLSA)	Gender-based socio-legal action research, lobbying and advocacy for policy change and law reform to improve the legal status of women in families and communities and to ensure that the law works for women. Offices in seven Southern African countries.
Zambia Association for Research and Development (ZARD)	Action oriented gender research, advocacy, lobbying, publishing and networking.
Movement of Community Action for the Prevention and Protection of Young People Against Poverty, Destitution, Disease and Exploitation (MAPODE)s	A community-based youth-at-risk focused non-Governmental Charity that focuses on protection and prevention interventions for young people's improved quality of life.

Notes

[1] See GIDD/Muyakwa S. L. (1998): Laws and Policies for Gender, Population and Development in Zambia, page 21.

[2] There are fears in some quarters that domesticating the CEDAW and starting work on the AU Women's Protocol at the same time may 'crowd' the gender agenda in Zambia.

[3] See Committee on Elimination of Discrimination against Women Twenty-seventh Session 551st and 552nd Meetings Report.

[4] The data presented is from ongoing work on 'Gender and the National Budget' being undertaken by Women Finance Cooperative Zambia.

23

Implications for the Protocol

Violence Against Women

Most respondents said that the penal code takes care of rape, assault and domestic violence. It was reported that there is no resolution for victims. A victim can only claim resolution if they are a public figure but should lodge the claim through the civil, and not the criminal, procedure. One respondent stated that implementation of the law is still not very strong. It was reported that there are no comprehensive statistics on the prevalence of rape, assault and domestic violence, except for those statistics reported to and maintained by the YWCA Women's Shelter project and the Zambia Police Service. It is evident that there are therefore many cases that are not reported to either the YWCA or the Zambian Police Service.

Respondents said that civil society organisations, particularly the YWCA, the Justice for Widows and Orphans Project and MAPODE, have conducted a series of training activities targeting law enforcement officers. The Zambian Police, through the Victim Support Unit, have also received tremendous support from UNICEF for both institutional development and capacity building.

The YWCA has been providing shelters and areas of safety for battered women. Government's only measure is the establishment of the Victim Support Unit (VSUs) and no shelters are provided per se. There are limitations, however, as the YWCA has a limited capacity to effectively cater for all the women in need. Churches and faith-based organisations are also providing some support in the form of safety and relief although this is also limited[1].

During the Sixteen Days of Activism, which takes place between 25 November and 10 December, some NGOs have sensitised the general public about GBV.

Many civil society organisations said that the African Women's Protocol would further enhance the rights of women, as it is a progressive Protocol. Others said that the Protocol should assist in implementing the gender policy and the CEDAW. Some emphasised that the Protocol is an extension of the other human rights instruments. One respondent stated that the Protocol would impact positively on the laws of marriage and inheritance, particularly in relation to traditional and customary practices.

The areas that will remain critical despite the Protocol are culture, religion, and political will. One respondent stated that:

> whereas article 18 of the ACHPR prohibits discrimination against women in the context of the family, it does not include explicit provisions guaranteeing the right of consent to marriage and to actual equality in the marriage, a situation that essentially leaves room for exploitation and injustice to women and their children.

The respondent further stated, "The Charter also places emphasis on traditional African values and traditions without addressing concerns that many customary practices, such as forced marriages and wife inheritance, continue to cause to both women and children."

GOVERNANCE

The respondents stated that Zambia has not adopted a quota system, in spite of it being a signatory to the SADC Declaration on Gender and Development, which stipulates that 30 per cent of decision-making positions should be reserved for women. The main reason for this can be attributed to the male dominance not just in government, but also in political parties. The respondents felt that there is no political will to establish a quota system, firstly, at the stage of candidate adoption and, secondly, in terms of appointments to decision-making positions. What is seen is tokenism – a few seats are allocated to women in order to keep them quiet[2]. It was, however, stated that submissions to the Constitution Review Commission and the ERTC include those on a quota system.

Some respondents stated that there has definitely been an increase in the presence of women in decision-making positions since 2001. One of the practical examples that can be cited, is that female parliamentarians have constantly raised the issue of gender and women's empowerment in parliament and they have even gone so far as to introduce a private member's motion in parliament on the process of gender mainstreaming, although this did not receive broad support from the rest of the parliamentarians. One female member of the Pan African Parliament said she brought up the issue of domesticating the CEDAW and the government has since started working on the exercise.

Another respondent said that it is apparent that a lot still remains to be done to improve participation of women in the electoral processes and high-level offices. There is no nationally shared vision on why women's participation is important. Voter education, on aspects of gender and women's participation, is important. The electoral practices should be reformed to make it conducive for everyone, including women, to easily participate.

One gender consultant stated that there is a need to fight from the inside, by getting women involved in politics. Another respondent from the government said that women voters need to support each other.

The African Women's Protocol provides a positive legislative framework regarding women's participation in governance. However, difficulties relating to women's participation were attributed to negative attitudes and beliefs. Some respondents said that there are a large number of rural based voters who, in most cases, retain strong cultural values, which subject women to secondary roles. The mindset of voters has to change in order for them to consider the merits of a candidate on a basis other than sex. Men need to be sensitised for them to effectively support women in the electoral process.

SEXUAL AND REPRODUCTIVE RIGHTS

The respondents said that there are no laws in Zambia that protect and treat people with AIDS, nor are there laws allowing women control over their own sexuality. All respondents said that, unless a panel of three doctors agrees that the abortion is necessary to ensure the safety of the mother or that of the unborn baby, abortion is illegal in Zambia.

On issues of culture and religion, all respondents felt that these teach women to be submissive to men and that contraceptive use is discouraged. The payment of lobola further domesticates the woman as the property of the husband. In addition, the church does not support contraception and is anti abortion.

It was reported that men are usually not involved in reproductive health activities. Furthermore, gay and lesbian rights are non-existent in Zambia, as these are regarded as illegal activities.[3]

It was reported that the African Women's Protocol would not only promote autonomy for women but would also allow women to make informed choices. Other respondents believe that the Protocol may improve on what other instruments have left out.

Awareness About the African Women's Protocol[4]

Policy Makers

The few policy makers interviewed in the course of this research project, exhibited serious gaps in their knowledge of the Protocol. The interviewee from the GIDD showed the highest level of awareness of the Protocol since there was awareness of its existence, even though the interviewee was unsure of its contents. The respondents from the Justice Ministry; the then Deputy Minister from the Ministry of Community development and Social Services, and the Gender Focal Point Person at the Ministry of Foreign Affairs[5] exhibited complete ignorance on the Protocol.

Civil Society Organisations

The regional civil society organisation, WILSA, appeared most conversant with the African Women's Protocol. WILSA uses the AU Women's Protocol to promote women's rights. An independent gender consultant/academic, Sara Longwe, was familiar with the Protocol. Mirab Kiremire of MAPODE was equally conversant with the Protocol and uses it in her work with girls in difficult circumstances. The other civil society organisations interviewed appeared completely ignorant of the Protocol.

Notes

[1] It should be noted that this is not a government response but is instead an NGO response.

[2] One deputy minister interviewed for this research said, "I do not agree in favouring women in politics. Let us compete and the people chose."

[3] It is important to note that although homosexuality is illegal in Zambia, this does not mean it does not exist.

[4] The research was conducted between Dec 2004 and April 2005 when awareness of the Protocol was low. The situation has since changed owing to popularisation of the Protocol by Women's Rights organisations. This situation is applicable to all areas discussed under the section on Awareness.

[5] The Gender Focal Point Person at the Ministry of Foreign Affairs, however, requested a copy of the AU Women's Protocol from the researcher for future reference.

24

Challenges

SOME RESPONDENTS STATED the main challenges for gender mainstreaming in Zambia as follows:

- Firstly, insufficient budgetary allocations for the implementation of the gender policy. Government has not committed all the necessary resources, which would make a significant impact on the gender inequalities Zambia is presently experiencing.

- Secondly, while policy pronouncements have been made on gender equality, this has not translated into concrete actions (e.g. land allocation remains largely gender blind).

- Thirdly, the NGP is a cover up since nothing is happening at ground level. It was further stated that because of the SADC's stipulation, which states that there must be 30 per cent women representation in decision-making areas, has a deadline, this may motivate the government to increase the number of women in decision-making.

- Finally, one respondent stated that immediate public awareness campaigns must be implemented to ensure that both the general public and relevant authorities know the societal benefits of the Protocol.

25

Achievements and Best Practices

THIS IS A LIST of achievements and best practices:

- The creation of the Ministry of Gender and Women in Development, the GIDD (which services the Ministry), the appointment of the Minister of Gender and Women in Development, the declaration of 8 March as a public holiday in honour of women and the appointment of Gender Focal Point Persons in all the line ministries.

- Government has put in place other measures that promote the rights of women. The Parliamentary Committee on Legal Affairs, Governance, Human Rights and Gender matters, which acts as an effective tool in monitoring the actions of government with regards to the rights of women and children. The recommendations of this parliamentary committee are implemented through legislative reforms and policy changes.

- Zambia is also going through Constitutional reforms that will see the Constitution having economic, social and cultural rights together with women's rights in the Bill of Rights. There have been legislative reforms to benefit women and children, for instance the penal code introduced stiffer penalties for sexual offences and introduced a new offence on trafficking in human beings especially children and women.

- The Zambia Law Development Commission undertook a study on the restatement of customary law whose general objective was to ascertain the current customary laws and their conformity and economic values in the country. In restating customary law, the study identified repugnant customs that should no longer be promoted, for example sexual cleansing after the death of a spouse.

- Government has also recorded some key delivery areas and strategies to ensure the acceleration of equality between women and men. For example, the promotion of participation of women in the social protection scheme, ensuring that 30 per cent of allocated titled land is reserved for women.

- The government is also implementing a governance program under which the component on Access to Justice is being pursued. Zambia is also part of the process to elevate the SADC Declaration on Gender and Development to a protocol with a provision for 50/50 power sharing between women and men in decision-making positions at all levels.

- Ratifying the CEDAW, the African Women's Protocol on the rights of women in Africa.

- Putting in place the VSUs in the police service.

- In 2006, the Government developed the Fifth National Development Plan (2006 – 2010) which outlines Zambia's development programme for the next five years. In the plan, gender has been mainstreamed within the existing macro and sectoral policies and programmes. The development also has a separate chapter on gender that allows for easy budgeting and programme implementation.

- There is a gender Consultative Forum which became operational in 2003. It is made up of government, civil society organisations and cooperating partners. It reviews progress on the Gender Policy activities.

- The formation of the Sector Advisory Group which has the mandate of prioritising programmes and allocating resources under the Fifth National Development Plan (FNDP).

- Gender mainstreaming in all government ministries by appointing Gender Focal Points. In addition, at district level the district administration will be responsible for implementing programmes and projects on gender through the Gender sub-committees of the DDCCS. Just like the provincial administrative establishment will be responsible for the implementation programmes and projects on gender, through the Gender Sub-committee of the PDCCS (FNDP).

- Section 108 of the Industrial and Labour Relations Act, Chapter 269 of the Laws of Zambia, prohibits any form of discrimination in employment on the grounds of sex, race, marital status, religion, political affiliation or tribal extraction.

26

Conclusions and Recommendations

CONCLUSIONS

SOME CONCLUSIONS, ARISING from the above analysis, regarding the level of awareness, significance and potential impact of the Africa Women Protocol in Zambia can be made. The conclusions are as follows:

- Zambia, like many other African countries, is a highly patriarchal society. Issues of gender equality and women's empowerment receive little or no attention in public policy and even less attention in terms of implementation.

- Many people in Zambia did not know of the African Women's Protocol at the time of conducting the research. The policy makers, CSOs and academics were not fully conversant with its provisions. The situation has since changed, but the challenge of translating the Protocol to benefit the lives of ordinary women and men still remains.

- In Zambia, there are strong gender-based CSOs and individuals that have been instrumental in advocating the establishment of gender machinery, the gender policy and the observance of international human rights and women's rights protocols in Zambia.

- Some civil society organisations see the potential of the Protocol as adding value to the existing array of tools that women and men in Zambia can use to bring about gender equality.

RECOMMENDATIONS

In view of the analysis and conclusions arising from this research, a number of concrete and action-oriented recommendations can be made about the AU Women's Protocol in Zambia. These are as follows:

- The government must be seen to take the lead role in gender reforms, law reforms and enforcement. It should sponsor and support gender oriented research and law reforms. Consequently, it needs to assign more resources to the Zambia Law Development Commission and employ at least two gender sensitive persons to focus on drafting gender law reforms in the Ministry of Justice and parliament. NGO efforts should merely supplement, not supercede, government efforts and donors should make this clear in providing funding. Women's rights must be ranked with political rights and democratic governance.

- The government must provide adequate resources, both human and financial, to implement a National Plan of Action for Gender Policy. These resources must be provided for in the national budget and timely disbursements should be ensured, a well resourced monitoring and evaluation system of the budget and its deliverable outputs should accompany this. These actions should be in line with the provisions made in the Africa Women's Protocol and the CEDAW on the provision of adequate budgetary and human resources to implement women's empowerment programmes.

- The leading women's NGOs and other development and civil rights NGOs should continuously lobby government to implement the gender policy effectively and efficiently and should hold government accountable for its implementation. These should undertake programmatic initiatives that link work on VAW, sexual and reproductive health services and livelihoods to the Protocol.

- Government, through the Ministry of Justice, should domesticate the provisions of all international, regional and sub regional instruments, for instance the CEDAW, the African Women's Protocol and the SADC GAD, in order to enhance the existing policy and legal framework that will result in ensuring the protection of women's rights.

- The government should popularise the Africa Women's Protocol. This will help strengthen the existing national legal and policy framework. Popularisation of the Protocol should be done through a joint effort amongst the major stakeholders, which include Ministries of Justice and Foreign Affairs as well as the Ministry of Gender and Women in Development and the GIDD, the Ministry of Community Development and Social Welfare and other stakeholders like the women's movement, women's rights Organisations and other civil society organisations.

- Oxfam GB Southern Africa should support efforts to popularise the AU Women's Protocol in Zambia.

Section Four

Mozambican Country Report
Alcinda Abreu and Angélica Salomão

Summary

THIS SECTION LOOKS AT the Mozambican situation in relation to women's rights. Chapter 27 contains the introduction; which provides the purpose of the research, the justification for the study and the study limitations.

Chapter 28 contains the research methodology, which involved both secondary and primary data collection. In addition, a national consultative workshop, which involved key policy makers from parliament and government line ministries, leading CSOs on women's rights, the academia, the media and grassroots CBOs, was held to validate and strengthen the research finding.

Chapter 29 provides the literature review; this discusses the general situation of women, the Constitution and the various measures undertaken by government to strengthen the mechanisms for strengthening gender and women's rights, the role undertaken by women's rights CSOs to promote women's rights; analyses the national policies and legislation on women's rights, decision-making and power sharing and Mozambique experience in relation to the use of international instruments.

Chapter 30 contains the challenges related to addressing gender and women's rights issues. The key issue highlighted is the discrepancy between the legal and policy framework on one hand, and the implementation of policies on the other, and the way these policies impact on the daily lives of ordinary women. Barriers related to weak implementation of policies relate to negative cultural aspects, limited gender expertise, budgetary constraints, HIV and AIDS and the weakening women's movement. This chapter examines the Mozambican policy framework in relation to the thematic areas for this study. With regard to VAW, this section looks at the forms, nature, extent and effects of violence and the various measures undertaken by the government and CSOs to address it. In addition, it provides a brief analysis of the African Women's Protocol in relation to VAW. With regard to governance, this section looks at the representation of women in public institutions (political and civil service), mechanisms for gender and women's rights. With regard to sexual and reproductive rights of women, this section looks at the situation of women in relation to sexual and reproductive rights and the various measures undertaken by the government to ensure this. The research indicates that the African Women's Protocol strengthens Mozambique's policy framework in relation to women's Rights.

Chapter 31 contains the conclusions and recommendations. The research concludes by stating that Mozambique has the environment to pursue the long road towards women's empowerment because there is a positive relationship between the government and women's rights organisations. A number of policy recommendations are suggested, which include: increased lobbying by women's rights organisations for increased representation of women in parliament, increased popularisation of the African Women's Protocol and the development of gender indicators to assess the achievements of the Protocol.

27

Introduction

MOZAMBIQUE IS A FORMER PORTUGUESE COLONY. In 1498, Vasco da Gama led the first European expedition to Mozambique. This resulted in the eventual colonisation of Mozambique for over 500 years by the Portuguese, the displacement of local leaders and the taking over of land and mineral resources (Henriksen, 1975).

In the late-nineteenth century, opposition to Portuguese rule arose among the Africans. This was however, fragmented along tribal, ethnic and regional ties. Three organisations, that is the Mozambique African National Union (MANU), the National Democratic Union of Mozambique (UDENAMO) and the National AU of Independent Mozambique (UNAMI), met in Dar-Es-Salaam under the auspices of the then Tanganyika President, Julius Nyerere. The three merged to form FRELIMO, under the leadership of Eduardo Mondlane in 1962 (ISS 2003: Henriksen, 1975). The goal of the FRELIMO was the "quick access to independence, the social and cultural development of the Mozambican women and the literacy of the Mozambican people". On 25 September 1964, FRELIMO launched a guerrilla war against the Portuguese that ravaged the northern part of the country. After three years of fighting, Eduardo Mondlane called for Mozambican society to be restructured on different lines to the colonial and traditional economic patterns (Henriksen, 1978: 441; Henriksen, 1975).

Women supported the armed struggle against Portuguese rule under the auspices of the Mozambique Women's Organisation (Organizacao da Mulher Mozambicana or OMM), which was established during the war. OMM was a wing of FRELIMO and operated within its framework (Arnfred, 2001). Eduardo Mondlane was assassinated in 1969, and his role was taken over by Samora Machel (Henriksen, 1975; ISS, 2003).

The war ended in 1974 after a military coup in Portugal. Mozambique gained their independence in 1975 under a one-party state, FRELIMO, led by Samora Machel. A transitional government, led by Prime Minister Joachim Chisano, was formed in September 1974, which led the country to independence (ISS, 2003).

In 1976, a civil war ensued launched by the Resistencia Nacional de Mozambique (RENAMO) (Agadjanian, 2001: 292). Depending on the historical accounts one comes across, the war lasted 13 – 16 years before it came to an end. According to Vines (1998), the war came to an end after 16 years of civil war. A cease-fire was signed on 4 October 1992 when the United Nations force, United Nations Operations in Mozambique (ONUMOZ), embarked on a disarmament exercise for the warring parties.

The war destroyed infrastructure and disrupted the social and economic life of the country. About one and a half million refugees fled to neighbouring countries. The war had a significant impact on present-day poverty levels in the country posing a challenge for post-war reconstruction and poverty alleviation (Clark, 1991; Bruck, 2001; Gaspar, 2002). The country held its first democratic elections in 1994, which were won by FRELIMO, although RENAMO gained a strong majority in the central and northern parts of the country.

Politically, Mozambique embraced socialism and FRELIMO's ideology was rooted in Marxist-Leninist terms and received support from socialist states prior to and after independence (Minter, 1978). According to their ideology, the conflict between Portugal and Mozambique was based on exploitation, that is to say that the colonisation of Mozambique by Portugal had been based on exploitation. This ideology is reported to have been independent of Europe and hence perceived as 'original' to the Mozambicans (Henriksen, 1978: 445). At this time, Mozambique formed close ties with the German Democratic Republic, Cuba, the People's Republic of Bulgaria, the Socialist Republic of Romania, and the People's Republic of China, the former Soviet Union and the Democratic Republic of Korea (Minter, 1978).

Agriculture is the main activity of the country, since it is the major contributor to the economy and is widely practiced in the central and northern parts of the country.

Labour migration is reported to have had an impact on agricultural production and the sexual division of labour. In the absence of men, women had to undertake agricultural production on their own (Berg, 1987). In 1909, the Mozambique Convention (revised in 1928 and 1930) was signed between Mozambique and South Africa, where the former was to supply an average of 100 000 workers (mostly for the mines) to the latter every year. After every six months on full salary, 60 per cent of Mozambican miners' wages were remitted to Portugal in gold bars for $35 an ounce. The remaining 40 per cent was paid to the workers in escudos at the end of their contracts. Interestingly, many workers were not aware that they were receiving low wages. Labour migration to South Africa declined after independence (Azevedo, 1980: 568).

A study conducted by Berg (1987) in the southern part of the country, reports that in the early nineteenth century, agricultural production was a major sustainable activity. However, labour migration to the plantations and mines in Southern Africa in the mid-nineteenth century reduced male power for agriculture. In the twentieth century, this was coupled with the labour withdrawal by Portuguese colonialists. These two processes are reported to have had a significant impact on agricultural production, as more labour-intensive crops that could adapt to the local climate were replaced with less labour-intensive, less climatically adapted crops. This is reported to have rendered peasant agricultural production dependant on wage labour (from migrant workers) for cash for the hire of ploughs and the purchase of seed. After independence in 1975, labour migration reduced drastically, posing a threat to agricultural production.

Poverty is associated with the 16 years of civil war that contributed to the decline in basic social services and increasing levels of poverty (World Vision, 2005: 29). The most affected parts are in the northern parts of the country. The war contributed to the decline of basic social services especially in health, education and agriculture. Access to quality healthcare services and education remains a challenge as a result of poverty exacerbated by the HIV and AIDS epidemic and the macroeconomic policy framework imposed by the IMF and the World Bank. HIV and AIDS remains a major barrier to development in Mozambique and have been declared an emergency by the government (World Bank, 2006).

With an estimated population of 19 million people, Mozambique is one of the poorest countries in the world with over 70 per cent of its inhabitants living in absolute poverty. The provinces most affected by poverty are Manica, Sofala, Tete and Inhambane.

Life expectancy is about 43 years and is being threatened by the HIV and AIDS pandemic (UNAIDS, 2004). In 2002, an average of 500 people were being infected daily, mainly through heterosexual intercourse (Manuel, 2005: 294). The national prevalence of HIV among adults 15–49 was 16.1 per cent in 2006. HIV infection in pregnant women is highest in the south and centre of the country (UNAIDS 2006). Women and girls are more vulnerable to HIV and AIDS than men, owing to a number of factors among which is their lack of control over their sexuality, lack of negotiation skills in matters relating to sex, VAW, low literacy levels and poverty (UNAIDS, 2004: 15).

The war had an effect on demographic patterns, with refugee migrations influencing the processes of urbanisation, population growth rates and other demographic characteristics. It is estimated that there were 4.7 million internal and external refugees during and after the war. Between 1993 and 1995, about 1.7 million refugees returned from abroad (75 per cent from Malawi, 14.5 per cent Zimbabwe and 10 per cent from South Africa, Tanzania, Zambia and Swaziland) and the three million internally displaced people returned to their homes, most of them to the central areas. These migration patterns are said to have contributed to the HIV-infection rate in Mozambique. About 45 per cent of the population is younger than 15 years of age, posing a threat to sustainable development. In addition, about 70 per cent of the population lives in the rural areas with less access to basic services (Gaspar, 2002: 5).

Literacy levels remain low in most of the country posing a serious challenge to development. The 2003 estimates showed that 53.6 per cent of Mozambique's adult population cannot read or write (Pridmore & Yates 2005: 492). There was an increase in gross primary enrolment rate to 92 per cent in 2000 and 110 per cent in 2003/2005. Girls' enrolment was 100 per cent, while for boys it was 121 per cent (World Bank, 2006). The gender gap in education is wide, since many women and girls are unable to read or write. Women constitute the majority of the illiterate population, with only 15 per cent of women in rural areas able to read and write. The gender disparity is exacerbated by negative cultural attitudes, beliefs and practices, such as early marriages, unequal gender division of labour in the family, limited role of women in decision-making areas and the lack of role models for young girls. Gender gaps in education pose a challenge for increased representation of women in formal employment, thus restricting their ability to fully contribute to development. In addition, accessibility to schools is compounded by the long distances to schools, inadequate learning materials, violence against girls in schools, inadequate meals at schools and the HIV and AIDS epidemic. According to Pridmore and Yates (2005: 492), 70 per cent of young people drop out of school by the age of 13 owing to the effects of HIV and AIDS.

Mozambique is generally divided into two systems of lineage:

matrilineal, prevailing in the northern and central parts, and patrilineal, in the southern part of the country. It is however, common to find the two systems side by side.

In matrilineal societies, descent is traced through the mother. It is common for marriage to be matrilocal, that is, for the man to move to the woman's family home/area. The societies are not matriarchal, in other words, women do not rule and they have less parental power over the children. Parental authority is exercised through the nearest male kin, such as the mother's uncles, brothers or cousins (Welch, Dagnino, & Sach. 1985:62). Lobola does not exist in such societies, though a symbolic payment is made to the bride's family. A marriage proposal is said to consist of a man paying some money to the girl, aunt or grandmother. He is expected to receive half the payment back as a sign of acceptance if not, it is considered a rejection. Upon agreement to the marriage, the man moves to the bride's family where he is obliged to build a house, prepare the fields, and contribute game and fish to the family. After that, he is expected to move out and stay with the wife close to her family. In the case of divorce, it is the man that moves out of the home. However, there is said to be considerable change taking place to traditional marriages within matrilineal societies (ibid: 63).

In patrilineal societies, the traditional marriage is patrilocal, that is, the woman moves to the man's home. Lobola is paid in the form of cattle, which is a form of economic advantage for the girl's family, compensation to the family for the loss of a family member and a symbol cementing the relationship between the two families (Jelle van den Berg, 1987:377). Lobola also has spiritual significance: it is a message sent to the ancestors to announce the departure of a family member to another family. The involvement of the parents, members of the community and the ancestral spirits is intended to contribute to the stability of the marriage, its mutual respect and its fidelity. However, owing to the decline in traditional values, this practice does not hold the same values that it had. Couples are reportedly not consulting their parents or involving them in their pending marriage anymore. Consequently, this has increased the instability in marriages, resulting in divorce, multiple sexual partners and the resultant exposure to the HIV infection (Bukali, 2002: 14). As a result of migrant labour to South Africa, lobola is reported to be cash and not cattle. (Ibid: 64). Among the Tsonga, the influence of trade and war in the nineteenth century in Delagao Bay changed bride wealth from cattle to imported hoes to British pounds. The hoes were not used for agriculture but were ritual objects imported from the Transvaal (present day provinces – Gauteng, Limpopo, parts of

Mpumalanga and North West in South Africa) and later from Europe (Berg, 1987: 377). In the patrilineal system, lobola is considered an important part of marriage. "It is a form of compensation for the parents of the bride, in exchange for the children (economic) that she will bear her husband and family" (Bukali, 2002:14).

Polygamy is common in Mozambique, with, according to the 1997 Demographic Health Survey, about 28 per cent of married women being in polygamous unions (Population Council, 2004). Polygamy refers to marriages where a man is concurrently married to more than one woman. There are however, ethnic differences; Sena/Ndau polygamy is at 40 per cent, followed by the Tsonga with 28 per cent. For the Macua it is 22 per cent, 20 per cent for the 'Other' ethnic group and 15 per cent for the Lomwe/Chuwabo. Although matrilineal ethnic groups have lower incidences of polygamy, there are differences between them. The Macua women are 48 per cent more likely to marry a polygamist than their Lomwe/Chuwabo counterparts. The high polygamy rates among the Macua could be attributed to the Moslem influence, as not only do they have matrilocal residence but polygamous men have to reside at their senior wife's family and visit the other wives elsewhere in turns (Arnaldo, 2004). Nationally, 19 per cent of girls aged 15 – 19 years are in polygamous marriages (Ibid).

Prior to December 2003, Mozambique had four official systems of marriage: customary, religious, civil and mutual consent union/cohabitation. By the time of Mozambique's independence in 1975, the Portuguese had established common laws that had little regard for local customs, as the majority of Mozambicans regulate their lives along customary practices. Both legal systems contained legislation and practices that disadvantage women. The new Family Law, which was introduced in 2003, has made progress in reconciling the two sets of laws, introducing legislation that will protect women from discrimination. The new law guarantees Mozambican women a broad range of rights which were previously non-existent. The minimum age for marriage has been raised to 18 years for both men and women. Prior to the legal reforms in December 2003, the minimum age for marriage was 14 years for females and 16 years for males. The new law allows women to inherit property in the case of divorce and legally recognises traditional marriages, which constitute the majority of marriages in Mozambique (Oxfam America, 2006: 1).

The Mozambique Constitution adopts the UN and African Charter on Human and Peoples' Rights. Article 35 and 36 state the principles of gender equality 37 to 39 state the both the right to protection and birthrights, which endorse the family as the backbone of society. Women play a critical role in the family.

The Mozambican Constitution states that all citizens have equal rights and are submitted to the same obligations; it also states that men and women are both equal before the law in all aspects of political, economic, social and cultural life. The Mozambican government recognises:

- Women's rights.
- That the right to health has to consider biological differences between man and women.
- That the expansion of health services should contribute to improve the health conditions of women.
- And that people in the countryside who do not have access to information on gender, the Protocol, or women's rights have the right this information.

28

Methodology

THE PURPOSE OF THIS STUDY was to inform Oxfam, partners, members of the civil society organisations and parliamentarians at national and AU level about the various implications of the African Women's Protocol. The objective of the national research was to:

- Collect primary and secondary data at country level.
- Identify the national position on the CEDAW and the SADC Gender Policy (ratification and domestication, lessons that can be learnt, areas of best practice or challenges on women's rights in relation to addressing VAW, sexual and reproductive rights, governance).

The research forms part of a regional policy study that was conducted in South Africa, Zambia and Mozambique. Data collection in Mozambique involved both secondary and primary sources. The research team examined key policy documents that relate to women's rights and a number of research reports that had been undertaken in Mozambique.

The research team conducted key informant interviews with representatives from the line ministries of Women and Social Action, parliamentarians, civil society organisations, and academicians and used a questionnaire, which involved 11 respondents.

In addition, a national consultative workshop was conducted on 15 April 2005. This involved key policy makers in government, line ministries and parliaments, CSOs, the academia and the media, who helped to disseminate, validate and strengthen the research findings and discuss the implications of the African Women's Protocol. Furthermore, it aimed to identify areas that different sectors can incorporate into their plans to further women's rights. The workshop discussed the implications on the implementation of the African Women's Protocol. Seventeen participants attended it.

At the end of the workshop, a national coalition was formed to lobby for ratification (now achieved) and the popularisation of the African Women's Protocol. This consisted of WILSA, Legal and Human Rights coalition, Women Law and Development, MULEIDE, Nhamai, FADAJ and Forum Mulher.

29

Literature Review

THE LEGAL SITUATION OF WOMEN IN MOZAMBIQUE

DESPITE ITS MEAGRE RESOURCES, Mozambique has been trying to bring about some positive changes in relation to the promotion of women's Rights. However, there is still a lot to be done to achieve equity and equality in the fulfilment of rights, particularly in view of the fact that the means of enforcing these rights are limited. Mozambique is one of the least developed countries in the world. It has an illiteracy rate of 54 per cent among the adult population (68 per cent of this is made up of women). The economy has grown from 7.1 per cent in 2003 to 7.2 per cent in 2004, with an inflation of 9.3 per cent in 2004. In the last six years, the poverty rate has fallen from 69.4 per cent to 54.1 per cent. However, the government has established the need to keep GDP between seven per cent and eight per cent.

In Mozambique, women constitute 52 per cent of the total population (72.2 per cent of which live in rural areas). They play an important role in the production and management of their families and their communities. Only 60 per cent of the population has access to sanitary services and 54 per cent to environmental sanitation. The average life expectancy of Mozambicans is 42.3 years of age (44 years old for women and 40.6 for men). It is estimated that the HIV and AIDS prevalence in the adult population is 16.6 per cent, which means that around 1.14 million people are infected with the virus.

The Constitution of the Republic establishes the universal principle of equality in Article 35 and the principle of gender equality in Article 36, which states that, "Men and women are equal under the law in all domains of political, economic, social and cultural life." In Article 26, the Constitution declares that foreigners, who have been married to a Mozambican man or woman for at least five years, can acquire Mozambican nationality and are entitled to it even in the event of a divorce or the death of their Mozambican spouse.

The promotion of women rights to increase the level of awareness of the society towards women's rights is one of the objectives mentioned in the government programme. The MMAS is the government mechanism for the advancement of women. The Minister of Women and Social Action leads the National Council for the Advancement of Women, created to promote gender equity and women's emancipation. The Council of Ministers has adopted a National Plan for the Advancement of Women 2002–2006, with the following priorities:

- Women, poverty and employment;
- Women, health and HIV/AIDS;
- Women's rights and violence;
- Women in power, at decision-making levels and in social communication;
- Women, environment and agriculture; and
- Institutional mechanisms for the advancement of women.

NGOs play also an important role in lobbing and advocating for women's human rights. There is, for example, a network called All Against Violence, lead by Forum Mulher. Organisations, such as Mulher, Lei e Desenvolvimento (MULEIDE); Organização da Mulher Moçambicana (OMM); Associação das Mulheres de Carreira Jurídica (AMCJP); Liga dos Direitos Humanos (LDH); and Associação dos Direitos Humanos (DHD), have developed services to provide legal education, training and assistance to women and men suffering from domestic violence and other violations to their rights.

ANALYSIS OF NATIONAL POLICIES AND LEGISLATION ON WOMEN'S RIGHTS

In the last few years, Mozambique has made positive developments in economic; political; social and cultural life. The government has established the Government Programme for 2005–2009 that gives priority to human and rural development for the next five years. It is based on six main goals out of which two stress the general rights of the people in the following ways:

- Reduction of the levels of absolute poverty through the promotion of rapid and sustainable economic growth focusing on education, health, and the development of infrastructures for water, sanitation, roads and communication.

- Social and economic development mainly directed at rural areas aiming to decrease regional imbalances.

Government policy is oriented at poverty reduction. The Government Programme for 2005–2009 states, "Poverty reduction is a challenge for all and conditions to promote human, economic and social development, in rural and urban areas" that must be made. It also says that, "The objective of reducing poverty levels must take in consideration the mainstreaming basic services to people in need." As a result, government action is directed towards improving the lives of the female population. Thus, women will be the centre of programmes aiming to provide equal opportunities and rights, by increasing their levels of education and reinforcing their roles as the educators of future generations, women will play a huge role in the socialisation of Mozambican men.

Key areas for action selected by the government are:

- Education;
- Health;
- Infrastructures;
- Agriculture;
- Rural development;
- Good governance, legality and justice; and
- Macroeconomic, financial and international trade policies.

It goes without saying that most of them favour the more deprived Mozambican population, with particular attention being paid to the situation of women. As far as human and social development is concerned, women's development is considered under women, family and social action.

One of the major challenges the government envisages is to set and implement an integrated policy of social action in order to tackle poverty, social exclusion and gender inequities that affect more and more people in Mozambican society.

Thus, women development deserves special attention by the 2005–2009 Government Programme. According to the programme, government will:

- Pursue social awareness on women's rights.
- Mainstream gender perspectives in the conception and analysis national development policies and strategies.
- Reinforce participation of women in decision-making bodies at all levels, particularly political, economic, social and cultural life, assuring equal opportunities and offering affirmative action when necessary.
- Promote participation of women in leadership roles and decision-making bodies at different levels.
- Promote the revision of legal tools that discriminate against women.
- Increase the level of education of women through measures that stimulate access and reward good performances at school.
- Encourage and participate in working groups to review existent laws, making proposals for new laws protecting citizens, in particular women, against domestic and sexual violence.

Under areas of governance, legality and justice, the programme states that the "Creation of indispensable conditions to materialise justice are essential in the process of consolidation of national unity, peace, stability and protection of human rights and the freedom of citizens." The principles that sustain this process are the protection, promotion and respect for human and women's rights in particular. In this regard, the programme states that government must "pursue the consolidation and enlargement of legal assistance and judiciary support to deprived citizens, particularly their defense in criminal processes". If one realises that women are among the most deprived citizens in the country, this paves the way for the protection of women.

There is high maternal mortality rate in the country. Therefore, in line with goals five and six of the Millennium Development Goals (i.e. these target reduction of maternal mortality and reverse the spread of HIV and AIDS), the National Strategy for Maternal Mortality and the National Strategic Plan to combating STI/HIV/AIDS pays attention to women as one of the vulnerable groups that need special consideration. In addition, the Mozambican government gives particular attention to girl enrolment at primary and secondary levels of education.

The national consultative workshop was held in Maputo on 15 April 2005 to disseminate the findings of the policy research to policy makers in Mozambique and identify areas that different sectors can incorporate into their plans to further women's rights. It also served the purpose of validating the research findings and strengthening the research report. It was attended by representatives from women's rights organisations, the academia, members of parliament and the media. The findings from the workshop have informed the Mozambique section of this publication.

Decision-Making and Power Sharing

The Government Programme for 2005-2009, prioritises human and rural development and includes some of these goals:

- Consolidation of national unity, peace, justice and democracy.
- Fight against corruption, bureaucratism and unrest.
- Reinforcement of sovereignty and international cooperation.

Mozambique's underwent elections in 2005. Under the new Assembleia da República (parliament), 35.7 per cent of the 250 members in government are women, 29 per cent of cabinet ministers are female (six ministers and four vice ministers), and, more importantly, the prime minister is a woman. Among the 11 provincial governors recently appointed, two are women and, at district level 13.2 per cent of the administrators are female.

The Gender National Policy was approved. Capacity building, to mainstream gender in different sectors, is under way, particularly in areas of gender planning, budgetary, gender sensitisation, lobbying and advocacy.

Experience with International Instruments

Mozambique ratified the CEDAW in June 1993, through Resolution No. 4193 of the Assembly of the Republic.

The CEDAW is being domesticated and has been incorporated in the labour law, land law and family law areas, as well in education, health and agriculture national policies.

The government of Mozambique has ratified the International Covenant on Civil and Political Rights and its second, optional protocol, as well as other major human rights treaties, including the Convention on the Rights of the Child and its optional protocol, which deals with the sale of children, child prostitution and children, the African Charter on the Rights and Welfare of the Child, the Convention on the Elimination of all forms of Racial Discrimination and the Convention Against Torture, the African Women's Protocol and signed the SADC GAD and its Addendum on VAW. These instruments contain important provisions and provide a framework for policy and legislation at national level.

Many of these international instruments require the government to submit periodic reports on the steps taken to implement them, including detailed data on the degree to which rights are being implemented and what the main constraints faced in the implementation process are. The ratification of the CEDAW provides a form of international accountability with regard to the rights of women. Thus, the ratification of the African Women's Protocol provides a form of regional accountability.

30

The African Women's Protocol

BACKGROUND

IN JUNE 1995, THE 31ST SESSION of the Assembly of the Heads of States and Governments of the OAU met in Addis Ababa in order to endorse recommendations made by the African Commission for Human and Peoples' Rights. It also gave the Commission the mandate to start the process of elaborating the African Protocol for Women Rights. After nine years of consultations and negotiations, among state members; NGOs women's rights movements and AU civil society groups, the draft was submitted to the AU heads of state.

The AU Heads of State Summit held in Maputo in July 2003, adopted the Protocol on the ACHPR on the Rights of Women. One year later, a campaign that joined civil society groups, women's rights activists and citizens started to mobilise support for the ratification of the Protocol, pressurising African governments to ratify and domesticate it in its national laws and policies. By July 2007, 43 countries had signed the Protocol, 21 of these countries had ratified.

The Protocol contains 32 articles addressing the following issues and rights:

- Definitions;
- Elimination of discrimination against women (article 2);
- Rights to dignity, life, integrity and security of the person;
- Elimination of harmful practices;
- Marriage, separation, divorce and annulment of marriage;
- Access to justice and equal protection before the law;

274

- Right to participation in the political and decision-making process; right to peace, education and training;
- Protection of women in armed conflicts;
- Economic and social welfare rights;
- Health and reproductive rights, the right to a healthy and sustainable environment;
- Right to food, security, adequate housing, positive cultural context and the right to sustainable development;
- Widows' rights;
- Right to inheritance;
- Special protection of elderly women, women with disabilities and women in distress;
- Remedies, implementation and monitory;
- Interpretation, signature, ratification and accession;
- Entry into force, amendment and revision;
- Status of the present Protocol and transitional provisions.

The African Women's Protocol calls upon member states to undertake measures to eliminate all forms of discrimination against women and practices that are prejudicial to women. In this context, the Protocol reaffirms and recognises women's rights as interdependent, inalienable and indivisible of human rights. To ensure these rights, the Protocol establishes the need to undertake internal and adequate legislative measures. The Protocol seeks:

- To include the principle of equality between men and women and the guarantee of its effective application in national Constitutions and legal instruments;
- To integrate gender perspectives in political and legal decisions, as well as in development plans and other spheres of life;
- To effectively promulgate and implement appropriate national, political and legal measures forbidding all forms of negative practices that put the health and welfare of women at risk;
- To take corrective measures and develop affirmative action in areas of discrimination against women;
- To adopt appropriate measures to prohibit the exploitation and degradation of women;

- To establish public education in order to eliminate negative cultural and traditional practices based ion the inferiority or superiority of either sex.

The African Women's Protocol is an important instrument for regional campaigns, which will aid the elimination of all forms of discrimination against women. The negotiation process was not easy, owing to a number of religious and cultural reservations manifested by some member states. The main contentious issues that featured in the negotiations concerned the minimum matrimony age for women; the fact that divorce, separation and annulments are only possible when determined by a court of law; equal rights for both men and women after separation; divorce and annulments with regard to the division of goods; women's freedom of choice in matters of contraception; and VAW in asylums, as well as those made against refugees. These acts should be seen as war crimes, genocides or crimes against humanity, and their actors should be judged in competent courts.

Other issues regarding the difficult negotiation process were related to the promotion of access to information, education and communication programmes for women, particularly those in rural areas. These include information about the right to abortions in cases where the conception was as a result of sexual violence, incest or, in the case where the pregnancy could put the mother's life at risk; widows' rights to the custody of their children, unless it resulted in prejudice against the interests and welfare of the children; and a widow's right to continue living in the couple's house if she inherits it.

COUNTRY POSITION

Mozambique defends the equal rights and opportunities for its people, and fights against all forms of discrimination against women. The Constitution of Mozambique was revised in December 2004 in order to accommodate the principle of gender equality (Article 36).

To ensure equal rights (defined in Article 35 of the Constitution), a National Gender Policy was developed as well as the National Plan of Action for the advancement of women. In addition, the sectors of education, health, agriculture, energy and mineral resources, water and housing, have developed strategies to mainstream gender equity in their programmes. In the five-year Government Programme, gender appears as a dominant issue, setting the framework for all the sectors to ensure:

- The promotion and increase of society's awareness of women rights;
- The reinforcement of gender perspectives in the conception and analysis of political strategies for national development;
- The elevation of the participation of women in all decision-making areas;
- The promotion of social justice.

The Republic of Mozambique signed the African Women's Protocol in December 2003 and ratified it on 9 December 2005.

RESEARCH FINDINGS

Awareness About the African Women's Protocol

At the time of the research, the African Women's Protocol was not a well-known document in most ministries and civil society groups, and in NGOs working in the area of human and women's rights. There were varying levels of awareness about its existence and most respondents were not aware of its content. The sector ministries of Foreign Affairs, Coordination of Social Action, and Health were aware about the Protocol.

Generic Aspects

The majority of respondents from NGOs stressed that their organisations promote and protect women's rights and gender equality. Examples in this regard come from two of the oldest and most active NGOs – Forum Mulher and MULEIDE.

The Forum Mulher Coordinator told researchers that their major focus were a) advocacy for women's rights in legislation and in policies and development programmes; b) production and dissemination of information on women's issues; c) capacity building of affiliated organisations for better performance in their work at grassroots level. Forum Mulher is the biggest umbrella association for women's rights in Mozambique and is a formal partner of the government.

The MULEIDE vice president spoke about the association's activities. MULEIDE promotes and protects women's rights. Besides information dissemination, MULEIDE opened cabinets for legal assistance and counselling. In 1992, MULEIDE lobbied for CEDAW ratification and supported the cabinet's decision to disseminate CEDAW. It has been involved in the fight against domestic violence since 1994 and campaigned for the All Against Violence NGO network. MULEIDE was the first NGO to pressurise government to adopt discussions on women's rights and gender equality. In conjunction with other human and women's rights associations, Forum Muller and MULEIDE were untiringly active in lobbying for the Law of the Family, which was passed in December 2004 as a result of formal partnerships between NGOs, civil society groups, and government. Integration of private organisations needs improvement.

NGOs play an important role in lobbying and advocating for women's Human rights. There is a network called All Against Violence, which is led by Forum Mulher. Organisations like MULEIDE, OMM, AMCJ, LDH, DHD have developed services to provide legal education, training and legal assistance to women and men suffering from domestic violence and other violations to their rights. While the government promotes a positive and enabling environment, NGOs, through their advocacy work, push for things to happen.

NGOs now form part of discussions concerning the Law Against Domestic Violence, Gender National Policy and other relevant topics. Many of the changes in attitude can be attributed to the work of NGOs. Through better coordination and more systematic planning, the work and roles of activists could be strengthened.

The Law of the Family, approved in 2004, considers aspects in favour of women and their rights. In decision-making bodies of the state, more and more women are taking part; parliament and the government have more women ministers than ever before. Owing to girl-child programmes within the Ministry of Education, primary and secondary schools are making efforts to enrol and retain more girls at school

Mozambique is one of the countries where the Gender Index was piloted, an important tool for monitoring progress on the continent, yet the country has not yet evaluated national gender mechanisms. The SADC Gender Declaration is another tool applied to measure the 30 per cent representation of women in decision-making bodies.

The Donor Gender team and the United Nations Gender Thematic Group have formed focal points in public institutions. This comprehensive group monitors the process and mainstreams gender in bilateral and multi-sector cooperation programmes. Sector reports and assessments of the National Council of the Advancement of Women activities and government programmes are mechanisms used to measure progress.

There are limited budgetary resources for gender, which is a major challenge for gender mainstreaming. To overcome this challenge, plans to build capacity for gender mainstreaming in the different sectors are underway, particularly in areas of gender planning, budget and in gender sensitisation, lobby and advocacy. Although gender perspectives in budgeting are still weak, improvements have been made. In 2004, government budget allocations for gender activities were about three per cent. However, as mentioned, donors participate in funding gender activities that do not have specific budget allocations.

The National Gender Policy was approved. The National Plan for the Advancement of Women is in place but there are a number of challenges for its implementation, budgetary constraints, the minimal coordination of activities between different sectors and the vague understanding of the importance of gender issues within institutions. A real drawback to gender progress stems from the fact that gender focal points in government institutions do not hold decision powers nor do they attend to decision-making boards, for this reason they lack the capacity to change things. This is a gap that needs to be seriously addressed. In addition, there is little involvement of the media. Government, parliament and society must attempt to strengthen the national gender machineries.

Recommendations from the National Consultative Workshop

A list of the most relevant and useful points that should be considered for more effective lobbing, advocacy and dissemination efforts are listed below:

- It is important to assure that the African Women's Protocol will not be a dead instrument.
- Plans to link Mozambican laws and the Protocol for effective interaction must be made.
- Civil society must sensitise parliament on gender-based issues.
- Since abortion is still a taboo topic in Mozambique, and is prohibited by the law, civil society organisations should use the African Women's Protocol, as a tool to lobby for the legalisation of abortion.
- Develop monitoring tools to assess progress of the implementation of the Protocol.

IMPLICATIONS OF THE AFRICAN WOMEN'S PROTOCOL

This section assesses the African Women's Protocol in relation to the thematic areas of governance, VAW and sexual and reproductive rights of women. Most of the issues presented here are a combination of interviews and discussions that arose during the national consultative workshop.

Governance

National and local government structures had been put in place, and national policies had been developed, though effective implementation was still a challenge owing to negative attitudes on women's rights, lack of physical infrastructure, low level of literacy especially in the rural areas, poor resource allocation and the lack of political will to deliver on women's rights.

The African Women's Protocol was perceived to be a tool to strengthen national frameworks and machineries on women's rights. National gender machineries were found to be weak, with little decision-making powers, under resourced and they are not taken seriously. In Mozambique, the women's rights machineries were found to be not as extensive as in South Africa. There is a Ministry for Women Affairs and Social Development, and a commission on women's rights chaired by the Prime minister, composed of sectoral ministers and NGOs.

The Protocol was also perceived as a tool that can be used to remind states to live up to the earlier commitments already made on women's rights. The women's movement was found to be weak and the Women's Protocol was perceived as a tool that can be used to re-awaken and strengthen the women's movement.

Violence Against Women (Article 1–5)

Mozambique has adopted many of the international instruments that tackle social justice and rights in order to improve the environment for the acceptance of Article 4 in the Protocol.

- Non-discrimination and gender equality principles were already contained in the national policy framework. In Mozambique, most of the issues in Article 4, nationality of women (5c), women's property rights (5f) and punishment for perpetuators of violence (4,2e), though a challenge, were found to be existent.

- New dimensions of VAW contained in the Protocol include: the right to a positive cultural environment (Article 17); the issues of trafficking of women (Article 4 (2g)). Mozambique recently introduced legislation on trafficking and peace education in schools (4,2d).

- Legislation on domestic violence, access to information, service and rehabilitation for victims of violence (4,2f) refugee status (4,2k) and nationality of children and Article 5 were found to be new dimensions to their context.
- Presently there is no law dealing with sexual abuse or sexual violation, but there is a proposal for the criminalisation of domestic violence.
- Forum Mulher and its umbrella NGOs must continue the work on women's rights. Dissemination of information about the African Women's Protocol should be a priority.

For the last five years, government has provided room to deal with this issue. The Ministry of Interior/Mozambican Policy has established a sector to deal with violence against women and children (Centros de Atendimento da Mulher e Criança nas Esquadras da Polícia). Although this implementation has not been widespread, some police stations throughout the country have officials who have been sensitised to take care of women who have been submitted to violence or abused.

Ministries of Social Action, Health, and Interior Affairs in coordination with civil society (NGOs and civil groups) are in the process of establishing shelters (at central and provincial levels) to accommodate victims of domestic violence.

Health and Reproductive Health (Article 14 of Protocol)

Most issues related to women's sexual and reproductive health were already in place in the national context. The right to control her fertility and decide whether to have children is a new challenge to women in the country. The right to health includes the right to sexual and reproductive health. At present, women's sexual and reproductive rights are still a dream. Article 14 (e) on the right to know your spouse's status will be a new dimension to Mozambique as well. Most women do not have a right to decide what methods of contraception to use. They are also not allowed to seek family planning support. Sexual and reproductive rights must therefore be promoted.

This means that:
- Information on family planning must be disseminated throughout the country, especially by the health sector. Associations and organisations working in human and women's rights could support the health sector to disseminate information for example on family planning.

- Information that family planning is free of charge has to be disseminated. Giving more women access to family planning is highly recommended.
- Information about HIV and AIDS and prevention must be made available and must be in accessible language.

Existing figures (made available by the Ministry of Health and 2003 Demographic Survey) show that coverage of family planning is 17.7 per cent and maternal mortality is one of the major problems in the health sector. The high levels of maternal mortality are owing to the unavailability of universal access to reproductive rights. Two aspects that affect family planning are the low coverage of family planning services and the fact that women are not encouraged to access these services.

Abortion is still a taboo topic. Although abortions can only take place after three doctors have confirmed the need for this procedure, there are still incidents where women seek illegal measures to terminate their pregnancies. Similarly, concepts, terms and attitudes that are not yet visible in Mozambican society are 'gay' and 'lesbian', though this does not mean that homosexuality does not exist.

Because of the dire need to implement sexual transmitted infections and HIV and AIDS prevention campaigns, the Ministry of Health and the National AIDS Council have to work in close proximity with several religious groups. Although they do not always agree with prevention techniques, such as the use of condoms and the right to control one's fertility, the collaboration is a positive one. Teenage pregnancy is a major concern. There are youth programmes in the Ministry of Health (Health of the Youth); Ministry of Youth; Ministry of Education; Youth National Council; and other youth organisations to address this issue. These aim to prevent girls from leaving school, preventing HIV infection and helping girls deal with and control their sexuality.

Positive Cultural Environment (Article 17)

During the national consultative workshop, Ms Angela Melo, AU Special Rapportuer on Women Rights, discussed social barriers that will affect the implementation of the African Women's Protocol. Negative traditional cultural values perpetuate discrimination against women. These are found in some laws that entrench patriarchy and disadvantaging women. She noted that women's roles are described according to men's superiority over women. She noted that though women are responsible for half of the world's production, they have little resources. The family, through the distribution of resources, separation and divorce, violence, widows's rights and inheritance, disadvantage women. She, therefore, called on the need to establish mechanisms for law implementation, the need to increase women's capacity to claim their rights and to encourage a culture that does not support silence over women's violence.

AWARENESS ABOUT THE AFRICAN WOMEN'S PROTOCOL

Organisations working with gender equality, empowerment and women's progress showed interest in participating in the different phases of the process from lobbying and dissemination to implementation. Most expressed the view that the government cannot work alone and they are willing to partner with the government to work on the African Women's Protocol.

Policy Makers

Government, in particular the Ministries of Women and Coordination of Social Action; Justice; Education; and Health should pursue the work in order to improve attitudes towards women's Rights and strengthen the framework for things to happen.

Civil Society Organisations

Lobby and advocacy are the main roles of civil society organisations. It was owing to this that the government ratified the Protocol. The focus then shifted to the domestication of the Protocol.

31

Challenges

ALTHOUGH SEVERAL CHALLENGES may exist, the fact that the African Women's Protocol was ratified is a positive sign. Information must be carefully disseminated so that citizens know the difference between national laws and the Protocol. The following challenges exist:

- The Mozambique policy framework is not fully aligned to women's international instruments.

- A number of studies exist within academia on abortion but as it is considered taboo; women's access to abortion services is limited.

- Negative traditional practices that impact on women's rights. It will be a challenge to implement Article 17 of the African Women's Protocol.

- How to ensure monitoring and evaluation of the Protocol. The gender machineries are over stretched with the periodical reporting on various instruments. For the African Women's Protocol, countries are required to submit reports after every two years. This is in addition to other periodic reports e.g. CEDAW and the BPFA. In addition, there is a gap between the impact of these reports and its various actors. Are the reports made use of by the different actors?

- The limited gender expertise within the gender machineries.

- Budgetary constraints for gender work.

- Limited use of the international instruments that pledge rights is linked to ignorance of the existence of such tools.

- The HIV/AIDS pandemic and its effect on women.

- The weakening of the women's movement in Mozambique.

The Mozambican case
Socio-Cultural Challenges

In Mozambique, socio-cultural challenges are the major issue facing the legitimatising of women's rights. In rural or urban areas, the situation does not vary significantly as both societies are regulated by the strong patriarchal structures. Women and men's roles are defined along cultural expectations.

Economic Dependence

Women grow and produce 60 to 80 per cent of food crops in the African continent, yet they do not control their economic resources. Traditional customary laws tend to maintain male dominance and are not friendly towards women, especially widows and divorcees. Even when the law (formal law) gives women access to land, the patriarchal structure does not make room for these entitlements. Cultural and social systems educate women to keep silent when she or her rights are violated.

The South African Case (as shared during the Mozambican Workshop)

Tradition is a heavy burden for women to deal with, but women are making visible improvements in the national arena. However, traditions that are prejudicial to women still exist. Inheritance is a problem that severely affects women. Lobola is one of the many topics that need to be discussed in more depth. In some communities, girls are forced to be women at an early age. But South Africa is discussing ways to tackle the issues and open doors in favour of women. However, attention should be paid to the fact that once traditional laws are adopted in legislation they become influential. Thus, aspects that favour prejudice have to be identified.

Section Five

Overall Summary

32

The Six Best Practices

- THE CONSTITUTION: THE PRINCIPLE of gender equality is established in the Constitution.
- The new Law of the Family: this is progressive as it establishes equal rights to both married women and men with regards to property rights, the rights to decision-making, to choose the family name, to domicile etc. Previously, the married women were required to reside at their husband's house, the children would assume the surname of their fathers, the husband was assumed to be the head of the household, women needed permission from their husbands to gain employment etc.
- The Land Law: provides equal rights to both women and men to access land. The constraint lies however, with the negative cultural land traditional practices that define unequal inheritance rights and prevent women from accessing and controlling land.
- The National Council for the Advancement of Women (CNAM), created to promote gender equity and women's emancipation. This is a government body that was established and is composed of different ministries, CSOs and the private sector.
- The National Gender Policy establishes the vision and mission of the government on gender issues. The guiding principles and objectives that the different sectors need to take into consideration in order to promote gender equality and women's rights in addressing poverty, such as the principles of non violence, non discrimination, equality, equity and gender mainstreaming. Its objective is to ensure that at all levels – political, economic, social and legal – women and men

289

participate and benefit equally and have equal opportunities.

- The National Plan for the Advancement of Women aims to contribute to the implementation of the gender policy and identify the different priorities regarding gender in the different sectors. It defines the priorities of the ministries that are represented at the National Council for the Advancement of Women (CNAM) with regards to ensuring gender equality.

33

Conclusions and Recommendations

CONCLUSIONS

IN MOZAMBIQUE, THERE is an environment to pursue the long road towards women's empowerment and strengthen awareness in regard to women's rights. The number of female parliamentarians in the Assembleia da República (35.7 per cent) and the number of female ministers (29 per cent) is very encouraging and paves the way to lobby for more reforms.

The working atmosphere between government and NGOs is encouraging. Government has recognised Forum Mulher – an umbrella NGO – as an important resource to deal with women's issues. The work undertaken by NGOs in the field of VAW and the field of legal education, training and legal assistance to women and men suffering from domestic violence and other violations to their rights that has been carried out by associations like MULEIDE, OMM, AMCJ, LDH and DHD has been remarkable. It paves the way to more work in the field of women's rights.

However, the popularisation of the Protocol has to be organised as a movement that has to start in urban areas and reach the countryside where most people live and where information relating to certain issues is insufficient.

RECOMMENDATIONS

There is still a lot to be done to achieve gender equality and women's empowerment. Strengthening of the women's movement is recommended.

In this regard, NGOs must work together with government institutions in order to:

- Promote persistent advocacy at all levels.
- Lobby for increased participation of women in decision-making and governing bodies.
- Lobby for increased access of more women and girls to education.
- Campaign for the extension of health services in rural areas.
- Strengthen gender mainstreaming in PARPA (Plan for the Absolute Poverty Reduction).
- Pave the way forward for gender departments/units in ministries.
- Disseminate and market the new Family Law, in support of a new positive environment towards women's situation.
- Re-establish the network fighting against VAW.
- Devise a strategy for the popularisation and implementation of the African Women's Protocol.
- Support the development of gender indicators to assess achievements of the Protocol.
- Support the development of monitoring and evaluation instruments to periodically assess achievements and make follow up of plans.
- Set up (realistic and consistent) strategies.
- Establish a pressure group for the implementation of the Protocol, which will lead the way forward (tasks assigned to FADAJ, LDH, MULEIDE, NHAMAI, WILSA).
- Establish partnership with media to support the dissemination of women's rights instruments.

34

The Way Forward: Some Practical Considerations for the Protocol

Rose Gawaya, Oxfam GB, Global Gender Advisor

WOMEN'S RIGHTS INSTRUMENTS can only be useful if they make a difference in the daily lives of ordinary women and men. This section proposes some of the ways in which women's human rights organisations and others interested in women's human rights can contribute to the way the African Women's Protocol can make a difference to ordinary women. Some of the ideas proposed here are derived from Oxfam GB's Southern African strategy on gender equality and women's rights. This reflects our overall direction in Southern Africa and we shall seek partnerships and alliances that seek to take this thinking forward.

Civil society organisations need to facilitate processes that enhance opportunities for ordinary women to use the African Women's Protocol to claim their rights. The policy research has shown that there is limited use of international human rights instruments to claim these rights. Using the African Women's Protocol to claim rights can only happen, if the women's movements and governments join hands to popularise the Protocol.

Popularisation of the Protocol should include a range of activities amongst which include:

- The simplification, translation and dissemination of the African Women's Protocol. The Protocol contains 32 articles and it needs to be made user friendly, depending on the different needs of different audiences. Therefore, it may be difficult to raise awareness on all aspects at the same time, especially to women in rural and semi urban settings. It is advisable, that the use of the Protocol is done in such a way, that thematic aspects are translated and related to the various aspects of work undertaken by civil society organisations and how they relate to the daily lives of women. Organisations working in the health sector, for example, can produce small booklets on Article 14, relate it to their work and show women how to access services related to reproductive health. Taking into account the low levels of women's literacy in most of the rural areas, creative ways of disseminating the African Women's Protocol need to be developed.

- Mobilising key actors in the formal decision-making structures such as government departments and within the communities to inform them existence of the Protocol, its relevance and how it relates to the different aspects of women's lives. For example, articles in the Protocol relating to food security and sustainable development can be used to relate to the daily activities that rural women are engaged in to address their livelihoods.

- Provision of information to women at the grassroots levels to access services e.g. those related to agricultural markets, HIV and AIDS, legal aid, credit etc.

- Providing legal awareness to inform women of the mechanisms and remedies available in case their rights have been violated.

- Support to women to access courts, the police and social service providers to claim their rights.

- Using key moments e.g. the International Women's Day to remind governments of their commitments to women.

The women's movement needs to lobby and advocate for the domestication of the African Women's Protocol. The research has shown that the Protocol can be used as a tool to strengthen the legal and policy framework related to women's rights in many countries. Domestication will require that aspects contained in the African Women's Protocol be incorporated in the national frameworks. The women's movements have to be alert and use opportunities such as constitutional review processes, review of national legislations and policies and development of policy guidelines to incorporate the various aspects contained in the African Women's Protocol. For example, in Zambia, WILSA and other women's rights organisations took advantage of the Constitutional review process to incorporate most of the provisions contained in African Women's Protocol in the draft Constitution. It is expected that once the Constitutional review process is completed, Zambia will have an improved legal framework on women's human rights. Domestication also requires states to set aside budgetary, human, material and other resources necessary for the implementation of the various aspects contained in the African Women's Protocol.

The women's movement needs to monitor the implementation of the African Women's Protocol. This is not to imply that there is no monitoring taking place. However, from the research findings, monitoring of other instruments like CEDAW and the BPFA mainly consists of countries producing periodical reports. In some cases, NGOs have produced shadow reports. The research has shown that there is limited use of these reports, and hence they seem to have little impact to improving the general functioning of machineries related to women's rights and to the daily lives of women.

Monitoring of the implementation of African Women's Protocol should take feminist and empowerment approaches. Monitoring should consist of three key elements. First, it should draw on feminist approaches to construct a transformative agenda. The concept of empowerment is said to consist of four major dimensions: power to, power over, power with and power within. 'Power to' refers to access to information, resources and services; 'power over' refers to actions that challenge gender inequalities, 'power with' refers to social mobilisation and a sense of belonging to a group or particular communities, and 'power within' refers to one's ability to resist oppression, injustice and take action against these.

Secondly, using an empowerment approach to monitoring implies constructing monitoring systems as a process where grassroots women engage in policy discourses. The critical voices of women at grassroots level need to inform policy process at local, national, regional and international levels. This is a radical approach where grassroots women speak for themselves, instead of being represented by professionals during policy discourses. The professionals should instead facilitate grassroots women to speak for themselves during policy debates and discussions. It is also radical in a way, as there will need for structural changes to the way policy debates are shaped. It requires flexibility from governments and other actors to construct their agendas in such a way that grassroots women do not feel intimidated. The norm of having 'men and women in uniform' and sometimes the extended security searches at policy venues needs to be done in such away, so as not to scare away grassroots women from places where policy agendas are set. Empowerment also requires providing translation and interpretation facilities to allow grassroots women to express themselves in the languages and ways that they understand most. This requires that other forms of expression enter the rooms of policy debates. The literacy level of women in Africa is generally low, so other forms of expressions, for example, through pictures, art and drama, need to enter the policy discourses.

Thirdly, monitoring the implementation of the African Women's Protocol implies that the demand and supply factors need to be addressed. On one hand, the demand dimension mainly focuses on creating an environment where women are aware of their rights and empowered to claim those rights. This requires women and human rights centred organisations to increase awareness of the Protocol at the grassroots level and inform women on where to find relevant information and services related to their needs. Creating demand for services requires that all four dimensions of empowerment be addressed. Women need to be provided with timely and relevant information to meet their different needs; there is a need to increase their self esteem and confidence for them to claim their rights; there is need to challenge injustice in all its forms; and a need for social mobilisation that builds a critical mass of women to demand the fulfilment of their rights.

On the other hand, the supply factor requires states to provide environments where women can exercise their rights. It also requires the strengthening of the capacity of public institutions to provide services to women in a timely and efficient manner. Strengthening the capacity of service providers can consist of a range of activities, including: raising awareness of the African Women's Protocol, training, improved coordination and effective service delivery within the various sectors, strengthening their human and technical capacity, and changing negative ideas and beliefs of service providers about women's rights.

35

Using Lobbying Opportunities Given by the UN Through CSW Meetings

Alice Banze, Oxfam GB, Regional Gender Advisor

THE COMMISSION ON THE Status of Women (CSW) is a functional commission of the United Nations Economic and Social Council. It is the main global policy-making forum for gender equality and the advancement of women. It sets the agenda on gender equality and identifies challenges and sets global standards. It holds meetings annually to monitor the progress of governments on gender equality and women's empowerment, particularly with regard to the Beijing Platform for Action. The CSW meetings provide a forum for learning, networking and fundraising for partner organisations.

CSW sessions are often strategic milestones within a continuum of programming for women's rights and gender equality. They facilitate the development of a political strategy and come up with concrete policy recommendations. They provide leadership to the women's movements as women from different walks of life organise and participate in these key global policy events that impact on gender work at the grassroots level. In the absence of global conferences, the CSW annual meeting is the only forum where women's movements from all over the world meet to organise, strategise and lobby the UN to influence governments on issues related to the status of women.

The theme for the 52nd Session of the Commission on the Status of Women, which was held from 25 February to 7 March 2008, was "Financing for Gender Equality and Women's Empowerment". This theme resonates with Oxfam's global work on essential services and the quality of aid, along with Southern Africa regional work on holding governments accountable for the implementation of women's human rights instruments. The women's movement sought to register concern on the importance of gender budgeting as an accountability tool at the national level. It highlighted the vital need to strengthen opportunities for local voices to be heard in national-level decision-making processes.

The meeting emphasised the importance of setting targets on resources allocated to gender equality as part of the bigger picture into which gender-responsive budgeting fits.

There is a need to strengthen the capacities of the women's movement by focusing on the rights-based approach. This will help ensure that key donors track the allocation of resources for gender. There is also a need to lobby different governments to ensure that government commitments made at the CSW are fulfilled. In addition, women's rights advocates must lobby for donors to assess their performance frameworks in relation to gender equality. National auditors must also be persuaded to include gender-specific indicators in their audits.

The CSW meeting provided Oxfam GB with the opportunity to share its work on the Protocol to the African Charter on Human and People's Rights on the Rights of Women as a result of the research undertaken in the Southern Africa Region. Oxfam GB launched programme insights on the African Women's Protocol. The insights highlight different experiences of Oxfam's support to civil society organisations and government stakeholders working with the African Women's Protocol.

It was clear that the Protocol is not a widely known instrument. Bringing it into the global policy arena on gender and women's rights was therefore critical. Countries involved in fighting gender inequality will also have to conduct research in their countries in order to facilitate the process of popularising, ratifying, domesticating and implementing the protocol.

Appendices

Appendix 1: List of Key Respondents

GENERAL

NAME	ORGANISATION
1. Christine Warioba	SADC
2. Gladys Mutukwa	WILDAF
3. Ms Angela Melo	ACHPR
4. Mr Nega Girmachew Lulessa	ACHPR
5. Ms Pamela Mhlanga	SARDC
6. Adv. Boogie Khutsoane	Centre for Human Rights (University of Pretoria)
7. Ms Mary Maboreke	AU Directorate
8. Mr Martin Nsibirwa	Centre for Human Rights (University of Pretoria)
9. Ms Irene Lomoyani	ECA Lusaka
10. Ms Mary Wandia	FEMNET
11. Hon Lois Bwambale	AU PAP
12. Adv. Madasa	AU PAP, ACDP
13. Hon. Miria Matembe	AU PAP
14. Ms Rumbidzai Kandawasuika-Nhundu	SADC Parliamentary Forum
15. Ms Souad Abdennebi	ECA (Addis Ababa)

SOUTH AFRICA

INTERVIEW NO.	NAME OF INTERVIEWEE	STRUCTURE/ORGANISATION REPRESENTED	MONTH/ YEAR OF INTERVIEW
Interview 1	Lulama Nongogo-Ngalwana	Gender Focal Point (GFP), Department of Justice	11/2004
Interview 2	Chana Majaki and Mmathari Masao	Director and Legal Director of the CGE respectively	11/2004
Interview 3	Susan Nkomo	Director of the National OSW	11/2004
Interview 4	Mr Sithole	Chair of Portfolio Committee on Foreign Affairs	12/2004
Interview 5	Dr Davids	Chair of the Portfolio Committee on Finance	12/2004
Interview 6	James Ngcule	Chair of the Portfolio Committee on Health.	01/2005
Interview 7	Sharon Ekambaram	Member of Treatment Action Campaign	11/2004
Interview 8	Cheryl Ayago	Coordinator of the VAW Network, Western Cape	11/2004
Interview 9	Penny Parenzee	Budget Information Service, Institute for Democratic Alternatives (IDASA)	11/2004

Interview No.	Name of Interviewee	Structure/Organisation Represented	Month/ Year of Interview
Interview 10	Pumla Mncayi	Director of Gender Advocacy Project (GAP)	11/2004
Interview 11	Sibongile Ndashe	Women's Legal Centre	12/2004
Interview 12	Sheila Meintjies	Political Science Department, University of the Witwatersand	12/2004
Interview 13	Cathi Albertyn	Director of Centre for Applied Legal Studies, University of the Witwatersand	11/2004
Interview 14	Dean Peacock	Engender Health	12/2004

ZAMBIA

Name	Institution	Position
1. Ms Matrine Chuulu	Women and Law in Southern Africa (WILSA)	Acting Regional Coordinator Tel: + 260 (0)253974/5; Cell: (0)97-777461
2. Ms Stellah M. Nkoma	Young Women's Christian Association of Zambia (YWCA)	Executive Director Tel: 260-1-255204/254751; Fax: 260-1-254751 E-mail: ywca@zamnet.zm
3. Col. Clement Mudenda	Legal Aid Clinic for Women	Former Executive Director Tel: 220595; Fax: 234747
4. Ms Caroline Thole	Zambia National Women's Lobby Group (ZNWLG)	Acting Executive Director Tel/ Fax: 260- 1- 255153; E- mail: nwlg@zamnet.zm
5. Hon. O. Nkumbula Liebenthal	Parliament	Member of the Pan African Parliament
6. Hon. Maybin Mubanga	Parliament	Member of the Pan African Parliament
7. Ms Sara Hlupekile Longwe	Self-employed	Consultant/Academician Tel: 283484; Fax: 226200
8. Mr Tobias Mulimbika	Gender in Development Division (GIDD)	Director for Social, Legal and Governance Tel: 260-1-251346- 67; Fax: 260-1-253493
9. Mr Rueben Lifuka	Dialogue Africa	Chief Executive Officer Tel: 260-1-256818; E-mail: rlifuka@coppernet.zm

Name	Institution	Position
10. Ms Getrude Imbwae	Ministry of Justice	Permanent Secretary. Tel: 260- 1- 252034. Fax: 253452. E- mail: mola@zamtel.zm
11. Mr Chrispin Matenga	University of Zambia	Lecturer – Development Studies Tel: 260 (0) 95902612
12. Ms Florence Chibwesha	Women's Finance Cooperative Zambia	Executive Director. Tel: 260-1-221628; 260-(0) 97773765 E- mail: fchibesha@yahoo.com
13. Mr Henry Malumo	Civil Society Trade Network of Zambia (CSTNZ)	Media Officer Tel: 260-1-97656832
14. Ms Merab Kiremire	MAPODE	Director Tel/ Fax: 260-1-290773 260-97-772537 E-mails: kiremire@zamnet; merabkiremire@yahoo.co.uk
15. Ms N. Mulikita	Gender Consultant	Consultant Based in South Africa
16. Ms E. Sinfukwe	Ministry Foreign Affairs	Gender Focal Point Person

MOZAMBIQUE

INSTITUTIONS/ORGANISATIONS	NAMES	NO. OF PEOPLE
Pan African Members of Parliament	• Verónica Macamo – First Vice President of the Assembly of the Republic	1
Regional Women's Organisations (WILSA, WILDAF)	• Elina Gomes, WILDAF	1
Leading national CSOs on gender/women rights	• Graça Samo – Forum Mulher Coordinator • Celeste Nobela – Vice President of MULEIDE • Zélia Langa – OMM • Beatriz Aguida – OMM • Mara Orlanda Lampião – AMMCJ • Augusta Lobo Ó da Silva – PROMUGE • M. Fátima Moçambique – AMORADE • Arlete Calane – AMME • Luís Chicune – ADEMO	9
MMAS	• Virgília Matabele – Minister • Sansão Buque – Deputy National Director for Women	2

Institutions/Organisations	Names	No. Of People
MINEC	<ul><li>Henrique Banse – Deputy Minister</li><li>Pedro Comissário – Ambassador</li><li>Amadeu da Conceição – Ambassador</li><li>Geraldo Saranga</li><li>Judite Taela</li><li>Felizmina Salégua</li><li>Maria Leonor Joaquim – Lawyer</li></ul>	7
MISAU		
Ministry of Justice	<ul><li>Dr. José Ibraimo Abudo – Former Minister of Justice</li><li>Ângela Melo – Lawyer and UA Commissioner</li><li>Albachir Macassar – Head of the Department of Promotion and Development of Human Rights</li></ul>	3
Members of parliament	<ul><li>Açucena Duarte</li><li>Maria Olívia Álvaro (Nampula)</li><li>Marta Zulimba (Tete)</li></ul>	3

Appendix 2: Checklist for Research Questions

Policy Research on African Union's Women's
Protocol for the Southern African Region

Checklist for National Researchers

Generic Questions (All Respondents)

1. What role does your organisation play in the promotion of and protection of women's rights and gender equality?
2. How effective has it been and how can its role be enhanced?

Baseline Information (Gender, Parliamentarians, Academicians, NGOs)

1. Has the country adopted a policy document on gender equality and the empowerment of women?
2. Is there a national plan of action to support its implementation?
3. What are the major achievements in the promotion of gender equality?
4. What are the main problems or constraints the country has encountered in implementing the policy document or action plan?
5. Where is the national mechanism for the promotion of gender equality located and what is its mandate?
6. What percentage of resources in the national budget does it receive?

7. What percentage of the budget is received from financial donors?

8. Have gender perspectives and concerns been taken into account in preparation of budgets at the national regional and local levels?

9. Are any efforts made to monitor budgetary allocations?

10. Who is responsible for monitoring and evaluating gender programs?

11. How are the different actors held accountable?

12. Has the country developed indicators for monitoring and evaluation?

13. Have any significant partnerships been established with NGOs, civil society groups or private sector organisations in support of gender equality?

14. Are they formal or informal?

15. What are the major achievements of the women's movement?

16. What are its major challenges?

17. Has any effort been made to actively engage men and boys in the promotion of gender equality?

18. If so what lessons could be learnt from these efforts?

CEDAW (Gender, Foreign Affairs, Justice, NGOs, Academicians)

1. Has the country signed, ratified and domesticated the CEDAW? If no to any of these, why not?

2. What was the major driving force of the decision to ratify the CEDAW?

3. Has the country entered any reservations?

4. If so, what impact have these had on the enjoyment of the rights spelt out under the CEDAW?

5. What effect has the CEDAW had on the national legislation, policy and practice?

6. Has the country honoured its reporting obligations under the CEDAW?

7. If so, were the reports publicised at the national level?

8. Did NGOs participate in their preparation? How?

9. What effect have the concluding comments of the Committee on the Elimination of Discrimination Against Women on state parties

reports had on the implementation of the CEDAW at national level?

10. What lessons can be learnt from the country's experience with the CEDAW's ratification and implementation?

The Protocol (All Respondents)

1. Is the country a signatory to the a) African Charter on Human and Peoples' Rights; b) the Protocol setting up the African Court on Human and Peoples' Rights or c) the Protocol African Charter on Human and Peoples' Rights on Women's Rights?

2. In what areas would the provisions of the AU Women's Protocol improve the existing legal and policy framework?

3. What are the procedures for ratifying the Protocol in your country? At what stage is the ratification process?

4. What specific actions can be taken to speed up the ratification of the Protocol?

5. What role can NGOs play in the process of ratification and subsequent implementation?

6. What gaps, ambiguities or controversial areas in the Protocol could hinder its effective use as a tool for the advancement of gender equality?

7. What role can your organisation play in the popularising the Protocol?

8. Has the mass media given any attention to the AU Protocol on Women's Rights?

Level of Awareness

9. How would you describe your level of awareness about the Protocol among the categories below on a scale of one to five?

    1. Never heard of it

    2. Aware it exists but ignorant of content

    3. Can describe at least two provisions

    4. Have read it

    5. Can use it to promote women's rights

Policy Makers
   a) gender machinery
   b) relevant sector ministries
   c) parliamentarians

Civil Society
   a) community based organisations
   b) human rights NGOs
   c) academia
   d) media

10. Who are the key actors and organisations in the country that the popularisation and ratification campaign should target?
11. What are the best methods of reaching each of them?
12. What specific actions do you recommend as a way forward for ensuring the popularisation, ratification and implementation of the Protocol?

Thematic Areas (Gender, Justice, Parliamentarians, NGOs, Academicians)

Violence Against Women

1. What are the current legislation and policies on a) rape; b) assault; and c) domestic violence?
2. Do they provide for any remedy or compensation for victims of violence?
3. Are there statistics on the prevalence of rape, assault and domestic violence?
4. Has any effort been made to sensitise law enforcement and medical officers on how to treat cases of VAW?
5. What measures has the Government taken to address this scourge?
6. Do battered women have access to shelters or areas of safety?
7. What role have NGOs played in preventing and combating VAW?

TARGET GROUP

INSTITUTIONS/ORGANISATIONS	No. OF PEOPLE
Pan African Members of Parliament	1
Gender, Family & Youth Committee of the PAP	1
Regional women's organisations (WILSA, WILDAF)	2
Leading CSOs on gender/women rights	3
MMAS. Ministério da Mulher e Coordenação da Acção Social	1
MINEC. Ministério dos Negócios Estrangeiros e Cooperação (Ministry of Foreign Affairs and Cooperation)	1
Minister for Parliamentary Issues/AR Committee on Social, Gender & Environment Issues	1
MPs	2
Ministry of Justice	1
Total	12

ACTIVITIES (INITIAL PLAN)

ACTIVITIES	RESPONSIBILITY	TIMEFRAME
Prepare a research plan of action	Researcher	11–12.11.04
Approve the plan of action and the contract	Oxfam	15.11.04
Provide national legislation relating to gender; CEDAW; SADC Gender Declaration; VAW; sexual and reproductive rights; marriage; HIV/AIDS; widow's rights and governance	Oxfam	16–17.11.04
Literature review	Researcher	15–20.11.04
Contact key informants for the interviews and the advisory team members	Oxfam	17–18.11.04
Interviews	Researcher	22–25.11.04
Data analysis	Researcher	25–30.11.04
Compile the draft report	Researcher	01–06.12.04
Send the draft report to the Oxfam Gender Officer	Researcher	08.11.04
Present to the advisory country committee	Researcher & Oxfam	13.12.04
Revise the report	Researcher	14–15.12.04
Present the final report to Oxfam	Researcher	16.12.04

313

8. In what ways will the AU Protocol advance the fight to prevent and eliminate VAW?

9. What areas will remain problems despite the provisions of the Protocol?

Governance

10. What are the current percentage of women in parliament, Cabinet, diplomatic missions and the top echelons of the judiciary and political parties?

11. Has the country adopted measures like quotas to enhance their representation?

12. Are there practical examples of how their presence has actually caused positive change in favour of women?

13. What lessons can be learned from their participation in electoral processes and in high-level offices?

14. What difficulties do you anticipate when attempts are made to implement the equal participation in elections and electoral processes called for in the Protocol?

Sexual and Reproductive Rights

15. Are there any provision in national legislation on the protection from and treatment for HIV/AIDS and other sexually transmitted infections that target women?

16. Under national legislation, do women have the right to control their fertility?

17. What percentage of women has the means to do so through access to family planning services?

18. What is the legal status of abortion in the country?

19. How do religion, culture and tradition affect the health reproductive rights?

20. To what extent has an effort been made to engage men in the promotion of sexual and reproductive rights?

21. What is the situation with regard to gay and lesbian rights?

22. What are the major issues on the subject?

23. What effect would the provisions in the Charter have on the enjoyment of health and reproductive rights in the country?

Appendix 3: Plan of Action of the Policy Research on the African Union Women's Protocol – Southern Africa Region

PURPOSE

To inform Oxfam, its partners, members of the civil society organisations and parliamentarians at the national and AU level, about the implications of the AU Women's Protocol at various levels.

OBJECTIVES

The objective of the national research is to:

- collect primary and secondary data at country level.
- identify national position on CEDAW and the SADC Gender Policy (ratification and domestication; lessons that can be learnt; areas of best practice or challenges on women rights in relation to addressing VAW; sexual and reproductive rights; marriage; governance and widow's rights).

METHODOLOGY

- Interviews of key informants.
- Literature review of national legislation related to gender and other policy documents.

Bibliography

African Commission on Human and Peoples' Rights: *Status on Submission* of *State Periodic Reports to the ACHPR as of May 2003*.

African Committee on Gender and Development, United Nations Economic Commission For Africa: *Assessing Women's Legal and Human Rights* (1999).

African Committee on Gender and Development, United Nations Economic Commission For Africa: The African Gender Development Index (October 2004).

African Union: *Protocol to the ACHPR on the Rights of Women in Africa* (11 July 2003).

Akina Mama Wa Afrika, compiled by Sharon Lamwaka and Sarah Mukasa (eds): *The Protocol to the African Charter on Human and Peoples' Rights on the Rights of Women in Africa: A Review of the Protocol and Its Relevance to Women in Africa* (September 2004).

Albertyn, C., Goldblatt, B., Hassim, S., Mbatha, L. and Meintjies, S: 'Women in South Africa: The Historical Context' in *Engendering the Political Agenda: A South African Case Study*. Gender Research Project of the Centre for Applied Legal Studies, University of the Witwatersrand, South Africa and the United Nations International Institute for Research and Training for the Advancement of Women, Dominican Republic (1999).

Albreu and Salamao: *Policy Research on the Protocol to the African Charter on Human and Peoples' Rights on the Rights of Women*, Mozambique Country Report (2005).

Assembleia da República: Lei No. 10/2004, de 25 de Agosto.

BRIDGE Report 63: *Gender and Monitoring: A Review of Practical Experiences*, a paper by Paola Brambilla / June 2001.

Catholic Commission for Justice and Peace / Muyakwa: S. L.: *Impact of the Land Act 1995 on the Livelihoods of the Poor and Peasants in Zambia: Lusaka*, Zambia (2003).

CEDAW/C/ZAM 3–4: *Consideration of Reports Submitted by State parties Under Article 18 of CEDAW, Third and Fourth Periodic Reports of Zambia* (12 August 1999).

Central Statistics Office: *2000 Census of Population and Housing*, Lusaka, Zambia (2003).

Centre for Applied Legal Studies: *Draft Report: African Gender and Development Index: South African Report.* University of the Witwatersrand, South Africa (2003–2004).

Center for Reproductive Health and Policy: *Women of the World: Laws and Policies Affecting their Reproductive Lives, Anglophone Africa, 2001 Progress Report.* Center for Reproductive Health and Policy, New York (2001).

Commission on Gender Equality: *The National Conference on Witchcraft Violence, 6–10 September 1998.* CGE, Johannesburg (1998).

Commission on Gender Equality: *Local Government Elections 2000 – A Gender Perspective.* CGE, Johannesburg (2001).

Commission on Gender Equality: *Annual Report April 2001 to March 2002.* CGE, Johannesburg (2002).

Commission on Gender Equality: *Annual Report 2002/2003.* CGE, Johannesburg (2003).

Commonwealth Secretariat: *South Africa Report of The Commonwealth Advisory Mission on National Machinery for Advancing Gender Equality.* London, United Kingdom (1995).

Committee on Elimination of Discrimination against Women: *Twenty-seventh Session 551st and 552nd Meetings Report* (2002).

Conselho de Ministros: *Programa do Governo 2005–2009*, Maputo, Abril de 2005.

Department of Health: *South Africa Demographic and Health Survey, 1998.* Ministry of Health, Pretoria (1998).

Department of Health: *Policy Guidelines for Youth and Adolescent Health.* Ministry of Health, Pretoria (2001).

Department of Health: *Saving Mothers: Second Report on Confidential Enquiries into Maternal Deaths in South Africa 1999–2000.* Ministry of Health, Pretoria (2000a).

Department of Health: *National Incomplete Abortion Study.* Ministry of Health, Pretoria (2000b).

Department of Health: *First Report of the National Committee on Confidential Enquiries into Maternal Deaths.* Ministry of Health, Pretoria (1999).

Doherty, T. and Colvin, M.: 'HIV/AIDS' in *South African Health Review 2003/4 9th Edition.* Health Systems Trust, Johannesburg and Durban (2004).

Division on the Advancement of Women: Department of Economic and Social Affairs: *Short History of the CEDAW Convention*, www.un.org/womenwatch/daw/cedaw/history.

FEMNET: *From OAU to AU and NEPAD: Strategies for African Women: Report of FEMNET's AU Regional Strategy Meeting*, 27–31 October 2003, Nairobi, Kenya.

Ficks, G., Meintjies, S. and Simons, M.: 'Introduction' in Fick, G., Meintjies, S and Simons, S (eds) *One Woman, One Vote The Gender Politics of South African Elections*. The Electoral Institute of Southern Africa, Johannesburg (2002).

Forman, L., Pillay, Y. and Sait, L.: 'Health Legislation 1994–2003 in *South African Health Review 2003/4 9th Edition*. Health Systems Trust, Johannesburg/Durban (2004).

Foster, Lesley Ann: 'Country Papers: South Africa' in *The First CEDAW Impact Study*. International Women's Rights Project, York University and The United Nations Division for the Advancement of Women, Geneva (1998).

Gender and Declaration: *A Declaration by Heads of State or Government of the SADC*, September 1997.

Gender in Development Division: *National Gender Policy*, Lusaka, Zambia (2000).

Gender in Development Division: *Strategic Plan of Action for the National Gender Policy (2004–2008)*, Lusaka, Zambia (2004).

Gender in Development Division: *Zambia's Progress Report on the Implementation of the Beijing Platform for Action 2000–2004*, Lusaka, Zambia (2004).

Gender in Development Division / Muyakwa, S. L.: *Laws and Policies for Gender, Population and Development in Zambia*, Lusaka, Zambia (1998).

Gender Manual Consortium: *Making Women's Rights Real: A Resource Manual on Women, Gender, Human Rights and the Law – Translating the rights that exist on paper into reality for South African women*. Gender Manual Consortium. Pretoria, South Africa (date unstated).

Government of Mozambique: *Report on the Decade of the Implementation of the Beijing Platform for Action*, (2005).

Governo de Moçambique: Balanço do Programa do Governo para 2000–2004, I Volume, Maputo, Maio de 2004.

Hassim, S.: "The Dual Politics of Representation: Women and Electoral Politics in South Africa" in Fick, G., Meintjies, S. and Simons, S. (eds): *One Woman, One Vote The Gender Politics of South African Elections*. The Electoral Institute of Southern Africa, Johannesburg (2002).

Holland-Muter, Susan: *Policy Research on the Protocol to the African Charter on Human and Peoples' Rights on the Rights of Women*, South Africa Country Report (2005).

International Labour Organisation / Ireland Aid / JUDAI: *Jobs, Gender and Small Enterprises in Africa: Preliminary Report. Women Entrepreneurs in Zambia*, Lusaka, Zambia (2002).

Into the Future: Gender and SADC, A report of the SADC Gender Strategic Workshop (January 1997) and the Ministerial Workshop on Gender (February 1997).

Landsberg-Lewis, Llana: *UNIFEM: Bringing Equality Home: Implementing the Convention on the Elimination of All Forms of Discrimination Against Women (CEDAW)* (1998).

Lomoyani, Irene: *Gender and Development in Southern Africa* (2005).

Mcpherson, Marilou, Bazilli, Susan, Moana, Erickson and Byrnes, Andrew: *The First Cedaw Impact Study* (2000).

Meintjies, S. and Simons, M.: 'Why Electoral Systems Matter to Women' in Fick, G., Meintjies, S. and Simons, S. (eds): *One Woman, One Vote The Gender Politics of South African Elections.* The Electoral Institute of Southern Africa, Johannesburg (2002).

Medical Research Council: *Policy Brief No. 5, June 2004. "Every six hours a woman is killed by her intimate partner": A National Study of Female Homicide in South Africa.* Medical Research Council, Pretoria and the Centre for the Study of Violence and Reconciliation, Johannesburg (2004).

Ministério da Mulher e Coordenação da Acção Social: *Balanço Preliminar do Programa do Governo 2000-2004 nas Áreas da Mulher, da Família e da Acção Social,* Maputo, Julho de 2004.

Muyakwa, Stephen: *Policy Research on the Protocol to the African Charter on Human and People's Rights on the Rights of Women,* Zambia Country Report (2005).

Nmeheille, Vincent O.: *Development of the African Human Rights System in the Last Decade:* Human Rights Briefs, Spring 2004.

Office on the Status of Women: *Celebrating 10 Years of Freedom: Women Building a Better South Africa and a Better World. A Review of South Africa's Progress in achieving its commitments to the United Nation's Beijing Platform of Action. A Discussion Document.* The Presidency, Pretoria (2004).

Office on the Status of Women: *Freedom: What has it meant for women of South Africa? Conversations amongst women – Dipuo Tsa basadi-lingxoxo Zamakhosikazi.* The Presidency, Pretoria (2003).

Organisation of African Unity: *African Commission on Human and People's Rights: Information Sheet No. 2, Guidelines of the Submission of Communications.*

Parenzee, P., Artz, L. and Moult, K. with contributions from Fedler, J., Carter, R. and Jacobs, T.: *Monitoring the Implementation of the Domestic Violence Act First research Report 2000–2001.* Institute of Criminology, University of Cape Town, Cape Town (2001).

Press Release WOM/1339: *Committee on the Elimination of Discrimination Against Women: 27th Session, 551st and 552nd Meeting: Experts on Women's Anti-Discrimination Committee Take Up Zambia's Report: Say Traditional Stereotypes Undermine Efforts At Ensuring Equality,* 4th June 2002, www.un.org/news/press/docs/2002/wom1339.doc.html.

Reproductive Rights Alliance: *Report on the Implementation of the Choice on Termination of Pregnancy Act (ACT No. 92 of 1996) 1997–2004.* RRA, Johannesburg (2004).

República de Moçambique: *Constituição da República,* Maputo, Desembro de 2004.

SADC Media Releases: *Media Briefing from the SADC Gender Program* by Christine Warioba, Gender Officer, www.sadc.iny/printout/php.

SARDC WIDSAA: *Towards Beijing + 10: Which way Southern Africa?* Lusaka, April 2004.

SARDC: *The African Gender and Development Index,* Moçambique (2004).

Semafumu, Rosemary: *East African Journal of Peace and Human Rights Journal, Vol5, No.2 1999: Uganda's Reporting Obligations Under the Convention on the Elimination of Discrimination Against Women,* pp 175-198 (1999).

Semalulu Nsibirwa, Martin: *African Human Rights Journal: A Brief Analysis of the Protocol to the African Charter on Human and Peoples' Rights on the Rights of Women.*

Sexual Harassment Education Project. *Report on the State of Sexual Harassment in the Workplace.* SHEP, Johannesburg (2003).

Smit, J., Beksinska, M., Ramkissoon, A., Kunene, B. and Penn-Kekana, L.: "Reproductive Health" in *South African Health Review 2003/4 9th Edition.* Health Systems Trust, Johannesburg and Durban (2004).

Steinberg, M., Johnson, S., Schierhout, G. and Ndegwa, D.: *Hitting Home: How Households Cope with the Impact of the HIV/AIDS Epidemic: A survey of households affected by HIV/AIDS in South Africa.* Keiser Family Foundation and Health Systems Trust, Durban (2002).

Tamale, Sylvia: *Teaching Resources, Feminist Legal Activism in the African Context,* www.gwsafrica.org/teaching/sylvia's.html.

UN: *Millennium Development Goals,* New York (2000).

UNAIDS: *Fact Sheet on Women, Girls and HIV/AIDS in South Africa.* UNAIDS, Geneva (2004a).

UNAIDS: *Report on the Global HIV/AIDS Epidemic 2002.* UNAIDS, Geneva (2002b).

UNAIDS: *Report on the Global AIDS Epidemic 2004.* UNAIDS, Geneva (2004c).

UNIFEM, GTZ and Federal Ministry for Economic Cooperation and Development: *Pathway to Gender Equality, CEDAW, Beijing and the MDGs.*

United Nations Commission for Africa ECA: *Sub-regional Decade Review Meeting on the Implementation of the Beijing Platform for Action (Beijing +10), Lusaka, Zambia 26–29 April 2004.*

United Nations: *Women 2000 and Beyond,* Committee on the Elimination of Discrimination against Women, 13 October 2004, *Statement to Commemorate the 25th anniversary of the Adoption of the Convention on the Elimination of All forms of Discrimination Against Women,* 2004.

Wandia, Mary: *Ratification of the Protocol to the African Charter on Human and Peoples' Rights on the Rights of Women in Africa: The Comoros, Rwanda and Libya lead the Way, FEMNET, 2004.*

Zambia Association for Research and Development / Muyakwa S. L.: *Zambia Country Profile on Women in Development:* Study Commissioned by Japan International Cooperation Agency, Lusaka, Zambia (1998).

Zambia Association for Research and Development: *Using the Democratic Process to Promote Women's Rights,* Lusaka, Zambia (1992).